The History of
the Devil

The History of the Devil

Paul Carus

MINT EDITIONS

The History of the Devil was first published in 1900.

This edition published by Mint Editions 2021.

ISBN 9781513299587 | E-ISBN 9781513223827

Published by Mint Editions®

MINT
EDITIONS
minteditionbooks.com

Publishing Director: Jennifer Newens
Design & Production: Rachel Lopez Metzger
Project Manager: Micaela Clark
Typesetting: Westchester Publishing Services

"Ich kann mich nicht bereden lassen,
Macht mir den Teufel nur nicht klein;
Ein kerl den alle Menschen hassen,
Der muss was sein!"

—GOETHE

Contents

Good and Evil as Religious Ideas 9

Devil Worship 12

Ancient Egypt 18

Accad and the Early Semites 26

Persian Dualism 39

Israel 49

Brahmanism and Hinduism 55

Buddhism 64

The Dawn of a New Era 81

Early Christianity 93

The Idea of Salvation in Greece and Italy 112

The Demonology of Northern Europe 135

The Devil's Prime 147

The Inquisition 167

The Age of the Reformation 184

The Abolition of Witch-Prosecution 200

In Verse and Fable 222

The Philosophical Problem of Good and Evil 237

GOOD AND EVIL AS RELIGIOUS IDEAS

T his world of ours is a world of opposites.

There is light and shade, there is heat and cold, there is good and evil, there is God and the Devil.

The dualistic conception of nature has been a necessary phase in the evolution of human thought. We find the same views of good and evil spirits prevailing among all the peoples of the earth at the very beginning of that stage of their development which, in the phraseology of Tylor, is commonly called Animism. But the principle of unity dominates the development of thought. Man tries to unify his conceptions in a consistent and harmonious Monism. Accordingly, while the belief in good spirits tended towards the formation of the doctrine of Monotheism, the belief in evil spirits led naturally to the acceptance of a single supreme evil deity, conceived as embodying all that is bad, destructive, and immoral.

Monotheism and Monodiabolism, both originating simultaneously in the monistic tendencies of man's mental evolution, together constitute a Dualism which to many is still the most acceptable world-conception. Nevertheless, it is not the final goal of human philosophy. As soon as the thinkers of mankind become aware of the Dualism implied in this interpretation of the world, the tendency is again manifested towards a higher conception, which is a purely monistic view.

Will Monism eliminate the idea of the Devil in order to make God the One and All? Or will it abolish both God and the Devil, to leave room only for a world of matter in motion? Will the future of mankind be, as M. Guyau prophesies, a period in which religion will disappear and give way to irreligion?

Those who do not appreciate the mission of Dualism in the evolution of human thought, and only know its doctrines to be untenable, naturally expect that the future of mankind will be irreligious, and there are freethinkers who declare that Atheism will supersede all the different conceptions of God. But this is not probable. The monistic tendencies of the age will not destroy, but purify and elevate religion. The Animism of the savage is a necessary stage of man's mental evolution: it appears as an error to the higher-developed man of a half-civilised period; but the error contains a truth which naturally develops into a more perfect conception of the surrounding world. Similarly, the religious ideas of the present time are symbols. Taken in their literal meaning, they are untenable, but understood in their symbolical nature they are seeds from which a purer conception of the truth will grow. The tendencies of philosophic thought prevailing today lead to a positive conception of the world, which replaces symbols by statements of fact and brings with it not a denial of religious allegories but a deeper and more correct conception.

A state of irreligion in which mankind would adopt and publicly teach a doctrine of Atheism is an impossibility. Atheism is a negation, and negations cannot stand, for they have sense only as confronted with the positive issues which they reject. Yet our present anthropomorphic view of God, briefly called Anthropotheism, which as a rule conceives him as an infinitely big individual being, will have to yield to a higher view in which we shall understand that the idea of a personal God is a mere simile. God is much more than a person. When we speak of God as a person, we ought to be conscious of the fact that we use an allegory which, if it were taken literally, can only belittle him. The God of the future will not be personal, but superpersonal.

But how shall we reach this knowledge of the superpersonal God? Our answer is, with the help of science. Let us pursue in religion the same path that science travels, and the narrowness of sectarianism will develop into a broad cosmical religion which shall be as wide and truly catholic as is science itself.

Symbols are not lies; symbols contain truth. Allegories and parables are not falsehoods; they convey information: moreover, they can be understood by those who are not as yet prepared to receive the plain truth. Thus, when in the progress of science religious symbols are recognised and known in their symbolical nature, this knowledge will not destroy religion but will purify it and will cleanse it from mythology.

We define God as "that authoritative presence in the All, which enforces a definite moral conduct." God is that something which constitutes the harmony of the laws of nature; God is the intrinsic necessity of mathematics and logic; God above all is what experience teaches us to be the inalienable features of righteousness, justice, morality. This presence is both immanent and transcendent: it is immanent as the constituent characteristic of the law that pervades the universe; it is transcendent, for it is the condition of any possible cosmic order; and in this sense it is supercosmic and supernatural.*

We do not say that God is impersonal, for the word "impersonal" implies the absence of those features which constitute personality; it implies vagueness, indefiniteness, and lack of character. God, however, as he manifests himself in the order of the universe is very definite. He is not vague but possesses quite marked qualities. He is such as he is and not different. His being is universal, but not indeterminable. His nature does not consist of indifferent generalities, but exhibits a distinct suchness. Indeed; all suchness in the world, in physical nature as well as in the domain of spirit, depends upon God as here defined, and what is the personality of man but the incarnation of that cosmic logic which we call reason? God, although not an individual being, is the prototype of personality; although not a person, thinking thoughts as we do, deliberating, weighing arguments, and coming to a decision, he is yet that which conditions personality; he possesses all those qualities which, when reflected in animated creatures, adds unto their souls the nobility of God's image, called personality. Therefore we say, God is not impersonal, but superpersonal.

While the idea of God has received much attention from philosophers and progressive theologians, its counterpart, the dark figure of the Evil One, has been much neglected. And yet the Devil is, after all, a very interesting personality, grotesque, romantic, humorous, pathetic, nay, even grand and tragic. And if we have to declare that the idea of God is a symbol signifying an actual presence in the world of facts, should we not expect that the idea of the Devil also represents a reality?

It is almost impossible to exhaust the subject, for it would take volumes to write an approximately complete history of demonology. Accordingly, we must confine ourselves to merely outlining some of the most salient features of the development of the belief in the Devil and the nature of the idea of evil.

---

* See the author's *Idea of God; Soul of Man,* p. 338 et seq.; *Fundamental Problems,* p. 152 *et passim; Primer of Philosophy,* p. 170 *et passim; The Monist,* Vol. III, pp. 357 et seq.; *Homilies of Science,* pp. 79–120.

Devil Worship

From a surveyal of the accounts gleaned from Waitz, Lubbock, and Tylor, on the primitive state of religion, the conviction impresses itself upon the student of demonology that Devil-worship naturally precedes the worship of a benign and morally good Deity. There are at least many instances in which we can observe a transition from the lower stage of Devil-worship to the higher stage of God-worship, and there seems to be no exception to the rule that fear is always the first incentive to religious worship. This is the reason why the dark figure of the Devil, that is to say, of a powerful evil deity, looms up as the most important personage in the remotest past of almost every faith. Demonolatry, or Devilworship, is the first stage in the evolution of religion, for we fear the bad, not the good.

Mr. Herbert Spencer bases religion on the Unknown, declaring that the savage worships those powers which he does not understand. In order to give to religion a foundation which even the scientist does not dare to touch, he asserts the existence of an absolute Unknowable, and recommends it as the basis of the religion of the future. But facts do not agree with Mr. Spencer's proposition. A German proverb says:

> *"Was ich nicht weiss*
> *Macht mich nicht heiss."*

Or, as is sometimes said in English:

> *"What the eyes don't see*
> *The heart doesn't grieve for."*

What is absolutely unknowable does not concern us, and the savage does not worship the thunder because he does not know what it is, but because he knows enough about the lightning that may strike his hut to be in awe of it. He worships the thunder because he dreads it; he is afraid of it on account of its known and obvious dangers which he is unable to control.

Let us hear the men who have carefully collected and sifted the facts. Waitz, in speaking in his *Anthropologie* (Vol. III, pp. 182, 330, 335, 345) of the Indians, who were not as yet semi-Christianised, states that the

Florida tribes are said to have solemnly worshipped the Bad Spirit, Toia, who plagued them with visions, and to have had small regard for the Good Spirit, who troubled himself little about mankind. And Martius makes this characteristic remark of the rude tribes of Brazil:

> "All Indians have a lively conviction of the power of an evil principle over them; in many there dawns also a glimpse of the good; but they revere the one less than they fear the other. It might be thought that they hold the Good Being weaker in relation to the fate of man than the Evil."*

Capt. John Smith, the hero of the colonisation of Virginia, in 1607, describes the worship of Okee (a word which apparently means that which is above our control) as follows:†

> "There is yet in Virginia no place discouered to bee so Savage in which the savages haue not a religion, Deare, and Bow and Arrowes. All thinges that were able to do them hurt beyond their prevention they adore with their kinde of divine worship; as the fire, water, lightning, thunder, our ordinance peeces, horses, &c. But their chiefe God they worship is the Diuell. Him they call *Oke*,‡ and serue him more of feare than loue. They say they haue conference with him and fashion themselues as neare to his shape as they can imagine. In their Temples they haue his image euill favouredly carued and then painted and adorned with chaines, copper, and beades, and couered with a skin in such manner as the deformity may well suit with such a God." (Original ed., p. 29.)
>
> "In some part of the Country, they haue yearely a sacrifice of children. Such a one was at *Quiyoughcohanock,* some 10 miles from *Iames* Towne, and thus performed.
>
> "Fifteene of the properest young boyes, betweene 10 and 15 yeares of age, they painted white. Hauing brought them forth,

---

* Quoted from Tylor, *Primitive Culture.* II, p. 325.

† "A map of Virginia. With a description of the covntrey, etc., written by Captaine Smith, etc. Oxford. Printed by Joseph Barnes. 1612."

‡ In the little dictionary of the language of the savages of Virginia which is printed in the same pamphlet, Captain Smith translates "Oke" simply by "gods."

the people spent the forenoone in dancing and singing about them with rattles.

"In the afternoone, they put those children to the roote of a tree. By them, all the men stood in a guard, every one hauing a Bastinado in his hand, made of reeds bound together. This [*these*] made a lane betweene them all along, through which there were appointed 5 young men to fetch these children. So every one of the fiue went through the guard, to fetch a child, each after other by turnes: the guard fearelessly beating them with their Bastinadoes, and they patiently enduring and receauing all; defending the children with their naked bodies from the vnmercifull blowes they pay them soundly, though the children escape. All this while, the women weepe and crie out very passionately; prouiding mats, skinnes, mosse, and drie wood, as things fitting their childrens funerals.

"After the children were thus passed the guard, the guard tore down the tree, branches and boughs, with such violence, that they rent the body and made wreathes for their heads, or bedecked their haire with the leaues. What else was done with the children was not seene; but they were all cast on a heape in a valley, as dead: where they made a great feast for al the company.

"The *Werowance* [chief] being demanded the meaning of this sacrifice, answered that the children were not all dead, but [only] that the *Oke* or *Divell* did sucke the blood from their left breast [of those], who chanced to be his by lot, till they were dead. But the rest were kept in the wildernesse by the yong men till nine moneths were expired, during which time they must not conuerse with any: and of these, were made their Priests and Coniurers.

"This sacrifice they held to bee so necessarie, that if they should omit it, their *Oke* or Divel and all their other *Quiyoughcosughes* (which are their other Gods) would let them haue no Deare, Turkies, Corne, nor fish: and yet besides, hee would make great slaughter amongst them.

"To divert them from this blind idolatrie, many vsed their best indeauours, chiefly with the *Werowances* of *Quiyoughcohanock*; whose devotion, apprehension, and good disposition much exceeded any in those Countries: who though we could not as yet preuaile withall to forsake his false Gods, yet this he did beleeue, that our God as much exceeded theirs, as our Gunnes did their Bowes and Arrows; and many times did send to the President, at *Iames* towne, men with presents, intreating them to pray to his God for raine, for his Gods would not send him any.

"And in this lamentable ignorance doe these poore soules sacrifice themselues to the Diuell, not knowing their Creator." (Original ed., pp. 32, 33, 34.)*

Similar practices prevailed among almost all the Indian tribes who inhabited the islands and the two continents of America a few centuries ago. M. Bernhard Picart's illustration†, drawn according to the report of Peter Martyr,‡ an eye-witness, proves that the tribes of Hispaniola, now commonly called Haiti, paid homage to the Supreme Being under the name of Jocanna, and their practices show that they were devil-worshippers of the worst kind. Even the most civilised Americans, the Mexicans, had not as yet outgrown this stage of religious belief. It is true that the idea of a white God of Love and Peace was not quite foreign to them, but the fear of the horrible Huitzilopochtli still prompted them to stain the altars of his temples with the blood of human victims.

Human sacrifices are frequently mentioned in the Bible. Thus the King of Moab, when pressed hard by the children of Israel, "took his eldest son that should have reigned in his stead and offered him for a burnt-offering upon the wall" (2 Kings, iv. 27). He succeeded by this terrible expedient in saving the city, for the biblical report continues: "And there was great indignation against Israel; and they [the Israelites] departed from him and returned to their own land."

The prophets were constantly preaching against the pagan practice of those Israelites who, in imitation of the religion of their neighbors, sought to "sacrifice their sons and daughters to devils," or let them "pass through the fire of Moloch to devour them"; but so near to the religious conception of the savage was even the purer faith of Israel that Jephtha still believed that God required of him "to offer his daughter up as a burnt offering." (Judges, xi. 29–40).

---

* See *The Works of Capt. John Smith* of Willoughby etc. Edited by Edward Arber. Birmingham, 1884, p. 74 ff.
† *The Religious Ceremonies and Customs of the Several Nations of the Known World.* III, p. 129.
‡ See his work, *De rebus oceanicis et novo orbe.*

The most civilised nations on earth still preserve in their ancient legends traces of having at an early period of their religious development immolated human beings in propitiation of angry deities. When the glory of Athens was at its climax, Euripides dramatically represented the tragic fate of Polyxena who was sacrificed on the tomb of Achilles in order to pacify the dead hero's spirit and thereby ensure the safe return of the Greek army.

Progress in civilisation led to a modification but not to a direct abolition of human sacrifices. We find among more advanced savages, and even at the dawn of a higher civilisation, a practice whereby the victim, be it a child, a virgin, or a youth is offered up without slaughtering, and has a chance either to escape by good luck or to be rescued by some daring deed. Traces of this conception are found in the tales of Perseus and Andromeda, of Palnatoke the marksman, who, like William Tell, shot an apple from his child's head, of Susano, in Japanese folk-lore, who slew the eight-headed serpent that annually devoured one of the daughters of a poor peasant, and similar ancient legends. At the same time human victims were supplanted by animals, as is indicated by various religious legends. Thus a hind was substituted for Iphigenia and a ram for Isaac.

Human sacrifices are one of the principal characteristic traits of Devil-worship, but not the only one. There are in addition other devilish practices which are based on the idea that the Deity takes delight in witnessing tortures, and the height of abomination is reached in cannibalism, which, as anthropology teaches us, is not due to scarcity of food, but can always be traced back to some religious superstition, especially to the notion that he who partakes of the heart or brain of his adversary acquires the courage, strength, and other virtues of the slain man.

The last remnants of the idea that the wrath of the Deity must be appeased by blood, and that we acquire spiritual powers by eating the flesh and drinking the blood of the victim still linger with us today in the mediæval interpretations of certain church dogmas, and will only disappear before the searching light of a fearless and consistent religious reformation. We must remember, however, that certain superstitions, at early stages of the religious development of mankind, are as unavoidable as the various errors which science and philosophy pass through in their natural evolution.

Religion always begins with fear, and the religion of savages may directly be defined as "the fear of evil and the various efforts made to escape evil." Though the fear of evil in the religions of civilised nations plays no longer so prominent a part, we yet learn through historical investigations that at an early stage of their development almost all worship was paid to the powers of evil, who were regarded with special awe and reverence.

Actual Devil-worship continues until the positive power of good is recognised and man finds out by experience that the good, although its progress may be ever so slow, is always victorious in the end. It is natural that the power that makes for righteousness is by and by recognised as the supreme ruler of all powers, and then the power of evil ceases to be an object of awe; it is no longer worshipped and not even propitiated, but struggled against, and the confidence prevails of a final victory of justice, right, and truth.

S et, or Seth, whom the Greeks called Typhon, the nefarious demon of death and evil in Egyptian mythology, is characterised as "a strong god (a-pahuti), whose anger is to be feared." The inscriptions call him "the powerful one of Thebes," and "Ruler of the South." He is conceived as the sun that kills with the arrows of heat; he is the slayer, and iron is called the bones of Typhon. The hunted animals are consecrated to him; and his symbols are the griffin (akhekh), the hippopotamus, the crocodile, the swine, the tortoise, and, above all, the serpent âpapi (in Greek "apophis"), who was thought to await the dying man in the domain of the god Atmu (also called Tmu or Turn), who represents the sun below the western horizon.

Set's pictures are easily recognised by his long, erect, and square-tipped ears and his proboscis-like snout, which are said to indicate the head of a fabulous animal called Oryx. The consort and feminine counterpart of Set is called Taour or Taourt. The Greeks called her Theouris. She appears commonly as a hippopotamus in erect posture, her back covered with the skin and tail of a crocodile.

Set is often contrasted with Osiris. Set was the deity of the desert, of drought and feverish thirst, and of the sterile ocean; Osiris represents moisture, the Nile, the fertilising powers and life. Plutarch says:

> "The moon (representing Osiris) is, with his fertilizing and fecundative light, favorable to the produce of animals and growth of plants; the sun, however (representing Typhon), is determined, with its unmitigated fire, to overheat and parch animals; it renders by its blaze a great part of the earth uninhabitable and conquers frequently even the moon (viz., Osiris)."

As an enemy to life, Set is identified with all destruction. He is the waning of the moon, the decrease of the waters of the Nile, and the setting of the sun. Thus he was called the left or black eye of the decreasing sun, governing the year from the summer solstice to the winter solstice, which is contrasted with the right or bright eye of Hor, the increasing sun, which symbolises the growth of life and the spread of light from the winter solstice to the summer solstice.

Set was not always nor to all Egyptians alike a Satanic deity. He was officially worshipped in an unimportant province west of the Nile, but this was the natural starting-point of the road to the northern oasis. The inhabitants, who were mostly guides to desert caravans, had good reasons to remain on friendly terms with Set, the Lord of the desert.

Further, we know that a great temple was devoted to Set, as the god of war, in Tanis, near the swamps between the eastern branches of the Delta, an important town of the frontier, and during the time of invasion the probable seat of the foreign dominion of the Hyksos and the Hyttites, who identified their own god Sutech with the Egyptian Set. But even among the Hyksos, Set was revered as the awful God of irresistible power, of brute force, of war, and of destruction.

There is an old wall-picture of Karnak, belonging to the era of the eighteenth dynasty, in which the god Set appears as an instructor of King Thothmes III in the science of archery.*

Sety I, the second king of the nineteenth dynasty, the shepherd kings, derives his name from the god Set—a sign of the high honor in which he was held among the shepherd kings; and indeed we are informed that they regarded Set, or Sutech, as the only true God, the sole deity, who alone was worthy of receiving divine honors.

If the time of the shepherd kings is to be identified with the settlement of Jacob's sons in Egypt, and if the monotheism of the Hyksos is the root of Moses's religion, what food for thought lies in the fact that the same awe of a fearful power that confronts us in life, changes among the Egyptians into the demonology of Set, and among the Israelites into the cult of Yahveh!

In spite of the terror which he inspired, Set was originally not merely an evil demon but one of the great deities, who, as such, was feared and propitiated.

Says Heinrich Brugsch (*Religion und Mythologie der alten Aegypter*, p. 706):

> "The Book of the Dead of the ancient Egyptians and the numerous inscriptions of the recently opened pyramids are, indeed, nothing but talismans against the imagined Seth and his

---

* See Lepsius, *Denkmäler*, Vol. V, p. 36. The picture is reproduced in outline by Adolf Erman in his *Life in Ancient Egypt*, Engl. trans., p. 282.

associates. Such is also, I am sorry to say, the greater part of the ancient literature that has come down to us."

When a man dies, he passes the western horizon and descends through Atmu's abode into Amenti, the Nether World. The salvation of his personality depends, according to Egyptian belief, upon the preservation of his "double," or his "other self," which, remaining in the tomb, resides in the mummy or in any statue of his body.

The double, just as if it were alive, is supposed to be in need of food and drink, which is provided for by incantations. Magic formulas satisfy the hunger and thirst of the double in the tomb, and frustrate, through invocations of the good deities, all the evil intentions of Set and his host. We read in an inscription of Edfu (Brugsch, *Religion und Mythologie der alten Aegypter*, p. 707):

> "Hail Ra, thou art radiant in thy radiance,
> While there is darkness in the eyes of Apophis!
> Hail Ra, good is thy goodness,
> While Apophis is bad in its badness!"

The dread of hunger, thirst, and other ills, or even of destruction which their double might suffer in the tomb, was a perpetual source of fearful anticipations to every pious Egyptian. The anxiety to escape the tortures of their future state led to the embalming of the dead and to the building of the pyramids. Yet, in spite of all superstitions and the ridiculous pomp bestowed upon the burial of the body we find passages in the inscriptions which give evidence that in the opinion of many thoughtful people the best and indeed the sole means of protection against the typhonic influences after death was a life of righteousness. This is forcibly expressed in the illustration of Chapter CXXV of the Book of the Dead, which is here reproduced according to Lepsius's edition of the Turin papyrus. (Republished by Putnam, *Book of the Dead*).

The picture of the Hall of Truth as preserved in the Turin papyrus shows Osiris with the atef-crown on his head and the crook and whip in his hands. Above the beast of Amenti we see the two genii Shai and Ranen, which represent Misery and Happiness. The four funeral genii, called Amset, Hapi, Tuamutef, and Kebhsnauf, hover over an altar richly laden with offerings. The frieze shows twelve groups of uræus snakes, flames and feathers of truth; on both sides scales are poised by a baboon who is the sacred animal of Thoth, and in the middle Atmu stretches out his hands over the right and left eye, symbolising sunset and sunrise, death and resurrection.

Mâ,* the goddess of truth and "the directress of the gods," decorated with an erect feather which is her emblem, ushers the departed one into the Hall of Truth. Kneeling, the departed one invokes the forty-two assessors by name and disclaims having committed any one of the forty-two sins of the Egyptian moral code. Omitting the names of the assessors, we quote here an extract of the confession. The departed one says:

"I did not do evil.—I did not commit violence.—I did not torment any heart.—I did not steal. I did not cause any one to be treacherously killed.—I did not lessen the offerings.—I did not do any harm.—I did not utter a lie.—I did not make any one weep.—I did not commit acts of self-pollution.—I did not fornicate.—I did not trespass.—I did not commit any perfidy.—I did no damage to cultivated land.—I was no accuser.—I was never angry without sufficient reason.—I did not turn a deaf ear to the words of truth. I did not commit witchcraft.—I did not blaspheme.—I did not cause a slave to be maltreated by his master.—I did not despise God in my heart."

Then the departed one places his heart on the balance of truth, where it is weighed by the hawk-headed Hor and the jackal-headed Anubis, "the director of the weight," the weight being shaped in the figure of the goddess of truth. Thoth, the ibis-headed scribe of the gods, reads Hor's report to Osiris, and if it announces that the weight of the heart is equal to truth, Thoth orders it to be placed back into the breast of the departed one, which act indicates his return to life. If the departed one escapes all the dangers that await him in his descent to Amenti, and if the weight of his heart is not found wanting, he is allowed to enter into "the boat of the sun," in which he is conducted to the Elysian fields of the blessed.

Should the evil deeds of the departed one outweigh his good deeds, he was sentenced to be devoured by Amemit (i.e., the devourer), which

---

* Also called Maâ't, or "the two truths," i.e., of the upper and of the nether world.

is also called "the beast of Amenti," or was sent back to the upper world in the shape of a pig.

While the double stays in the tomb, the soul, represented as a bird with a human head, soars to heaven where it becomes one with all the great gods. The liberated soul exclaims (Erman, *ib.*, p. 343 et seq.):

"I am the god Atum, I who was alone,

"I am the god Ra at his first appearing,

"I am the great god who created himself, and created his name 'Lord of the gods, who has not his equal.'

"I was yesterday, and I know the tomorrow. The battlefield of the gods was made when I spoke.

"I come into my home, I come into my native city.

"I commune daily with my father Atum.

"My impurities are driven out, and the sin that was in me is conquered.

"Ye gods above, reach out your hands, I am like you, I have become one of you.

"I commune daily with my father Atum."

Having become one with the gods, the departed soul suffers the same fate as Osiris. Like him, it is slain by Set, and like Osiris, it is reborn in Hor who revenges the death of his father. At the same time the soul is supposed frequently to visit the double of the departed man in the tomb, as depicted in the tomb of the scribe Ani.

The Abode of Bliss (in Egyptian *Sechnit aanru,* also written *aahlu),* as depicted in the Turin papyrus of the Book of the Dead, shows us the departed one with his family, and Thoth, the scribe of the gods, behind them, in the act of sacrificing to three gods, the latter being decorated with the feather of truth. He then crosses the water. On the other side, he offers a perfuming pan to his soul which appears in the shape of a man-headed bird. There are also the three mummy-form gods of the horizon, with an altar of offerings before the hawk, symbolising Ra, "the master of heaven." In the middle part of the picture the departed one ploughs, sows, reaps, threshes, stores up the harvest, and celebrates a thanksgiving with offerings to the Nile. The lower part shows two barks, one for Ra Harmakhis, the other one for Unefru; and the three islands: the first is inhabited by Ra, the second is called the regenerating place of the gods, the third is the residence of Shu, Tefnut, and Seb.

A very instructive illustration of Egyptian belief is afforded us in the well-preserved tomb of Rekhmara, the prefect of Thebes under Thothmes III of the eighteenth dynasty, the inscriptions of which have been translated into French by Ph. Virey and were published in 1889 by the *Mission Archéologique Française.*

The visitor to the tomb enters through a door on the eastern end; when proceeding westward, we see Rekhmara on the left wall pass from life to death. Here he attends to the affairs of the government, there he receives in the name of Pharaoh the homage of foreign princes; further on he organises the work of building magazines at Thebes. He superintends the artists engaged at the Temple of Ammon and is then buried in pomp. At last he assumes the appearance of the Osiris of the West and receives sacrifices in his capacity as a god. We are now confronted with a blind door through which Rekhmara-Osiris descends into the West and returns to life toward the East as the Osiris of the East. Through funeral sacrifices and incantations his double is again invested with the use of the various senses; he is honored at a festival and graciously received by Pharaoh; in a word, he acts as he did in life. When we return to the entrance where we started, Rekhmara receives the offerings of his family and inspects the progress of the works to which he attended in life.

In the tomb of Rekhmara, Set receives offerings like other great gods. The departed one is called the inheritor of Set (Suti), and is purified by both Hor and Set. As an impersonation of Osiris, the departed one is approached and slain by Set, who then is vanquished in the shape of sacrificial animals which are slaughtered. But when the departed one is restored to the use of his senses and mental powers, Set again plays an important part, and appears throughout as one of the four points of the compass, which are "Hor, Set, Thoth, and Seb."*

According to the original legend, Set represented the death of the sun, and as a personality he is described as the murderer of Osiris, who was finally reconciled with Hor. He remained, however, a powerful god, and had important functions to perform for the souls of the dead. Above all, he must bind and conquer the serpent Apophis (Apap), as we read in the *Book of the Dead* (108, 4 and 5):

---

* *Le Tombeau de Rakhmara,* by Ph. Virey. Paris: Le Roux. 1889.

"They use Set to circumvent it [the serpent]; they use him to throw an iron chain around its neck, to make it vomit all that it has swallowed."

In the measure that the allegorical meaning of the Osiris legend is obliterated, and that Osiris is conceived as a real person who as the representative of moral goodness, succumbs in his struggle with evil and dies, but is resurrected in his son Hor, Set is more and more deprived of his divinity and begins to be regarded as an evil demon.

The reign of Men-Kau-Ra, the builder of the third pyramid of Gizeh (according to Brugsch, 3633 B.C., and according to Mariette, 4100 B.C.), must have changed the character of the old Egyptian religion. "The prayer to Osiris on his coffin lid," says Rawlinson (Vol. II, p. 67), "marks a new religious development in the annals of Egypt. The absorption of the justified soul in Osiris, the cardinal doctrine of the Ritual of the Dead, makes its appearance here for the first time."

According to the older canon Set is always mentioned among the great deities, but later on he is no longer recognised as a god, and his name is replaced by that of some other god. The Egyptians of the twenty-second dynasty went so far as to erase Set's name from many of the older inscriptions and even to change the names of former kings that were compounds of Set, such as Set-nekht and others. The crocodile-headed Ceb (also called Seb or Keb) and similar deities, in so far as their nature was suggestive of Set, suffered a similar degradation; and this, we must assume, was the natural consequence of an increased confidence in the final victory of the influence of the gods of goodness and virtue.

Plutarch, speaking of his own days, says (*On Isis and Osiris*, Chapter XXX) that:

"The power of Typhon, although dimmed and crushed, is still in its last agonies and convulsions. The Egyptians occasionally humiliate and insult him at certain festivals. They nevertheless propitiate and soothe him by means of certain sacrifices."

Set, the great and strong god of prehistoric times, was converted into Satan with the rise of the worship of Osiris. Set was strong enough to slay Osiris, as night overcomes the light of the sun; but the sun is born again in the child-god Hor, who conquers Set and forces him to make the old serpent of death surrender its spoil. As the sun sets to rise again, so man dies to be reborn. The evil power is full of awe, but a righteous cause cannot be crushed, and, in spite of death, life is immortal.

Accad and the Early Semites

About the year 3000 B.C., long before the rise of the Semitic nations, among whom the Babylonians, Assyrians, Israelites, and later the Arabians, were most prominent, there lived in Mesopotamia a nation of great power and importance, which is known by the name of Accad. And, strange to say, the Accadians were not a white, but a dark race. They are spoken of as "blackheads" or "blackfaces"; yet we need not for that reason assume that they were actually as black as the Ethiopians, for the bilingual tablets found in the mounds of Babylonia speak also of them as *Adamatu** or red-skins, which makes it probable that they were reddish-dark or brown. How much the Semites owe to the Accadians, whose dominion ceased about 1500 B.C., and whose language began to die out under the reign of the Assyrian king Sargon (722–705), we may infer from the fact that many religious institutions, legends, and customs among the Semites were of Accadian origin.

Thus we know for certain that in their mode of determining the time they already possessed the institution of a week of seven days, and that the Sabbath was their holy day of rest. The literal meaning of the original Accadian word is explained as "a day on which work is unlawful," and the Assyrian translation *Sabattu* signifies "a day of rest for the heart." Further, the legends of creation, of the tree of life, and of the deluge, mentioned in Genesis and also in Assyrian records, were well known to the Accadians, and from the conventional form of the tree of life, which in the most ancient pictures bears fircones, we may infer that the idea is an old tradition which the Accadians brought with them from their former and colder home in the fir-covered mountains of Media. In addition we have reminiscences of Accadian traditions in many Hebrew names, which proves beyond the shadow of a doubt the long-lasting influence of the ancient civilisation of Accad. The rivers of paradise, mentioned in Genesis, are Babylonian names. Thus, the Euphrates, or *Purat,* is the curving water; Tigris is *Tiggur*, the current; Hid-Dekhel, "the river with the high bank," is another name for the

---

* A popular etymology connected this word *Adamatu* with *Adamu* or *Admu,* "man," which later, as Rawlinson pointed out, reappears in the Bible as the name of the first man. See *The Chaldean Account of Genesis,* by George Smith, p. 83.

Tigris, which in inscriptions is called *Idikla* or *Idikna;* Gihon has been identified by some Assyriologists with *Arakhtu* (Araxes), and by Sir H. Rawlinson with Jukha; and King Sargon calls Elam "the country of the four rivers."

The names of the rivers of Eden indicate that the people with whom the legend of paradise originated must have lived on the banks of the Euphrates and Tigris. Under these circumstances we are surprised to find that the cultivated portion of the desert lands west of the Euphrates was called *Edinna,** a name that sounds very much like Eden.

About the time of Alexander the Great, a Babylonian priest by the name of Berosus wrote an interesting book on the history and religion of Babylon. It is now lost, but as various Greek authors, Alexander Polyhistor, Apollodorus, Abydenus, Damascius,† and Eusebius have largely quoted from his reports, we know quite a good deal about the information he gave to the world concerning his country.

All this was very interesting, but there was no evidence of the reliability of Berosus's records. The Babylonian legends might have been derived from the Old Testament. However, since the successful excavations of the Assyrian stone-libraries we have the most positive evidences as to the source and the great age of these traditions. A great part of them have come down to us from the old Accadians.

We know that the Babylonians possessed several legends which have been received into the Old Testament, the most striking ones being the legend of the deluge, of the tower of Babel, of the destruction of corrupt cities by a rain of fire (reminding us of Sodom and Gomorrah), of the babyhood adventures of King Sargon I. (reminding us of Moses), and of the creation of the world. The name of Babel, which is in Assyrian *bab-ilant,* or *babilu,* i.e. the Gate of God, is a Semitic translation of the Accadian *Ka-dingirra-ki,* with the same meaning; literally: "Gate + of God + the place." The etymology of the name Babel from *balbel,* "to confound," which is suggested both in the Assyrian account of the story and in Genesis, is one of those popular etymologic errors which are frequently found in ancient authors.

---

* Sir Henry Rawlinson believes that Gân Eden or the Garden of Eden is Gan-Duniyas (also called Gan-Duni), meaning "enclosure," which is a name of Babylonia in Assyrian inscriptions.

† See Cory's *Ancient Fragments,* pp. 51–56.

In the legend of the destruction of the cities there occur several names which indicate an Accadian source. The legend of the deluge* agrees in all important details with the analogous story in Genesis. It is the eleventh part of a larger epic celebrating Izdubar,[†] a sun-hero and an Assyrian Hercules, who goes through the twelve signs of the Zodiac, the eleventh being Aquarius, corresponding to the eleventh month of the Accadians, called "the rainy."[‡]

Who has not yet seen, even in our most modern cathedrals, pictures and statues of the four Evangelists adorned with the four representative beings of the animal creation? Matthew is accompanied by an angel or a winged man, Mark by a lion, Luke by a steer, and St. John by an eagle. The creatures represent the cherubim of the Old Testament, who by the early Christians were conceived as the guardians and heavenly prototypes of the Gospel-writers. But these symbols are not original with the Jews; they are of a more venerable age than even the Old Testament; for we find them on the walls of the ancient royal palaces of Nineveh, and there can be no doubt about it that the Jewish conception of the cherubim is the heirloom of a most hoary antiquity.

About Sargon I, king of Agade, who, according to a tablet of King Nabonidus, lived 3754 B.C. and built a temple to Samas, Mr. E. A. Wallis Budge says in his *Babylonian Life and History*, p. 40:

> "A curious legend is extant respecting this king, to the effect that he was born in a city on the banks of the Euphrates, that his mother conceived him in secret and brought him forth in a humble place; that she placed him in an ark of rushes and closed it with pitch; that she cast him upon the river in the water-tight ark; that the river carried him along; that he was rescued by a man called Akki, who brought him up to his own trade; and that from this position the goddess Istar made him king."

---

* See George Smith, *The Chaldean Account of Genesis*, edited by Prof. A. H. Sayce, p. 304, and also Dr. Paul Haupt's habilitation lecture *Der keilinschriftliche Sint fluthbericht*, Leipzig, 1881.

[†] This is the commonly adopted form of the name; although the proper transcription is Gilgamesh. He is also called "Gistubar." The literal meaning of the word is "mass of fire." See Lenormant's *Histoire Ancienne de l'Orient*, V, p. 199.

[‡] Some of the pictures of the Zodiac are strikingly like those which modern charts employ; for instance the centaur and the scorpion, which can be seen on an Assyrian bas-relief in the British Museum reproduced in Lenormant's *Histoire Ancienne de l'Orient*, V, p. 180.

As to the Assyrio-Babylonian origin of these legends there can be no doubt. The best authorities agree—

> "that Chaldea was the original home of these stories and that the Jews received them originally from the Babylonians." (Smith Sayce, *The Chaldean Account of Genesis*, p. 312.)

The numerous illustrations that have been found or early Assyrian and Babylonian seals prove—

> "that the legends were well known and formed part of the literature of the country before the second millennium b.c." (*Ib.*, p. 331.)

It is probable that all the old Chaldean legends existed in several versions. Of the creation story we possess two accounts which vary considerably; but one of them, which is narrated on seven tablets, is of special interest to us, not only on account of its being the main source of the first chapter of the Old Testament, but also because we possess in it one of the oldest documents in which the existence of the Evil One is mentioned. He is called in Assyrian *Tiamtu*, i.e., the deep, and is represented as the serpent that beats the sea, the serpent of the night, the serpent of darkness, the wicked serpent, and the mighty and strong serpent.

The derivation of the biblical account of Creation from Assyrian sources can as little be doubted as that of other legends, not only because of its agreement in several important features, and in many unimportant ones, but also because sometimes the very words used in Genesis are the same as in the Assyrian inscriptions. We find in both records such coincidences as the creation of woman from the rib of man and the sending out of birds from the ark to ascertain whether the waters had subsided. First the birds returned at once, then they returned, according to the cuneiform tablet-inscriptions of the Assyrians, with their feet covered with mud; at last they returned no more. Further, the Hebrew *Mehûmâh*, confusion, chaos, is the Assyrian *Mummu*, while the Hebrew *tehôm*, the deep, and *tohû*, desolate, correspond to the Assyrian *Tiamtu* (= *Tiamat*).

Our excavators have not as yet found a report of the fall of man and of the serpent that seduced Adam and Eve to taste the fruit of the tree of life. There is, however, a great probability that some similar legend existed, as we are in possession of pictures which represent two persons seated under a tree and a serpent nearby.

The tree of life is an idea which must have been very popular among the Assyrians and Babylonians, for their artists do not tire of depicting it in every form. It may date back to that remote period when the fruits of trees constituted an important part of the food by which human life was sustained.[*]

Tiamat is the original watery chaos from which heaven and earth were generated. Babylonian philosophers see in it the mother of the world and the source of all things, while in mythology it appears as the representative of disorder and the mother of the monsters of the deep.

After a long struggle Tiamat was conquered, as we read in the fourth tablet of the creation-story, by the Sungod, Belus or Bel-Merodach. The struggle, however, is not finished, for the demon of evil is living still and Bel has to fight the seven wicked storm-demons who darken the moon. He kills dragons and evil spirits, and the reappearance of divine intelligence in rational creatures is symbolised in the myth that Bel commanded one of the gods to cut off his, i.e. Bel's head, in order to mix the blood with the earth for the procreation of animals which should be able to endure the light.

We here reproduce a brief statement of the Babylonian story of the creation, in which Tiamat plays an important part. Professor Sayce says (*Records of the Past,* New Series, Vol. I, pp. 128–131):

> "A good deal of the poem consists of the words put into the mouth of the god Merodach, derived possibly from older lays. The first tablet or book, however, expresses the cosmological doctrines of the author's own day. It opens before the beginning of time, the expression 'at that time' answering to the expression 'in the beginning' of Genesis. The heavens and earth had not yet been created, and since the name was supposed to be the same as the thing named, their names had not as yet been pronounced.

---

[*] It is noteworthy that *fagus,* the beechtree, and φηγός, the oak, which are both etymologically identical with the English word *beech* and the German *Buche,* mean "eating" or "the tree with eatable fruit." The word *acorn,* which is not derived from oak, but is connected with *acre,* the field, means "harvest or fruit"; it has no connexion with the German *Eichel* (acorn), but it is the same as the German *Ecker,* which is the name of the beechtree fruit.

A watery chaos alone existed, Mummu Tiamat, 'the chaos of the deep.' Out of the bosom of this chaos proceeded the gods as well as the created world. First came the primæval divinities, Lakhmu and Lakhamu, words of unknown meaning, and then An-sar and Ki-sar, 'the upper' and 'lower firmament.' Last of all were born the three supreme gods of the Babylonian faith, Anu the sky-god, Bel or Illil the lord of the ghost-world, and Ea the god of the river and sea.

"But before the younger gods could find a suitable habitation for themselves and their creation, it was necessary to destroy 'the dragon' of chaos with all her monstrous offspring. The task was undertaken by the Babylonian sun-god Merodach, the son of Ea, An-sar promising him victory, and the other gods providing for him his arms. The second tablet was occupied with an account of the preparations made to ensure the victory of light over darkness, and order over anarchy.

"The third tablet described the success of the god of light over the allies of Tiamat. Light was introduced into the world, and it only remained to destroy Tiamat herself. The combat is described in the fourth tablet, which takes the form of a poem in honor of Merodach, and is probably an earlier poem incorporated into his text by the author of the epic. Tiamat was slain and her allies put in bondage, while the books of destiny which had hitherto been possessed by the older race of gods were now transferred to the younger deities of the new world. The visible heaven was formed out of the skin of Tiamat, and became the outward symbol of Ansar and the habitation of Anu, Bel, and Ea, while the chaotic waters of the dragon became the law-bound sea ruled over by Ea.

"The heavens having been thus made, the fifth tablet tells us how they were furnished with mansions for the sun, and moon, and stars, and how the heavenly bodies were bound down by fixed laws that they might regulate the calendar and determine the year. The sixth tablet probably described the creation of the earth, as well as of vegetables, birds, and fish. In the seventh tablet the creation of animals and reptiles was narrated, and doubtless also that of mankind.

"It will be seen from this that in its main outlines the Assyrian epic of the creation bears a striking resemblance to the account of it given in the first chapter of Genesis. In each case the history of the creation is divided into seven successive acts; in each case the present world has been preceded by a watery chaos. In fact the self-same word is used of this chaos in both the Biblical and Assyrian accounts—*tehôm, Tiamat*—the only difference being that in the Assyrian story 'the deep' has become a mythological personage, the mother of a chaotic brood. The order of the creation, moreover, agrees in the two accounts; first the light, then the creation of the firmament of heaven, subsequently the appointment of the celestial bodies 'for signs and for seasons and for days and years,' and next, the creation of beasts and 'creeping things.' But the two accounts also differ in some important particulars. In the Assyrian epic the earth seems not to have been made until after the appointment of the heavenly bodies, instead of before it, as in Genesis, and the seventh day is a day of work instead of rest, while there is nothing corresponding to the statement of Genesis that 'the spirit of God moved upon the face of the waters.' But the most important difference consists in the interpolation of the struggle between Merodach and the powers of evil, as a consequence of which light was introduced into the universe, and the firmament of the heavens was formed.

"It has long since been noted that the conception of this struggle stands in curious parallelism to the verses of the Apocalypse (Rev. xii, 7–9): 'And there was war in heaven: Michael and his angels fought against the dragon; and the dragon fought and his angels, and prevailed not; neither was their place found any more in heaven. And the great dragon was cast out, that old serpent, called the Devil, and Satan, which deceiveth the whole world.' We are also reminded of the words of Isaiah, xxiv. 21, 22: 'The Lord shall punish the host of the high ones that are on high, and the kings of the earth upon the earth. And they shall be gathered together, as prisoners are gathered in the pit, and shall be shut up in the prison.'"

The Babylonians worshipped many deities, but their favorite god was Bel, who is frequently identified with Merodach, on account of his struggle with Tiamat.

Bel-Merodach is one of the great trinity of Anu, Ea, and Bel, which on an ancient cylinder is pictured as hovering above the tree of life before which two human forms, apparently king and queen, are seen in an attitude of adoration.

The Babylonian trinity was thought to be male and female, and it is noteworthy that the female representative of the divine father Anu, the god-mother Anna, also called Istar, was worshipped under the symbol of a dove, which in a purer and nobler form reappears in Christianity as an emblem of most significant spirituality.

Bel-Merodach is the Christ of the Babylonians, for he is spoken of as the son of the god Ea, the personification of all knowledge and wisdom. Professor Budge says:

> "The omnipresent and omnipotent Marduk (Merodach) was the god 'who went before Ea' and was the healer and mediator for mankind. He revealed to mankind the knowledge of Ea; in all incantations he is invoked as the god 'mighty to save' against evil and ill."
>
> —*Babylonian Life and History,* p. 127

The struggle between Bell-Merodach and Tiamat was a favorite subject with Assyrian artists. In one of them, which is now preserved in the British Museum, the Evil One is represented as a monster with claws and horns, with a tail and wings, and covered with scales.

Concerning the Evil One and hell, as conceived by the Babylonians, Mr. Budge says, pp. 139, 140:

> "Their Hades was not so very far different from Sheol, or the 'pit' of the Bible, nor the Devil much to be distinguished from the Satan we read of."
>
> "The Babylonian conception of hell is made known to us by a tablet which relates the descent of Istar thither in search of her lovely young husband, Tammuz. It has been stated that the same word for Hades, i.e. Sheol, as that used in the Hebrew Scriptures, has been found in Babylonian texts; but this assertion has been made while the means for definitely proving it do not at present exist. The lady of the Babylonian Hades was called Nin-kigal, and the place itself had a river running through it, over which spirits had to cross. There was also 'a porter of the waters' (which reminds us of the Charon of the Greeks), and it had seven gates. The tablet mentioned above tells us that—

1. To the land of no return, to the afar off, to regions of corruption.
2. Istar, the daughter of the Moon-god, her attention firmly
3. fixed, the daughter of the Moon-god, her attention fixed
4. the house of corruption, the dwelling of the deity Irkalla (to go)
5. to the house whose entrance is without exit
6. to the road whose way is without return
7. to the house whose entrance is bereft of light
8. a place where much dust is their food, their meat mud.
9. where light is never seen, where they dwell in darkness
10. ghosts (?) like birds whirl round and round the vaults
11. over the doors and wainscoting there is thick dust.

"The outer gate of this 'land of no return' was strongly guarded and bolted, for the porter, having refused to grant Istar admission, the goddess says—

> 'Open thy gate and let me enter in;
> If thou openest not the gate, and I come not in,
> I force the gate, the bolt I shatter,
> I strike the threshold, and I cross the doors,
> I raise the dead, devourers of the living,
> (for) the dead exceed the living.'

"There is another name for Hades, the signs which form it meaning 'the house of the land of the dead.' A gloss gives its pronunciation as *Arali*. Such, then, is the Babylonian hell. It is difficult to say where they imagined their Hades to be, but it has been conjectured by some that they thought it to be in the west."

Besides Tiamat there were in Assyrian and Babylonian mythology innumerable demons whose names are known through the inscriptions and whose portraits are preserved on statues, bas-reliefs, and cylinders. The magic formulae which were employed to ward off their influence are always uttered seven times in the Sumero-Accadian language which was deemed more sacred on account of its age, for it had become unintelligible for the common people and remained in use only for liturgic purposes. The Assyrians expected to frighten demons away by showing them their own shape and by exhorting them to destroy themselves mutually in an internecine combat. Lenormant briefly sets forth the demonology of the Assyrians *Histoire ancienne de l'Orient*, V, p. 494.

"In the army of the Good as well as in the army of Evil, there obtains a hierarchical system of more or less powerful spirits according to their rank. The texts mention the *ekim* and the *telal* or warrior; the *maskin* or trapper; the *alal* or destroyer; the *labartu*, the *labassu*, the *ahharu*, kind of ghosts, phantoms, and vampires. Frequently the *mas*, the *lamma*, and the *utuq* are quoted; and a distinction is made between the good and the evil *mas*, the good and the evil *lamma*, the good and the evil *utuq*. There are also the *alapi* or winged bulls, the *nirgalli* or winged lions, and the innumerable kinds of heavenly archangels. The gods *Anna* and *Ea*, called the spirit of heaven (*zi an na*) and the spirit of the earth (*zi ki a*), as the gods of every science, are commonly invoked in incantations as alone able to protect mankind against the attacks of the evil spirits. The monuments of Chaldea prove the existence of an extremely complex demonology the exact gradation of which is not yet sufficiently known."

Concerning the Devil of the disease-engendering southwest wind Lenormant says (*ibid.* V, p. 212):

"The Louvre possesses the image of a horrible demon in upright posture, with a dog's head, eagle's feet, lion's paws, and a scorpion's tail. Half of the head shows the skull fleshless. He has four spread wings. A ring at the top of the head served to suspend the figure. On the back of the statue is the inscription *in sumero-accadian*, indicating that it represents the demon of the southwest wind and that it should be placed at the door or the window for the sake of warding off his injurious influence. The southwest wind in Chaldea comes from the deserts of Arabia, and its burning breath parches everything, producing the same ravages as the khamsin in Syria and the simoon in Africa."

The Nirgalli are described by the same scholar as follows (*ibid.* V, p. 215):

'At Kuyunjik, in the palace of Asurbanipal, we see in several corners a series of monsters with human bodies, lions' heads, and eagles' feet. They appear in groups of two, combating one another with daggers and clubs. They, too, are demons and express in the language of the sculptor the formula so frequently met with in incantation: 'The evil demons should get out, they should mutually kill one another.'"

There is an ancient bronze tablet which shows the picture of the world in the clutches of the Devil. Lenormant, when speaking of the Chaldean conception of hell, alludes to this remarkable piece of antiquity and describes it as follows:

"A bronze plate in the collection of M. De Clercq contains in a synoptic world-picture a representation of hell, and it is necessary that we here give a description of it. One side of the bronze plate is entirely occupied by a four-footed monster, with four wings, standing on eagle's claws. Raising himself on his hind feet, he looks as though he intended to jump over the plate against which he leans. His head reaches over the border as over the top of a wall. The face of the wild and roaring monster towers, on the other side of the plate, above a picture which is divided into four horizontal strips representing the heavens, the earth, and hell. In the top strip one sees the symbolic representations of the celestial bodies. Underneath appears a series of seven persons clad in long robes and having heads of a lion, a dog, a bear, a ram, a horse, an eagle, and a serpent. These are the celestial genii called *igbigs*. The third strip exhibits a funeral scene, which undoubtedly happens on earth. Two personages dressed in the skin of a fish, after the fashion of the god Anu, are standing at the head and foot of a mummy. Further on there are two genii—one with a lion's head, the other with a jackal's head—who threaten one another with their daggers, and a man seems to flee from this scene of horror. The picture of the fourth strip is bathed in the floods of the ocean, which according to the traditional mythology of the Chaldeans reaches underneath the foundations of the earth. An ugly monster, half bestial, half human, with eagles' wings and claws, and a tail terminating in a snake's head, stands on the shore of the ocean, on which a boat is floating. This is the boat of the deity Elippu, frequently mentioned in the religious texts and probably the prototype of the boat of Charon in Greek mythology. In the boat is a horse which carries upon its back a gigantic lion-headed deity, holding in her hands two serpents; and two little lions jump to her breast to suck her milk. In the corner there are fragments of all kinds, human limbs, vases, and the remainders of a feast.

"Thus this little bronze tablet contains the picture of the world such as the imagination of the Chaldeans represented it to be: the gods and the sidereal powers, angels and demons, ighigs and anunnaks, the earth and men, with supernatural beings who exercise a direct influence upon them: the dead protected by certain demons and attacked by others according to the philosophical conception of good and evil, and the antagonism of the two principles which constitutes the basis of the Assyrio-Chaldean religion. Anu protects the dead in the same way as does the Egyptian Osiris. There is the subterranean river reminding one of the Styx and Acheron of the Greeks as well as of the subterranean Nile of Amenti." (p. 291.)

It goes without saying that the old biblical legends, far from losing their value by being proved to be much older, gain an additional value; they are now more interesting to us than ever. Formerly the biblical account of the creation was thought to be the very beginning of the religious evolution of man, but now we know that it is merely a milestone on the road. It is neither the beginning nor the end. It is simply the summary of a long history of anxious inquiry and speculation, which would have remained forgotten had we not discovered the Assyrian tablets bearing witness to the aspirations that preceded the composition of the Old Testament. But there is one thing which seems strange: the Chaldean belief in the immortality of the soul found no echo in the literature of the Jews. Did they refuse to incorporate it into the Hebrew world-conception because they disbelieved it; or did they merely ignore it because they were too realistic and would not allow themselves to be carried away by illusions even of the loftiest kind?

The civilisation of Assyria and Babylon was more brilliant, more powerful, and more cosmopolitan than the civilisation of Israel. Nevertheless, there is this important difference between the religious legends and speculations of these two nations, that while the

Assyrian tablets are polytheistic and mythological, the Hebrew text is monotheistic. The mythological ornaments of the original story have been chastened and simplified. Without being blind to the poetic beauties of the original, which in its way is not less venerable than the later Hebrew version, we must say that the latter is a decided improvement. Its greater simplicity and freedom from fantastic details gives it a peculiar soberness and grandeur which is absolutely lacking in the Assyrian myth of the creation.

While unequivocally recognising the superiority of the Hebrew account, we must, however, mention in justice to the Assyrian and Babylonian civilisation that monotheism was by no means an exclusively Jewish belief. There were monotheistic hymns of great strength and religious beauty, both in Egypt and in Babylon, long before the existence of the people of Israel, and it is not impossible that what Sir Henry Rawlinson calls "the monotheistic party" of Babylon or their brethren in Egypt were the founders of Jewish monotheism. It is certain that the philosophers of Egypt and Babylonia were not without influence upon the development of the Israelitic religion.

Egyptian and Babylonian monotheists apparently suffered the popular mythology as a symbolical expression of religious truth, while in later periods the religious leaders of the Jews had no patience with idolators, and, becoming intolerant of polytheism, succeeded in blotting out from their sacred literature the popular superstitions of their times; some vestiges only were left, which are now valuable hints indicating the nature of the text before it was changed by the hands of later redactors.

Persian Dualism

The transition from Devil-worship to Godworship marks the origin of civilisation; and among the nations of antiquity the Persians seem to have been the first who took this step with conscious deliberation, for they most earnestly insisted upon the contrast that obtains between good and evil, so much so that their religion is even today regarded as the most consistent form of dualism.

The founder of Persian dualism was Zarathustra, or, as the Greeks called him, "Zoroaster"—a name which in its literal translation means "golden splendor."

Zoroaster, the great prophet of Mazdaism (the belief in Mazda, the Omniscient One), it is rightly assumed, was not so much the founder of a new era as the concluding link in a long chain of aspiring prophets before him. The field was ripe for the harvest when he appeared, and others must have prepared the way for his movement.

Zoroaster is in all later writings represented as a demigod, a fact which suggested to Professor Darmesteter the idea that he was a mythical figure. Nevertheless, and although we know little of Zoroaster's life, we have the documentary evidence in the "Gathas" that he was a real historical personality.

Prof. A. V. Williams Jackson in an essay "On the Date of Zoroaster"[*] arrives at the conclusion that he lived between the latter half of the seventh and the middle of the sixth century, and Dr. E. W. West[†] points out that the calendar reform, in which the old Persian names of the months were supplanted by Zoroastrian names, was introduced in the year 505 B.C. This proves that the kings of the Achæmenian dynasty were Zoroastrians.[‡] Professor Jackson says:

---

[*] *Journal of the American Oriental Society,* Vol. XVII, p. 96.

[†] In a letter to Professor Jackson alluded to on p. 20 of his essay.

[‡] The story that Croesus's life was saved through Zoroastrian influences upon the mind of Cyrus, as told by Nicolaus Damascenus who wrote in the first century B.C., is quite probable. We read (in fragm. 65, Müller, *Fragm. Hist. Gr.,* iii, 409) that religious scruples rose in addition to other considerations, and the words of Zoroaster (Ζωροάστρου λόγια) were called to mind that the fire should not be defiled. Therefore the Persians shouted that the life of Croesus should be spared. Compare Harlez, *Avesta traduit,* Introd., pp. xliv, lxvii.

"The kingdom of Bactria was the scene of Zoroaster's zealous ministry, as I presume. Born, as I believe, in Atropatene, to the west of Media, this prophet without honor in his own country met with a congenial soil for the seeds of his teaching in eastern Iran His ringing voice of reform and of a nobler faith found an answering echo in the heart of the Bactrian king Vishtaspa, whose strong arm gave necessary support to the crusade that spread the new faith west and east throughout the land of Iran. Allusions to this crusade are not uncommon in Zoroastrian literature. Its advance must have been rapid. A fierce religious war, which in a way was fatal to Bactria, seems to have ensued with Turan. This was that same savage race in history at whose door the death of victorious Cyrus is laid. Although tradition tells us the sad story that the fire of the sacred altar was quenched in the blood of the priests when Turan stormed Balkh, this momentary defeat was but the gathering force of victory; triumph was at hand. The spiritual spark of regeneration lingered among the embers and was destined soon to burst into the flame of Persian power that swept over decaying Media and formed the beacon-torch that lighted up the land of Iran in early history."

The Gathas are hymns; they are a product of the fifth and sixth centuries before Christ, the authenticity of which is sufficiently proved not only by the later Persian literature, the Pahlavi books, but also by Greek authors, especially by passages quoted in Plutarch and Diogenes Laertes from Theopompus, who wrote at the end of the fourth century before Christ. The Gathas profess to be written by Zoroaster who appears in them not as a demigod but as a struggling and suffering man, sometimes elated by the grandeur of his aspirations, firmly convinced of his prophetic mission, and then again dejected and full of doubt as to the final success of the movement to which he devoted all his energies. Says Prof. L. H. Mill, the translator of the Gathas:

"Their doctrines and exhortations concern an actual religious movement taking place contemporaneously with their composition; and that movement was exceptionally pure and most earnest.

"That any forgery is present in the Gathas, any desire to palm off doctrines upon the sacred community in the name of the great prophet, as in the Vendidad and later Yasna, is quite out of the question. The Gathas are genuine in their mass."

There were two religious parties in the days of Zoroaster: the worshippers of the daêvas or nature-gods, and the worshippers of Ahura, the Lord. Zoroaster appears in the Gathas as a priest of the highest rank who became the leader of the Ahura party. Zoroaster not only degraded the old nature-gods, the daêvas, into demons, but also regarded them as representatives of a fiendish power which he called *Angrô Mainyush*, or *Ahriman*, which means "the evil spirit," and *Druj*,* i.e., falsehood.

The Scythians in the plains of Northern Asia, the most dangerous neighbors of Persia, worshipped their highest deity under the symbol of a serpent, and it was natural that the snake Afrasiâb,† the god of the enemy, became identified with the archfiend Ahriman.

The Persians are often erroneously called fire worshippers, but it goes without saying that as the sun is not a god and cannot, according to Zoroaster, in and for itself receive divine honor or be worshipped, so the flame which is lit in praise of Ahura Mazda is a symbol only of him who is the light of the soul and the principle of all goodness.

Zoroaster taught that Ahriman was not created by Ahura, but that he was possessed of independent existence. The evil spirit, to be sure, was not equal to the Lord in dignity, nor even in power; nevertheless, both were creative, and both were original in being themselves uncreated. They were the representatives of contradictory principles. And this doctrine constitutes the dualism of the Persian religion, which is most unmistakably expressed in the words of the thirtieth Yasna.‡

"Well known are the two primeval spirits correlated but independent; one is the better and the other is the worse as to thought, as to word, as to deed, and between these two let the wise choose aright."

---

* *Druj*, fiend, is always feminine, while *Ahriman* is masculine.
† The Turanian form of Afrasiâb, was probably Farrusarrabba.
‡ Compare *Sacred Books of the East*, XXXI, p. 29.

Ahura Mazda, the Omniscient Lord, reveals himself through "the excellent, the pure and stirring word."* On the rock inscription of Elvend, which had been made by the order of king Darius, we read these lines†:

> *"There is one God, omnipotent Ahura Mazda,*
> *It is He who has created the earth here;*
> *It is He who has created the heaven there;*
> *It is He who has created mortal man."*

The noble spirit of Zoroaster's religion appears from the following formula, which was in common use among the Persians and served as an introduction to every liturgic worship:‡

"May Ahura be rejoiced! May Angrô be destroyed by those who do truly what is God's all-important will.

"I praise well-considered thoughts, well-spoken words, and well-done deeds. I embrace all good thoughts, good words, and good deeds; I reject all evil thoughts, evil words, and evil deeds.

"I give sacrifice and prayer unto you, O Ameshâ-Spentâ!§ even with the fulness of my thoughts, of my words, of my deeds, and of my heart: I give unto you even my own life.

---

* "The creative Word which was in the beginning" (Ahuna-Vairyo, Honover) reminds one not only of the Christian idea of the λόγος ός ήν έν άρχή, but also of the Brahman *Vâch* (word, etymologically the same as the Latin *vox*), which is glorified in the fourth hymn of the Rig Vêda, as "pervading heaven and earth, existing in all the worlds and extending to the heavens."

† Translated from Lenormant's French rendering, *l. c.,* p. 388.

‡ Cf. *Sacred Books of the East,* Vol. XXII, p. 22.

§ The six *Ameshâ-Spentâ* (the undying and well-doing ones) are what Christians might call archangels. Originally they had been seven, but the first and greatest among them, Ahura Mazda, came to overshadow the divinity of the other six. They remained powerful gods, but he was regarded as their father and creator. We read in *Yast,* XIX, 16, that they have "one and the same thinking, one and the same speaking, one and the same doing, one and the same father and lord, who is Ahura Mazda."

At first the Ameshâ Spentâ were mere personifications of virtues, but later on they were entrusted with the government of the various domains of the universe. *Haurvatât* and *Ameretât* (health and immortality) had charge of waters and trees. *Khshathrem Vairîm* (perfect sovereignty), represented the flash of lightning. His emblem being molten brass, he was revered as the master of metals. *Asha Vahita* (excellent holiness), the moral world-order as symbolised by sacrifice and burnt-offering, ruled over the fire. *Spenta Armaití* (divine piety) continued to be regarded as the goddess of the earth, which position,

"I recite the 'Praise of Holiness,' the *Ashem Vohu:**

"'Holiness is the best of all good. Well is it for it, well is it for that holiness which is perfection of holiness!

"'I confess myself a worshipper of Mazda, a follower of Zarathustra, one who hates the daêvas (devils) and obeys the laws of Ahura.'"

Lenormant characterises the God of Zoroaster as follows:

"Ahura Mazda has created *asha,* purity, or rather the cosmic order; he has created both the moral and material world constitution; he has made the universe; he has made the law; he is, in a word, creator (*datar*), sovereign (*ahura*), omniscient (*mazdâo*), the god of order (*ashavan*). He corresponds exactly to Varuna, the highest god of Vedism.

"This spiritual conception of the Supreme Being is absolutely pure in the Avesta, and the expressions that Ormuzd has the sun for his eye, the heaven for his garment, the lightning for his sons, the waters for his spouses, are unequivocally allegorical. Creator of all things, Ormuzd is himself uncreated and eternal. He had no beginning and will have no end. He has accomplished his creation work by pronouncing 'the Word,' the 'Ahuna-Vairyo, Honover,' i.e., 'the Word that existed before everything else,' reminding us of the eternal Word, the Divine Logos of the Gospel." *Histoire Ancienne de l'Orient,* V, p. 388.

Concerning Ahriman, Lenormant says:

"The creation came forth from the hands of Ormuzd, pure and perfect like himself. It was Ahriman who perverted it by his infamous influence, and labored continually to destroy and overthrow it, for he is the destroyer (*paurou marka*) as well as

---

according to old traditions, she had held since the Indo-Iranian era; and *Vohu Manô* (good thought) superintended the creation of animate life. (See Darmesteter, *Ormuzd et Ahriman,* Paris: 1877. pp. 55, 202–206. Comp. *Encyclopædia Britannica, s. v.* "Zoroaster," and *Sacred Books of the East,* Vol. IV, p. LXXI, et seq.) For an exposition of the modern Parseeism of India see Mr. Dosabhai Framji Karaka's *History of the Parsis,* London, 1884.
* Says Darmesteter: "The 'Ashem Vohu' is one of the holiest and most frequently recited prayers."

the spirit of evil. The struggle between these two principles, of good and of evil, constitutes the world's history. In Ahriman we find again the old wrathful serpent of the Indo-Iranian period, who is the personification of evil and who in Vedism, under the name of *Ahi*, is regarded as an individual being. The myth of the serpent and the legends of the Avesta are mingled in Ahriman under the name of *Aji Dahâka*, who is said to have attacked Atar, Traêtaona, and Yima, but is himself dethroned. It is the source of the Greek myth that Apollo slays the dragon Python. The Indo-Iranian religion knows only the struggle that was carried on in the atmosphere between the fire-god and the serpent-demon Afrasiâb. And it was, according to Professor Darmesteter, the doctrine of this struggle, which, when generalised and applied to all things in the world, finally led to the establishment of dualism."

Says James Darmesteter, the translator of the Zend-Avesta:

"There were two general ideas at the bottom of the Indo-Iranian religion; first, that there is a law in nature, and secondly, that there is a war in nature (*Sacred Books of the East*, IV, p. lvii).

The law in nature proves the wisdom of Ahura, who is therefore called Mazda, the Wise. The war in nature is due to the intrusion of Ahriman into the creation of Ahura.

The fire sacrifice was accompanied by partaking of the haoma drink, a ceremony which reminds us on the one hand of the soma sacrifice of the Vedic age in India and on the other hand of the Lord's Supper of the Christians. We know through the sacred scriptures of the Persians that little cakes (the *draona*) covered with small pieces of holy meat (the *myazda*) were consecrated in the name of a spiritual being, a god or angel, or of some great deceased personality, and then distributed among all the worshippers that were present. But more sacred still than the draona with the myazda is the haoma drink which was prepared from the white haoma plant, also called gaokerena. Says Professor Darmesteter: "It is by the drinking of gaokerena that men, on the day of the resurrection, will become immortal."

The way in which the Persian sacrament of drinking the gaokerena was still celebrated in the times of early Christianity, must have been very similar to the Christian communion, for Justinus, when speaking of the Lord's Supper among the Christians, adds "that this very solemnity, too, the evil spirits have introduced in the mysteries of Mithra."

After death, according to the Zoroastrian doctrine, the soul must pass over *cinvato peretush*, that is, the "accountant's bridge," where its future fate is decided. This bridge stretches over the yawning abyss of hell, from the peak of Judgment to the divine Mount Alborz, and becomes, according to the most common statements of the doctrine, broad to the good, a pathway of nine javelins in breadth, while to the wicked it is like the edge of a razor. Evil doers fall into the power of Ahriman and are doomed to hell; the good enter *garô demâna*, the life of bliss; while those in whom good and evil are equal, remain in an intermediate state, the *Hamêstakâns* of the Pahlavi books, until the great judgment-day (called *âka*).

The most characteristic features of the Persian religion after the lifetime of Zoroaster consist in the teaching that a great crisis is near at hand, which will lead to the renovation of the world called *frashôkereti* in the Avesta, and *frashakart* in Pahlavi. Saviours will come, born of the seed of Zoroaster, and in the end the great Saviour who will bring about the resurrection of the dead. He will be the "son of a virgin" and the "All-conquering." His name shall be the Victorious (*verethrajan*), Righteousness-incarnate (*astvat-ereta*), and the Saviour (*saoshyañt*). Then the living shall become immortal, yet their bodies will be transfigured so that they will cast no shadows, and the dead shall rise, "within their lifeless bodies incorporate life shall be restored." (Fr. 4. 3.)[*] The Persian belief in the advent of a saviour who will make mankind immortal seems to reappear in an intenser form in the days of John the Baptist and Jesus of Nazareth, who preached that the kingdom of heaven is near at hand. St. Paul still believed that the second advent of Christ would take place during his own life-time. The dead who sleep in the Lord will be resurrected, and the bodies of those that are still in the flesh will be transfigured and become immortal.

The influence of Zoroaster's religion upon Judaism and early Christianity cannot be doubted. Not only does the original text of the book of Ezra directly declare that "Cyrus, the King, built the house of

---

[*] For a concise statement of the Persian religion, which in many respects foreshadows the Christian doctrines of a Saviour and of the bodily resurrection of the dead, see Prof. A. V. Williams Jackson's excellent article, "The Ancient Persian Doctrine of a Future Life," published in the *Biblical World*, August, 1896.

the Lord in Jerusalem, where they worship him with the eternal fire" (διὰ πυρὸς ἐνδελεχοῦς), but there are many Jewish ceremonies preserved to the present day, which bear a close resemblance to the ritual of ancient Mazdaism. In addition there is a documentary evidence preserved in "The Arabic Gospel of the Infancy" (Chapter 7), that the Magi came from the East to Jerusalem according to a prophecy of Zoroaster.

The Persian world-conception, like the religion of the Jews, was too abstract to favor any artistic development.* Therefore we do not possess representations of either good or evil spirits which are exclusively and peculiarly Persian. Even the picture of Ahura Mazda (as we find it on various bas-reliefs) is not based upon a conception that could be said to be regarded as original. The figure from which the bust of the god of light and goodness rises can be traced to Assyrian emblems, and may, for all we know, be of Accadian origin. There is, for instance, an Assyrian cylinder which represents a worshipper standing before the idol of a god. Behind him is the tree of life and a priest carrying in his left hand a rosary, while the deity hovers above them in a similar shape to the Ahura-Mazda pictures of the Persians.

Ahura Mazda is pictured as a winged disc without any head, in the style of Chaldean sun-pictures, in a cameo representing him as worshipped by two sphinxes, between whom the sacred haoma plant is seen (see p. 59). In another cameo (see p. 59) he appears as a human figure without wings, rising from a crescent that hovers above the sacrificial fire. Above him is a picture of the sun, and before him stands a priest or a king in an attitude of adoration.

There are some magnificent representations of Ahura-Mazda on ancient Persian monuments, which claim our special attention. There is a loftiness and majesty about his appearance, which lifts his picture above the Assyrian conception of deities. In his hands he holds either a ring or the short royal staff of rulers, appearing at the top like a lotus flower.

Prof. A. V. Williams Jackson explains the ring in the hands of Ahura Mazda as "the Circle of Sovereignty,"† and interprets the loop with streamers in which the figure floats as a variation of the same idea,

---

* For Persian art see Marcell Dienlafoy's work *L'art antique de la Perse,* in which for the present purpose the title vignette and the illustrations on p. 4 are of interest.
† See his article on "The Circle of Sovereignty," in the *American Oriental Society's Proceedings,* May, 1889.

for in some of the pictures it appears as a chaplet, or waist-garland with ribbons.[*]

It is not possible that the loop with streamers is originally a disc representing the disc of the sun after the fashion of Egyptian temple decorations. At any rate, there are a great number of Assyrian sculptures of the same type which are unequivocally representations of the sun. A cylinder (published in Lajard's *Culte de Mithra*, plate XLIX, No. 2) illustrating the myth of god Isdubar's descent to Hasisatra, shows the two scorpion-genii of the horizon watching the rise and the setting of the sun. Here the sun appears, like the figure from which Ahura Mazda rises, as a winged disc with feather-tail and streamers. In addition, we find the same picture in the deity that protects the tree of life, which can only signify the benign influence of the sun on plants (see p. 36); and the old Babylonian cylinder representing Merodach's fight with the evil spirit that darkens the moon (see p. 37), shows the feathered dial in this same conventional shape covered with clouds.[†]

A representation of Ahriman has not yet been discovered among the Persian antiquities. There is, however, a bas-relief in Persepolis which depicts the king in the act of slaying a unicorn. The monster is very similar to the Assyrian Tiamat (see p. 41), and we cannot doubt that the Persian sculptor imitated the style of his Assyrian predecessors.

We have little information concerning the origin of Zoroaster's dualism, but we can nevertheless reconstruct it, at least in rough outlines. For there are witnesses left, even today, of the historical past of the old Persian religion. A sect called the Izedis are the fossil representatives of the Devil-worship that preceded the purer notions of the Zoroastrian worship prevailing in the Zend-Avesta. Following the authority of a German traveller, Tylor says (*Primitive Culture*, Vol. II, p. 329):

> "The Izedis or Yezidis, the so-called Devil-worshippers, still remain a numerous though oppressed people in Mesopotamia and adjacent countries. Their adoration of the sun and horror of defiling fire accord with the idea of a Persian origin of their religion (Persian "*ized*" = God), an origin underlying more

[*] See K. O. Kiash, *Ancient Persian Sculptures;* and also Rawlinson, *J. R. A. S.,* X, p. 187. Kossowicz, *Inscriptions Palaeo Persicae Achaemeniodorum,* p. 46 et seq.

[†] There is no need of enumerating other cylinders and bas-reliefs of the same kind, as they are too frequently found in Assyrian archæology. See for instance the illustrations in Lenormant, *l. l.* V, pp. 177, 230, 247, 296, 299, etc.

superficial admixture of Christian and Moslem elements. This remarkable sect is distinguished by a special form of dualism. While recognising the existence of a Supreme Being, their peculiar reverence is given to Satan, chief of the angelic host, who now has the means of doing evil to mankind, and in his restoration will have the power of rewarding them. 'Will not Satan then reward the poor Izedis, who alone have never spoken ill of him, and have suffered so much for him?' Martyrdom for the rights of Satan! exclaims the German traveller, to whom an old white-bearded Devil-worshipper thus set forth the hopes of his religion."

This peculiar creed of the Izedis is similar to the religion of Devil-worshipping savages in so far as the recognition of the good powers is not entirely lacking, but it is, as it were, a merely negative element; the positive importance of goodness is not yet recognised. It is probable that the Persians in prehistoric times were as much Devilworshippers as are the Izedis. The daêvas, the deities of the irresistible forces of nature, were pacified by sacrifices. A recognition of the power of moral endeavor as represented in the personified virtues, the Ameshâ Spentâ, was the product of a slow development. Thus in Persia the Devil-worship of the daêvas yielded to the higher religion of God-worship; and this change marks a decided step in advance, resulting soon afterwards in the Persians' becoming one of the leading nations of the world.

Israel

Azazel, the God of the Desert

THE PRIMITIVE STAGES OF THE Hebrew civilisation are not sufficiently known to describe the changes and phases which the Israelitic idea of the God-head had to undergo before it reached the purity of the Yahveh conception. Yet the Israelites also must have had a demon not unlike the Egyptian Typhon, for the custom of sacrificing a goat to Azazel, the demon of the desert, suggests that the Israelites had just emerged from a dualism in which both principles were regarded as equal.

We read in Leviticus xvi:

> "And Aaron shall cast lots upon the two goats; one for the Lord, and the other for Azazel. And Aaron shall bring the goat upon which the Lord's lot fell, and offer him for a sin-offering. But the goat on which the lot fell for Azazel, shall be presented alive before the Lord, to make atonement with him and to let him go to Azazel in the desert."

The name *Azazel* is derived from *aziz*, which means strength, and *El*, God. The god of war at Edessa is called *Asisos* (Ἄσιϛος), the strong one. *Bal-aziz* was the strong god, and *Rosh-aziz*, the head of the strong one, is the name of a promontory on the Phœnician coast. *Azazel*, accordingly, means the Strength of God.

The mention of Azazel must be regarded as a last remnant of a prior dualism. Azazel, the god of the desert, ceased to be the strong god, and became a mere shadow of his former power, for the scapegoat is no longer a sacrifice. Yahveh's goat alone is offered for a sin-offering, while the scapegoat carries out into the desert the curse of the people's sin, and thus the worship of Azazel changed into a mere recognition of his existence.

These sacrificial ceremonies, however, which, on account of their being parts of religious performances, were only reluctantly discarded, are the lingering vestiges in Hebrew literature of an older dualism in which the power of evil received an equal share of worship with the power of good.

Superstitions

THE OLD TESTAMENT CONTAINS MANY noble ideas and great truths; indeed it is a most remarkable collection of religious books, than which there is none more venerable in the literature of the world. Yet there are tares among the wheat, and many lamentable errors were, even by some of the leaders of the old Israelites, regarded as essential parts of their religion. The writers of the Bible not only made God responsible for, and accessory to, the crimes which their own people committed, e.g., theft (Exodus xi.), and murder and rape (Numbers xxxi. 17–18); but they cherished also the same superstitions that were commonly in vogue among savages. Thus the custom of burying people alive under foundation stones is mentioned as having been sanctioned by the God of Israel. When Jericho was destroyed at the special command of God, all its inhabitants were slain, "both man and woman, young and old, and ox and sheep and ass," with the sole exception of Rahab, a disreputable woman who had betrayed the city into the hands of the enemies of her countrymen. And Joshua adjured the people, saying:

> "Cursed be the man before the Lord, that riseth up and buildeth this city Jericho: he shall lay the foundation thereof in his first born and in his youngest son shall he set up the gates of it."

Jericho, however, was sure to be rebuilt sooner or later, for, being the key to Palestine, and commanding the entrance into the country from the desert routes, it was too important both for commercial and strategic purposes to be left in ruins; and the man who undertook the work was still superstitious and savage enough to heed Joshua's curse: We read in the first Book of Kings, with reference to the reign of Ahab (Chap. xvi. 34):

> "In his days, Hiel the Bethelite built Jericho; he laid the foundation stones thereof in Abiram, his first born, and set up the gates thereof in his youngest son, Segub, according to the word of the Lord which he spake by Joshua, the son of Nun."

The terrible witch-prosecutions which in the Middle Ages harassed Christianity have their root in passages of the Old Testament.

The laws of Exodus (xxii. 18) provide capital punishment for witchcraft, and the same command is repeated in Leviticus, where we read:

"The soul that turneth after such as have familiar spirits, and after wizards, I will even set my face against that soul, and will cut him off from among his people." (Lev. xx. 6.)

"A man also or a woman that hath a familiar spirit, or that is a wizard, shall surely be put to death; they shall stone them with stones: their blood shall be upon them." (Lev. xx. 27.)

In spite of the severity of the law against wizards and witches, the Israelites were always inclined to resort to their help. Saul, who had done his best to exterminate soothsayers (1 Sam. xxviii. 9), when in greatest anxiety, called on the witch of Endor.

It is evident from various passages that the Israelites believed in evil spirits dwelling in darkness and waste places. (See Lev. xvii. 7; Deut. xxx. 17; *ib.* xxxii. 17; 2 Chron. xi. 15; Isaiah xiii. 21; *ib.* xxxiv. 14; Jer. 1. 39; Psalms cvi. 37.) Their names are *Seirim* (chimeras or goat-spirits), *Lilith* (the nightly one), *Shedim* (demons). The *Seirim* remind us of Assyrian pictures which represent evil spirits in the shape of goats. It is difficult to say whether these various demons of the Hebrews are to be regarded as the residuum of a lower religious stage preceding the period of the monotheistic Yahveh cult, or as witnesses to the existence of superstitions which certainly haunted the imagination of the uncultured not less in those days than they do now in this age of advanced civilisation.

Apparently the rise of a purer religion was slow and the habits of a savage age were long-lingering. The vestiges of devil-worship with several of its most bestial rites and even human sacrifices* continued to exist even when a more radiant light began to shine in the world.

Satan

WHEN AZAZEL BEGAN TO BE neglected, Satan rose into existence. The belief in a God of Evil was replaced by the belief in an evil demon. And Satan, the tempter and originator of all evil, was naturally

---

* See pp. 10–12 of this book.

identified with the serpent that "was more subtil than any beast of the field" (Genesis iii. 1).

Satan, the fiend, as a name in the sense of Devil, is rarely mentioned in the Old Testament. The word Satan, which means "enemy" is freely used, but, as a proper name, signifying the Devil, appears only five times. And it is noteworthy that the same event is, in two parallel passages, attributed, in the older one to Yahveh, and in the younger one, to Satan.

We read in 2 Samuel xxiv. 1:

> "The anger of the Lord was kindled against Israel, and he moved David against them to say, Go, number Israel and Judah."

The same fact is mentioned in 1 Chron. xxi. 1:

> "Satan stood up against Israel and provoked David to number Israel."

In all the older books of Hebrew literature, especially in the Pentateuch, Satan is not mentioned at all. All acts of punishment, revenge, and temptation are performed by Yahveh himself, or by his angel at his direct command. So the temptation of Abraham, the slaughter of the first-born in Egypt, the brimstone and fire rained upon Sodom and Gomoriah, the evil spirit which came upon Saul, the pestilence to punish David—all these things are expressly said to have come from God. Even the perverse spirit which made the Egyptians err (Isaiah xix. 14), the lying spirit which was in the mouths of the prophets of Ahab (1 Kings xxii. 23; see also 2 Chron. xviii. 20–22), ignorance and indifference (Isaiah xxix. 10), are directly attributed to acts of God.

The prophet Zechariah speaks of Satan as an angel whose office it is to accuse and to demand the punishment of the wicked. In the Book of Job, where the most poetical and grandest picture of the Evil One is found, Satan appears as a malicious servant of God, who enjoys performing the functions of a tempter, torturer, and avenger. He accuses unjustly, like a State's attorney who prosecutes from a mere habit of prosecution, and delights in convicting even the innocent, while God's justice and goodness are not called in question.

It is noteworthy that Satan, in the canonical books of the Old Testament, is an adversary of man, but not of God; he is a subject of God and God's faithful servant.

The Jewish idea of Satan received some additional features from the attributes of the gods of surrounding nations. Nothing is more common in history than the change of the deities of hostile nations into demons of evil. In this way Beelzebub, the Phœnician god, became another name for Satan; and Hinnom (i.e. *Gehenna*), the place where Moloch had been worshipped, in the valley of Tophet, became the Hebrew name for hell in place of the word *Sheol*, the world of the dead under ground. The idol of Moloch was made of brass, and its stomach was a furnace. According to the prophets (Is. lvii. 5; Ez. xvi. 20; Jer. xix. 5), children were placed in the monster's arms to be consumed by the heat of the idol. The cries of the victims were drowned by drums, from which ("toph," meaning drum) the place was called "Tophet." Even the king, Manasseh, long after David, made his son pass through the fire of Moloch (2 Kings xxi.).* Josiah endeavored to make an end of this terrible practice by defiling Tophet, in the valley of the children of Hinnom (2 Kings xxxiii 10).

Thus the very name of this foreign deity naturally and justly became among the Israelites the symbol of abomination and fiendish superstition.

The historical connexion of Israel's religion with the mythologies of Assyria and Babylon, begins now to be better understood; since we have learned to decipher the ancient cuneiform records. There are many most significant reminiscences of Bel Merodach's combat with Tiamat left in the Old Testament, and Hermann Gunkel after having given a literal translation of the several passages with explanatory comments says (*Schöpfung und Chaos*, p. 88):

"Nowhere in extant literature is the myth of Yahveh's combat with the dragon actually narrated. Judaism, the distinctive work of which was the collection of the canon, did not admit myths that savored of heathendom. Nevertheless, the fact that in all the passages that speak of the dragon the myth is not portrayed but simply presupposed, proves that it was very well known and very popular with the people. The absence of the myth in the canon,—

---

* There is no reason to doubt the Biblical reports concerning Moloch, for Diodorus (20, 14) describes the cult of the national god of Carthage, whom he identifies with the Greek "Kronos," in the same way; so that in consideration of the fact that Carthage is a Phœnician colony, we have good reasons to believe this Kronos to be the same deity as the Ammonite Moloch, who was satiated by the same horrible sacrifices.

and this in the interest of the Christian reader need not be deplored,—is distinct and conclusive evidence that we possess in our Old Testament a fragment only of the old religious literature.

"The myth was from the very beginning in Israel a hymn to Yahveh. The Yahveh-hymn therefore is the favorite place for making reference to the dragon-myth,—of which we have a beautiful instance in Psalm lxxxix. The poet that portrays Yahveh's oppression of humanity (Job xl. et seq.; ix. 13; xvi. 13; also Psalm civ.); the prophet that terrorises the sinning people with pictures of Yahveh's omnipotence (Am. ix.); he that arouses the people languishing under a foreign dominion (Isaiah li. 9 et seq.): all make direct reference to Yahveh's power even over the dragon."*

It is noteworthy that the seven-armed candlestick of the arch of Titus contains on its base figures of dragons, which we may justly assume to be Leviathan, Behemoth, and Rahab, the mythological monsters of Israel.

---

* It may be added that the references in the passages in question are absolutely unintelligible unless interpreted by some such light as that given by Gunkel. To the reader without a commentary they are sealed utterances, for the mere translation in our Bible offers no help to their understanding.

Brahmanism and Hinduism

I ndia, the primitive home of religion and philosophy, exhibits as strong a tendency for monism as the Persian nation has shown for dualism. But the ancient monism of India is apt to lose itself in pantism,—a theory according to which the All alone (or rather the conception of the absolute as the All) is possessed of reality, while all concrete existences are considered as a mere sham, an illusion, a dream.*

The polytheism of the popular Hinduism† is practically a pantheism in which the various deities are regarded as aspects of the One and All in which a discrimination between good and evil is entirely lost sight of. Thus the struggle between good and evil is contemplated as a process of repeated God-incarnations made necessary, according to the idea of the Brahmans, by the appearance of tyranny and injustice, lack of reverence for the priests, encroachments of the warrior caste on the supremacy of the Brahmans, or some other disorder. While the enemies of the gods—giants, demons, and other monsters—are not radically bad, and cannot be regarded as devils in the sense of the Christian Satan, the Brahman gods in their turn are by no means the representatives of pure goodness. Not only do they frequently assume shapes that to the taste of any Western nation would be exceedingly ugly and diabolical, but the same deities who in one aspect are beneficent powers of life, are in another respect demons of destruction.

Brahm, the highest god of Brahmanism, represents the All, or the abstract idea of being. He is conceived as a trinity which is called Trimurti, consisting of Brahma, Vishnu, and Siva.

Brahma, the first-originated of all beings, the lord of all creatures, the father of all the universes, is the divine mind who is the beginning of all. He is called *Aja*, the not-born, because he has originated, but was not begotten.

Brahma originated from *tat*, i.e., undifferentiated being, in which he existed from eternity in an embryonic form.

---

* Pantism, the theory of the All (from πᾶν, root ΠΑΝΤ), is different from Pantheism, the theory which identifies the All (πᾶν) with God (θεός).
† Sir Monier-Monier Williams distinguishes between Brahmanism, the old faith of the Indian Aryas, and Hinduism, the modern form of this same religion, as it developed after the expulsion of Buddhism from India.

Brahma's consort, Sarasvati, also called Brahmi or Brahmini, is the goddess of poetry, learning, and music.

Brahma is the creator of man. We are told in the Yajurveda that the god produced from himself the soul, which is accordingly a part of his own being, and clothed it with a body—a process which is reported in the reverse order in the Hebrew Genesis, where Elohim creates first the body and then breathes the life into the body, which makes of man a living soul.

Brahma is pictured with four heads and four hands, in which he holds a spoon, a sacrificial basin, a rosary, and the Vedas. One of the four hands is frequently represented as empty. He sits on a lotus which grows from Vishnu's navel, representing the spirit that broods over the waters.

Brahma keeps the first place in the speculations of philosophers, where he is identified with the life-breath of the world, the Atman or self that appears in man's soul, but he has not exercised a great influence on the people. The gods of the people must be less abstract, more concrete and more human. Thus it is natural that Vishnu, the second person of the trinity, the deity of avatars or incarnations, is, for all practical purposes, by far more important than Brahma.

Vishnu appears in the following ten incarnations:*

In the first incarnation, called the Matsya-Avatar, Vishnu assumes the form of a fish in order to recover the Vedas stolen by evil demons and hidden in the floods of a deluge that covered the whole earth. This incarnation is of interest because we read in the *Pistis Sophia* (one of the most important gnostic books) that the books of Ieou, which were dictated by God to Enoch in paradise, were preserved by Kalapatauroth from destruction in the deluge.†

In order to enable the gods to procure the immortality-giving drink, amrita, Vishnu appeared as an immense tortoise in the kurm-avatar, his second incarnation. He lifted on his back the world-pillar, the mountain Mandaras, and the world-serpent, Vasuki (or Anantas, i.e., infinite), was wound about it like a rope. The gods seized the tail, the demons (daityas) the head, and they began to churn the ocean, which produced Vishnu's gem, Kaustubha; Varunani, the goddess of the sea;

---

* Since it is our intention to be brief, we do not enter in this exposition of the ten avatars into any details that could be omitted and neglect to mention the variants of the myths.

† Ms., p. 354, English translation from Schwartze's latest translation by G. R. S. Meade, p. 354.

PAUL CARUS

the Apsaras, lovely sprites, corresponding to the Greek nymphs; Indra's horse, with seven heads; Kamadhenu, the cow of plenty; Airavata, Indra's elephant; the tree of abundance; Chandra, the god of the moon; Sura, the goddess of wine; and, finally, Dhanvantari, the Indian Æsculapius, who is in possession of the water of life. The serpent began now to spit venom, which blinded the demons, while the gods drank the Amrita.

Varunani, when conceived as goddess of beauty, is called Lakshmi or Shri; and it is noteworthy that like Aphrodite of the Greeks she originates from the froth of the ocean.

The third incarnation is the Varaha-avatar, in which Vishnu, in the shape of a wild boar, kills, with his tusks, the demon Hiranyaksha, who threatened to destroy the world.

Hiranyaksha's brother, Hiranya-Kasipu, had a son by the name of Prahlada, who was a pious devotee of Vishnu. The unnatural father tried to kill his son, but the latter escaped all danger because he did not cease to pray to Vishnu. When Hiranya-Kasipu expressed a doubt of Vishnu's omnipresence, mockingly declaring that he could not possibly be in a column to which he pointed, the wrathful god decided to punish the scoffer. The column rent in twain, and Vishnu, proceeding from its interior in the shape of a monster half man half lion, tore Hiranya-Kasipu to pieces. This fourth incarnation is called the Narasinhaavatar. Its moral is to impress upon the people the sad fate of those who do not believe in Vishnu.

Pralada's grandson, Balis, was a pious king, but on that very account dangerous to the gods, for he was just about to complete the hundredth grand sacrifice, by which he would have acquired sufficient power to dethrone Indra. Vishnu came to the assistance of the god of heaven and appeared before Balis as a dwarf in guise of a Brahman mendicant. Balis honored him with presents and promised to fulfil his desire, whereupon the dwarf requested three paces of ground. This was gladly granted under a rigid oath that would be binding on gods and men. Then the dwarf assumed a huge shape and stepped with the first pace over the whole earth, with the second over the atmosphere, with the third into the infinity of the heavens. This is the reason why Vishnu is called Tripadas, or Trivikramas, the three-paced god. Thus Balis was prevented completing the hundredth sacrifice, and Indra was again safe on his throne. This dwarf incarnation is called the Vamana-avatar.

The sixth incarnation, called the Parashura avatar, is historical in its character, for it reflects the struggles between the warrior-caste and the Brahmans for supremacy. It is said that Jamadagni, a pious Brahman, had received from the gods the miraculous cow, Kamadugha (or Surabhi), which provided him, his wife, Renuka, and their son, Rama, with every luxury. Karttavirya, a king of the warrior-caste, visits him, and seeing the wealth of the Brahman, tries to take the cow from him, but the cow kills all who dare to approach her, and rises into heaven, whereupon Karttavirya in his wrath slays the pious Jamadagni. Rama, the son of the murdered Brahman, invokes Vishnu's help for the punishment of the wicked king, and the god not only presents him with a bow and a battle-ax, which latter is called in Sanskrit *paracus,* the Greek πέλεκυς (hence the name of this avatar), but also incarnates himself in Rama. Karttavirya is described as being in possession of a thousand arms, wielding a thousand weapons, but Rama, endowed with the divine powers of Vishnu, conquers him after a decisive struggle.

The Rama Chandra avatar has taken a firm hold on the Indian mind, and is described in the Ramayana, an epic which is the Hindu Odyssey, to the narrative of which the legend of Rama bears a great resemblance.

Rama Chandra lived with his wife Sita (frequently regarded as an incarnation of Lakshmi) and with his half-brother Lakshmana in the wilderness of the south, where he had withdrawn in order to obey his father, who had unjustly banished him and appointed Bharata, another son of his, as heir to the throne. The demon-king, Ravana, waged war against Rama, and carried off Sita while he and his brother were hunting. It is impossible to relate here Rama's adventures in detail, how he fought with giants and demons, how the monkey kings, Lugriva and Hanuman, became his allies, how Hanuman jumped over to Lanka, the island of Ceylon, to reconnoitre the enemy's country, how the monkeys built a bridge over the strait by throwing stones into the water, how Rama pursued Ravana to Lanka, and finally how he vanquished Ravana and recovered his faithful wife Sita.

Like the sixth avatar, the Rama Chandra avatar probably contains historical reminiscences. It also resembles both the Trojan War and the Gudrun Saga, the epics of Western nations that relate the story of an abducted wife. The mythical part of all these stories describes the wanderings of the sun god in search of his consort, the moon.

In his eighth incarnation, the Krishna avatar, Vishnu has reached the ideal man-god of the Hindus. Kansa, called Kalankura (i.e., crane), the tyrant of Mathura, receives the prophecy that the eighth son of his sister, Devaki, will take his throne. He therefore decides to kill all the children of his sister. Her eighth son, Krishna, however, was an incarnation of Vishnu, who spoke at once after his birth, comforted his mother, and gave directions to his father, Vasudeva, how to save him. Vasudeva carried the infant, protected by the serpent king, over the river Jamuna, and exchanged him in Gokula for a girl which Yasuda had just borne to the cowherd Nanda. Kansa seized at once the girl baby, but before he could kill her she raised herself into the air, explained to the wrathful king that Krishna had been saved, and disappeared in the form of lightning. Kansa now decided to have all the babies in his empire killed, but Krishna escaped again. A demon nurse was sent to poison him with her venomous milk, but he bit and killed her, while his stepfather decided to remove to a more distant country in order to escape the continued hostilities of the king. Krishna slew the huge serpent, Kali-naga, overcame the giant Shishoo-polu, killed the monster bird that tried to peck out his eyes, and also a malignant wild ass. He also burnt the entrails of the alligator-shaped Peck-Assoort who had devoured him, and choked Aghi-Assoor, the dragon who attempted to swallow him. When Krishna had grown to youth he became the favorite of the lasses of Gokula. When he played the flute every one of the dancing girls believed that the swain whom she embraced was Krishna himself. He fell in love with the country girl Radha, the story of which is sung in the Jagadeva's poem, Gitagovinda. He protected the cowherds against storm and fire, and finally marched against Kansa, killed him and took possession of his throne.

Krishna plays also a prominent part in the Mahabharata, the Iliad of the Hindus, which describes the war between the Kurus and the Pandus,* both descendants of Bharata and both grandchildren of Vyasa. Dhritarashtra, the father of the Kurus, was king of Hastinapur, but being blind, Bhishma, his uncle, reigned in his stead. After a test of the faculties of the young princes, in which the Pandu Arjuna, the skilled bowman and the Hindu Tell, showed himself superior to all the others, the oldest Panduprince, Yudhishthira, was installed as heir apparent. The Kurus, however, who managed to remain in power, tried to burn the Pandus, but they escaped and lived for some time in the disguise of mendicant Brahmans. Having allied themselves, by

---

* The Pandus are also called Pandavas, and the Kurus Kamavas.

marriage with Draupadi,* the daughter of Drupada, king of Panchala, with a powerful monarch, the Pandus reappeared at Hastinapur and induced Dhritarashtra to divide the kingdom between his sons, the Kurus, and his nephews, the Pandus; but at a festival, held at Hastinapur, Yudhishthira, the chief of the Pandus, staked in a game of dice his kingdom, all his possessions, and Draupadi herself, and lost everything. The Kurus promised their cousins to return their share of the kingdom after thirteen years, if they would live twelve years with Draupadi in the forest and remain another year in exile; but when this period had elapsed the Kurus refused to give up the country or any part of it, and thus the war became unavoidable. Then Duryodhana, the Kuru prince, and Arjuna, the main hero of the Pandus, called on Krishna for succor and assistance. Krishna decided not to take an active part in the fight himself, but left to Arjuna, whom he had seen first, the choice between his (Krishna's) company as a mere adviser or his (Krishna's) army of a hundred million warriors. Arjuna chose Krishna himself, and left the hundred million warriors to his rivals, the Kurus. The two armies met on the field of Kurukshetra, near Delhi. During the battle, as we read in the Bhagavadgita, Krishna accompanies Arjuna as his charioteer and explains to him the depth and breadth of the religious philosophy of the Hindus. The Pandus conquer the Kurus, and Yudhishthira becomes king of Hastinapur. After sundry additional adventures the Pandus die and go to heaven, where they find that rest and happiness which is unattainable on earth.

The Mahabharata, like the Wars of the Roses, shows neither party in a favorable light; but the epic is written from the standpoint of the Pandus, whose demeanor is always extolled, while the Kurus are throughout characterised as extremely unworthy and mean.

Krishna is the Hindu Apollo, Orpheus, and Hercules in one person, and there is no god in the Hindu Pantheon who is dearer to the Brahman heart than he. Many of his adventures, such as his escape from the Hindu Herod, the massacre of babes, his transfiguration, etc., reappear

---

* That the five Pandus held Draupadi in common as their wife, proves the high antiquity of the story. Polyandry was apparently a practice not uncommon in ancient times. It prevails still today among the less cultured hill tribes. But being at variance with the Aryan customs of the age in which the Mahabharata was versified, Vyasa (the Homer or "arranger" of the poem, and its supposed author) tries to explain it allegorically by declaring that Draupadi is Lakshmi, and the five Pandu brothers represent five different forms of one and the same Indra.

in a modified form in Buddhist legends and bear some resemblance to the events told of Christ in the New Testament.

In his ninth incarnation Vishnu appears as Buddha, the enlightened one, to be a teacher of morals, of purity, charity, and compassionate love toward all beings. It is difficult to state the differences between the Buddha avatar of the Brahmans and the Buddha of the Buddhists. The latter, there can be no doubt, was a historical personality, by the name of Gautama, the son of Shuddhodana of the warrior caste, while the former is a mere ideal figure of ethical perfection. Burnouf* proposes to regard both as quite distinct, and he is right, but we need not for that reason deny that, on the one hand, the ideal of a Buddha avatar was a prominent factor in the formation of Buddhism, while on the other hand Gautama's teachings have, since the rise of Buddhism, powerfully affected and considerably modified the Buddha ideal of the Brahmans. Whatever may be the historical relation between the Hindu Buddha and the Buddha of the Buddhists, this much is sure: the Buddha has been received by the Brahmans as one of the members of the Hindu Pantheon.

The Hindu deity that is nearest in spirit to the Buddha avatar is Jagannath, the god of love and mercy.

The tenth avatar has not yet been completed. Vishnu is expected to appear on a winged white horse to reward the virtuous, convert the sinners, and destroy all evil.

The horse has one foot raised, and when it places its foot down, the time of the incarnation will find its fulfilment.

The third person of the Indian trinity is Siva, the Auspicious One, representing the end of the world and its regeneration. He is commonly represented by the *linga* as a symbol of the creative faculty and by the all-devouring fire, the tongued flame of which is pictured in a triangle turning its point upwards Δ.

Sir Monier Monier Williams (in *Brahmanism and Hinduism*, p. 68) says of this deity, which is "more mystical and less human than the incarnated Vishnu," that his symbol, the linga, is "never in the mind of a Saiva (or Siva-worshipper) connected with indecent ideas, nor with sexual love." The linga, or, as the Romans called it, the phallus, the male organ of generation, becomes at the first dawn of civilisation, almost among all the nations of the world, an object of great awe and

---

* *Histoire du Buddhisme,* I, p. 338.

reverence. As the symbol of the creative principle it is regarded as the most essential attribute of both the God-Creator himself and all those who hold authority in his name. The linga develops in the hand of the medicine man into a wand, in the hand of the priest into a staff, and in the hand of the king into a sceptre. The yoni, or female organ, is regarded as the symbol of Siva's consort, Parvati, and is worshipped in connexion with the linga by the sect of the Sactis. Perforated rocks are considered as emblems of the yoni, through which pilgrims pass for the purpose of being regenerated, a ceremony in which Hindus place great faith for its sin-expelling significance. (See Charles Coleman, *The Mythology of the Hindus*, p. 175.)

Siva's consort, Kali, is one of the greatest divinities of India. She is the goddess of a hundred names, representing not only the power of nature, but also the ruthless cruelty of nature's laws. She is called Parvati, the blessed mother, and Durga, which means "hard to go through," symbolising war and all kinds of danger. She is in the pantheon of modern Hinduism the central figure; and in spite of the universality of Brahma in philosophical speculations, in spite of the omnipresence of Vishnu and his constant reincarnations as told in ancient myths and legends, in spite of the omnipotence of Siva, and the high place given him in Hindu dogmatology, she is the main recipient of Hindu worship all over the country. As Kali she is identified with time, the all-devourer, and is pictured as enjoying destruction, perdition, and murder in any form, trampling under foot even her own husband. There is scarcely a village without a temple devoted to her, and her images can be seen in thousands of forms. Her appearance is pleasant only as Pavarti; in all other shapes she is frightful, and it is difficult to understand the reverence which the pious Hindu cherishes for this most diabolical deity, who among the Buddhists of Thibet is changed into a devilish demon under the name of mKha'sGroma.

The Pantheism which lies at the bottom of the whole Hindu mythology finds expression in the worship of HariHara, who is a combination of Vishnu and Siva. In the Mahatmya, or collection of temple legends of the HariHara, a town in the province of Mysore, Isvara says:*

---

* The legends of the shrine of HariHara, translated from the Sanskrit by Rev. Thomas Foulkes.

"There are heretics among men who reject the Vedas and the Shastras, who live without purificatory ceremonies and established rules of conduct, and are filled with hatred of Vishnu: so also there are heretical followers of Vishnu, who are similarly filled with hatred of Shiva. All these wicked men shall go to hell so long as this world endures. I will not receive worship from any man who makes a distinction between Vasudeva and my own divinity: I will divide every such man in two with my saw. For I have assumed the form of HariHara in order to destroy the teaching that there is a difference between us: and he who knows within himself that HariHara is the god of gods, shall inherit the highest heaven."

HariHara is depicted as a combination of the two gods in one figure, which is half male and half female, for according to the Southern version of the legend Vishnu assumed the form of a beautiful woman who was embraced so fervently by Siva that both became one.

There are in Hindu mythology innumerable other deities, among whom Indra, the thunder-god, is the greatest, as the hero among the gods of secondary rank, reminding us of the Thor of the Norsemen; but Varuna, the Hindu Kronos, Agni the god of fire, have also at times been very prominent.

There are in addition gods of third degree, such as Kama, the Hindu Amor, Ganesa, the elephant-headed god of wisdom,* and Karttikeya,† the leader of the good demons, on the peacock, both sons of Siva, and others. In addition, we have a great number of devas, sprites, and goblins. Some of them are good, as the Gandharvas, others at least not naturally ill-intentioned, as for instance the Apsaras (a kind of Hindu elves), but most of them are dangerous and demoniacal. Such are the general mischief-makers, the Asuras, the Pretas, or ghosts, the Bhutas, or spook-spirits, the baby-killing Grahas, the Rakshasas, who are either giants or vampires, not to mention all the other demons of less power and importance.

---

* Ganesa, which means the lord (*isa*) of hosts (*gana*), is originally Siva himself, and he was invoked under that name by writers of books to drive away evil demons.

† Karttikeya is also called Subrahmanya and Skanda.

Buddhism

Buddhism is a religious revolution against the evils that are dominant in Brahmanism. Gautama Shakyamuni, who claimed to be the Enlightened One, the Buddha, rejected bloody sacrifices, the authority of the Vedas, trust in rituals and the caste system, and taught a religion of moral endeavor which was to be obtained by enlightenment, or the bodhi. He recognised the existence of evil and sought salvation in the radical abolition of all selfishness through the extension of an all-comprehensive love toward all creatures.

The many-sidedness of Buddhism is well illustrated in the Buddhistic conception of evil and of a final escape from evil, which is taught to the thinker in the shape of a philosophy, and to the uneducated masses in the garb of a poetical myth, affording the artist a good opportunity for representing deep thoughts in allegorical form.

Mara, the Evil One

EVIL IS PERSONIFIED IN MARA, the Buddhist Devil, who represents temptation, sin, and death. He is identified with Namuche, one of the wicked demons in Indian mythology with whom Indra struggles. Namuche is the mischievous spirit who prevents rain and produces drought. The name Namuche means "not letting go the waters." However, Indra, the god of thunder-storms, forces him to surrender the fertilising liquids and restores the life-bringing element to the earth.

Mara is also called Papiyan* the Wicked One or the Evil One, the Murderer, the Tempter. In addition he is said to be Varsavarti,† meaning "he who fulfils desires." Varsavarti, indeed, is one of his favorite names. In his capacity as Varsavarti, Mara personifies the fulfilment of desire or the triple thirst,‡ viz., the thirst for existence, the thirst for pleasure, the thirst for power. He is the king of the Heaven of sensual delight.

---

* *Papiyan* means "more or very wicked"; it is the comparative form of the Sanskrit, *papin*, wicked.

† *Varsavarti* is Sanskrit. The Pâli form is *Vasavatti*, derived from *vasa*, wish, desire. Childers explains the word as "bringing into subjection." Mara is also called Paranimmita Vasavatti, which means "bringing into subjection that which is created by others."

‡ Pâli *tanha*; Sanskrit, *trishna*.

There is a deep truth in this conception of Mara as Varsavarti. It means that the selfishness of man is Satan and the actual satisfaction of selfishness is Hell.

This reminds us of one of Leander's *Märchen*, in which we are told that once a man died and awoke in the other world. There St. Peter appeared before him and asked him what he wanted. He then ordered breakfast, the daily papers, and all the comforts he was accustomed to in life, and this kind of life lasted for many centuries until he got sick of it and began to swear at St. Peter and to complain of how monotonous it was in Heaven, whereupon St. Peter informed him that he was in Hell, for hell is where everybody has his own sweet will, and heaven is where everybody follows God's will alone. Similarly, according to the Buddhist conception, the heaven of sensual delight is hell, the habitation of the Evil One.

In the Dhammapada, Mara is not so much a person as a personification. The allegorical nature of the Evil One is plainly felt in every passage in which Mara's name occurs. We read, for instance:

"He who lives looking for pleasures only, his senses uncontrolled, immoderate in his food, idle and weak, him Mara will certainly overthrow as the wind throws down a feeble tree."

Buddhism in its original and orthodox purity knows nothing of devils except Mara, representing the egotistical pleasures, sensuality, sin, and death; but Buddhist mythology from the ancient Jatakas down to the most modern folklore of China and Japan has peopled the universe with evil spirits of all kinds, such as the demons of thunder and lightning, to personify the various ills of life and the dangers that lurk everywhere in nature.

While the evil consequences of sin are depicted in the tortures of Hell which are similar to the Christian belief, the final escape from evil is expressed in the belief that all good Buddhists will be reborn in the Western Paradise.

Mara, the Enemy of Buddha

IN THE LIFE OF BUDDHA, Mara plays an important part. He is that principle which forms an obstacle to the attainment of Buddhahood. Having told how, in the night of the great renunciation, the deity of the door swung the gate open to let the future Buddha out, the Jataka continues:

> "At that moment Mara came there with the intention of stopping the Bodisat; and standing in the air, he exclaimed, 'Depart not, O my lord! in seven days from now the wheel of empire will appear, and will make you sovereign over the four continents and the two thousand adjacent isles. Stop, O my lord!'"

The prince refused to listen to Mara's wily insinuation.

When Buddha, in his search for enlightenment, had tried for seven years to find the right path in asceticism and self-mortification, his health began to give way and he was shrunken like a withered branch. At this moment Mara drew near and suggested to him the thought of giving up his search for enlightenment. We read in the Padhana Sutta:*

> "Came Namuche speaking words full of compassion: 'Thou art lean, ill-favored, death is in thy neighborhood. Living life, O thou Venerable One, is better! Living, thou wilt be able to do good works. Difficult is the way of exertion, difficult to pass, difficult to enter upon.'
>
> "To Mara, thus speaking, Bhagavat said: 'O thou friend of the indolent, thou wicked one, for what purpose hast thou come here? Even the least good work is of no use to me, and what good works are required ought Mara to tell? I have faith and power; and understanding is found in me. While thus exerting myself, why do you ask me to live? While the flesh is wasting away the mind grows more tranquil, and my attention, understanding, and meditation becomes more steadfast. Living thus, my mind does not look for sensual pleasures. Behold a being's purity!
>
> "Lust thy first army is called; discontent thy second; thy third is called hunger and thirst; thy fourth desire; thy fifth is called sloth and drowsiness; thy sixth cowardice; thy seventh doubt; thy eighth hypocrisy and stupor, gain, fame, honor, and what celebrity is falsely obtained by him who exalts himself and despises others. This, O Namuche, is thine, the Black One's fighting army. None but a hero conquers it, and whoever conquers it obtains joy. Woe

---

* *Scared Books of the East.* Vol. X, second part, pp. 69–71.

upon life in this world! Death in battle is better for me than that I should live defeated.

"Seeing on all sides an army arrayed and Mara on his elephant, I am going out to do battle that he may not drive me from my place. This army of thine, which the world of men and gods cannot conquer, I will crush with understanding, as one crushes an unbaked earthen pot with a stone.

"Having made my thoughts subject to me and my attention firm, I shall wander about from kingdom to kingdom training disciples. They will be zealous and energetic, obedient to the discipline of one free from lust, and they will go to the place where there is no mourning.

"And Mara said: 'For seven years I followed Bhagavat, step by step, but found no fault in the Perfectly Enlightened and Thoughtful One.'"

When Buddha went to the Bo-tree Mara, the Evil One, proposed to shake his resolution, either through the allurements of his daughters or by force. "He sounded the war cry and drew out for battle." The earth quaked, when Mara, mounted on his elephant, approached the Buddha. The gods, among them Sakka, the king of the gods, and Brahma, tried to stay Mara's army, but none of them was able to stand his ground, and each fled straight before him. Buddha said:

"'Here is this multitude exerting all their strength and power against me alone. My mother and father are not here, nor a brother, nor any other relative. But I have these Ten Perfections, like old retainers long cherished at my board. It therefore behooves me to make the Ten Perfections my shield and my sword, and to strike a blow with them that shall destroy this strong array.' And he remained sitting and reflected on the Ten Perfections."

—*Buddhism in Translations*
By H. C. Warren, pp. 77–78

Mara caused a whirlwind to blow, but in vain; he caused a rain-storm to come in order to drown the Buddha, but not a drop wetted his robes; he caused a shower of rocks to come down, but the rocks changed into bouquets; he caused a shower of weapons—swords, spears, and arrows—to rush against him, but they became celestial flowers; he caused a shower of live coals to come down from the sky, but they, too, fell down harmless. In the same way hot ashes, a shower of sand, and a shower of mud were transmuted into celestial ointments. At last he caused a darkness, but the darkness disappeared before Buddha, as the night vanishes before the sun. Mara shouted: "Siddhattha, arise from the seat. It does not belong to you. It belongs to me." Buddha replied: "Mara, you have not fulfilled the ten perfections. This seat does not belong to you, but to me, who have fulfilled the ten perfections." Mara denied Buddha's assertion and called upon his army as witnesses, while Buddha declared: "I have no animate witnesses present;" but, stretching out his right hand towards the mighty earth, he said: "Will you bear me witness?" And the mighty earth thundered: "I bear you witness." And Mara's elephant fell upon its knees, and all the followers of Mara fled away in all directions. When the hosts of the gods saw the army of Mara flee, they cried out: "Mara is defeated! Prince Siddhattha has conquered! Let us celebrate the victory!"

When Buddha had attained enlightenment, Mara tempted him once more, saying:

"Pass away now, Lord, from existence! Let the Blessed One now die! Now is the time for the Blessed One to pass away!"

Buddha made reply as follows:

"I shall not die, O Evil One! until not only the brethren and sisters of the order, but also the lay-disciples of either sex shall have become true hearers, wise and well trained, ready and learned, versed in the Scriptures, fulfilling all the greater and the lesser duties, correct in life, walking according to the precepts,—until they, having thus themselves learned the doctrine, shall be able to tell others, of it, preach it, make it known, establish it, open it, minutely explain it and make it clear,—until they, when others start vain doctrines, shall be able by the truth to vanquish and refute it, and so to spread the wonder-working truth abroad!

"I shall not die until this pure religion of mine shall have become successful, prosperous, wide-spread, and popular in all its full extent, until, in a word, it shall have been well proclaimed among men!"

When, shortly before Buddha's death, Mara repeated his words as quoted above, "Pass away now, Lord, from existence," Buddha answered:

"Make thyself happy; the final extinction of the Tathagata shall take place before long."

Mara in Buddhist Art

IN THE VARIOUS SCULPTURES REPRESENTING scenes of Buddha's life there is a figure holding in his hand a kind of double club or vajra—i. e., thunderbolt, as it is usually called. Since the expression of this man with the thunderbolt decidedly shows malevolence, the interpretation naturally suggested itself that he must be one of Buddha's disciples who was antagonistic to his teachings. The common explanation of this figure, accordingly, designated him as Devadatta, the Buddhistic Judas Iscariot, who endeavored to found a sect of his own, and who according to Buddhistic legends is represented as an intriguer bent on the murder of Buddha. The various representations of this figure, however, are not altogether those of a disciple who tries to outdo Buddha in sternness and severity of discipline, but frequently bear the character of a Greek faun, and resemble, rather, Silenus, the foster-father of Bacchus, representing all kinds of excesses in carousing and other pleasures. Moreover, the same figure with the thunderbolt appears in representations of Buddha's entering Nirvana, at a time when Devadatta had been long dead. Alfred Grünwedel, for these reasons, proposes to abandon the traditional interpretation of the thunderbolt-bearer as Devadatta, and it appears that he has found the right interpretation when he says:*

"This figure which accompanies Buddha from the moment he leaves his father's house until he enters Nirvana, and who waylays him in the hope of awakening in him a thought of lust or hatred or envy, who follows him like a shadow, can be no one but Mara Papiyan, the Wicked One, the demon of passion. The thunderbolt in Mara's hand is nothing but the old attribute of all Indian gods. In his capacity as the god of pleasure, Mara is especially entitled to this attribute of the Hindu gods. As

---

* *Buddhistische Kunst in Indien.* Berlin: Speman, p. 87.

Vasavatti he reigns in the highest domain of the pleasure heaven, surrounded by dancing girls and musicians."

It seems probable that the contrast in which Mara or Varsavarti stands to the Buddha began by and by to be misunderstood. For the thunderbolt-bearer Vajrapani is gradually changed into a regular attendant of Buddha, and the Vajra, or thunderbolt, is now interpreted as an attribute of Buddha himself. Thus it happened that among the northern Buddhists the Vajra became the indispensable attribute of the lamas. It is called Dorje in Tibet and Ojir in Mongolia.

THE ATTACK OF MARA UPON Buddha under the bo-tree is a favorite subject of Buddhist artists, who gladly avail themselves of this opportunity to show their ingenuity in devising all kinds of beautiful and hideous shapes. Beautiful women represent the temptations of the daughters of Mara, and the hideous monsters describe the terrors of Mara's army.

In Buddhistic mythology Mara, the Evil One, is, in harmony with the spirit of Buddha's teachings, represented as the Prince of the World. It is Mara who holds the wheel of life and death (*Chavachakra*, i.e., wheel of becoming) in his hands, for all living beings reside in the domain of death. The hand of death is upon every one who is born. He is the ruler in the domains of the *nidanas,* the twelve links of the chain of causation, or dependent origination.

The Twelve Nidanas

THE TWELVE NIDANAS ARE A very old doctrine, which possibly goes back to Buddha himself, and may contain elements that are older. While the general meaning of the chain of causation is clearly indicated by the first and last links, which imply that ignorance, not-knowing, or infatuation is at the bottom of all evil, there are great difficulties in the interpretation of the details, and Mr. Warren thinks that it is a combination of two chains of causation representing similar thoughts. He says:

"The Buddhist Sacred Books seem to claim Dependent Origination as the peculiar discovery of the Buddha, and I suppose they would have us understand that he invented the whole formula from beginning to end. But it is to be observed that the formula repeats itself, that the human being is brought into existence twice—the first time under the name of consciousness, and name and form and by means of ignorance and karma, the second time in birth and by means of desire (with its four branches called attachments) and karma again, this time called existence.* Therefore, though Buddhaghosa is at great pains to explain this repetition as purposely intended for practical ends, yet one is much inclined to surmise that the full formula in its present shape is a piece of patchwork put together of two or more that were current in the Buddha's time and by him— perhaps expanded, perhaps contracted, but at any rate made into one. If the Buddha added to the formula of Dependent Origination, it would appear that the addition consisted in the first two propositions. For ignorance, of course, is the opposite of wisdom, and wisdom is the method for getting rid of ignorance."

—*Buddhism in Translations,* p. 115

Whatever may have been the original wording, the traditional formula of the causation of evil has been, without change, faithfully preserved in the triumphal progress of Buddhism from India to Japan. One of the oldest passages in which the twelve nidanas are enumerated is found in the *Questions of King Milinda,* p. 79, where we read:

"By reason of ignorance came the Confections,† by reason of the Confections consciousness, by reason of consciousness name-and-form, by reason of name-and-form the six organs of sense, by reason of them contact, by reason of contact sensation, by reason of sensation thirst, by reason of thirst craving, by reason of craving becoming, by reason of becoming birth, by reason of birth old age and death, grief, lamentation, sorrow, pain, and despair. Thus is it that the ultimate point in the past of all this time is not apparent."

—Translated by T. W. Rhys Davids in
Sacred Books of the East, Vol. XXXV

The Samyutta Nikaya enumerates as the second nidana "karma," i.e., action. The passage reads:

---

* The Visudhi Magga declares karma-existence is equivalent to existence.
† Confection is a bad translation of *Sankhâra,* formation or deed-form. See *The Dharma,* pp. 16–18.

"On ignorance depends karma;

"On karma depends consciousness;

"On consciousness depend name and form;

"On name and form depend the six organs of sense;

"On the six organs of sense depends contact;

"On contact depends sensation;

"On sensation depends desire;

"On desire depends attachment;

"On attachment depends existence;

"On existence depends birth;

"On birth depend old age and death, sorrow, lamentation, misery, grief, and despair. Thus does this entire aggregation of misery arise.

"But on the complete fading out and cessation of ignorance ceases karma;

"On the cessation of karma ceases consciousness;

"On the cessation of consciousness ceases name and form;

"On the cessation of name and form cease the six organs of sense;

"On the cessation of the six organs of sense ceases contact;

"On the cessation of contact ceases sensation;

"On the cessation of sensation ceases desire;

"On the cessation of desire ceases attachment;

"On the cessation of attachment ceases existence;

"On the cessation of existence ceases birth;

"On the cessation of birth cease old age and death, sorrow, lamentation, misery, grief, and despair. Thus does this entire aggregation of misery cease."

—Buddhism in Translations,
Warren, p. 166

The Pali terms are: (1) *avijja* (ignorance), (2) *sankhara* (organised formation) or *kamma* (Karma), (3) *vinnyana* (sentiency), (4) *nama-rupa* (name and form, i.e., individuality), (5) *salayatana* (the six fields, i.e., the five senses and mind), (6) *phasso* (contact), (7) *vedana* (sensation), (8) *tanha* (thirst), (9) *upadana* (craving), (10) *bhava* (growth), (11) *jati* (birth), (12) *jaramarana,* etc. (old age, death, sorrow, etc.).

It seems that we have three chains of causation combined into one. One chain explains that Karma, i.e., deed or activity, produces first *vinnyana* (sentiency), and then *nama-rupa* (name and form, or personality); the other begins with sensation, as known in the six senses or *salayatana,* which by contact *(phasso)* produces first consciousness *(vedana)* and then thirst *(tanha).* The third group, which may be the peculiarly Buddhistic addition to the two older formulas, is founded in the first, or first and second, and the four concluding links of the traditional chain, stating that ignorance *(avija)* produces blindly in in its random work organisations *(sankharas).* These sankharas or elementary organisms are possessed of craving *(upadana), which leads to conception (bhava)* and birth *(jati),* thus producing old age, death, sorrow, and misery of any kind.

The Wheel of Life

LIFE IN ITS ETERNAL ROTATION is represented in Buddhist mythology as a wheel that is held in the clutches of the Evil One.

Judging from a communication of Caroline A. Foley (in the *Journal of the Royal Asiatic Society,* 1894, p. 389), the allegory of the world-wheel, the wheel of life, must be much older than is commonly thought, for it is mentioned already in the *Divyavadana,* pp. 299–300. Caroline Foley says:

> "There it is related how Buddha instructed Ananda to make a wheel *(cakram karayitavyam)* for the purpose of illustrating what another disciple, Maudgalyayana, saw when he visited other spheres, which it seems he was in the habit of doing. The wheel was to have five spokes *(pancagandakam),* between which were to be depicted the hells, animals, pretas, gods, and men. In the middle a dove, a serpent, and a hog, were to symbolise lust, hatred, and ignorance. All round the tire was to go the twelve-fold circle of causation *(pratityasamutpado)* in the regular and in the inverse order. Beings were to be represented 'as being born in a supernatural way *(aupapadukah),* as by the machinery of a waterwheel, falling from one state and being produced in another.' The wheel was made and placed in the 'grand entrance gateway' *(dvarakoshtake),* and a bhikshu appointed to interpret it."

Samsara, or the circuit of life, the eternal round of birth, death, and rebirth, as summarily expressed in the doctrine of the twelve nidanas or twelve-linked chain of causation, is painted around the tire of the wheel.

How carefully the Buddhistic conception of Mara, as the Prince of the world, holding in his clutches the wheel of life, has been preserved, we can learn from a comparison of an old fresco in the deserted caves of Ajanta, Central India,* with Tibetan and Japanese pictures of the same subject.† All of them show in the centre the three causes of selfhood, viz., hatred, spite, and sloth, symbolised in a serpent, a cock, and a pig. They are also called the three fires, or the three roots of evil, which are *raga* (passion), *doso* (sin), *moho* (infatuation). The Hindu picture exhibits six divisions,—the realm of gods, the realm of men, the realm of nagas (or snakes),‡ the realm of paradise, the realm of ghosts, and the realm of hell. The Tibetan picture shows the same domains, only less distinctly separated, while the Japanese picture shows only five divisions. In order to show the omnipresence of the Buddha as the principle that sustains all life, the Japanese picture shows a Buddha statue in the hub, while in the Hindu wheel every division contains a Buddha figure. This Buddha in the world is the Buddha of transformations, *Nirmana-Kaya*, representing the tendency of life toward enlightenment. Outside of the wheel two other Buddha figures appear. At the right-hand corner there is Buddha, the teacher, in the attitude of expounding the good law of righteousness. It is the *Dharma-Kaya*, the Buddha embodied in the dharma, i.e. the law, religion, or truth. In the left-hand corner there is Buddha in the state of rest, represented as *Sambhoga-Kaya*, the Buddha who has entered into Nirvana and attained the highest bliss.

The twelve nidanas are an essential element in the Buddhist wheel of life, and are commonly represented by twelve little pictures either on the tire or surrounding the tire.

On the Japanese wheel, which exhibits the nidanas more clearly than the older wheels, the series begins at the bottom, rising to the left-hand side and turning down again on the right-hand side.

The first nidana (in Pali *Avijja*), ignorance, is pictured as a passionate man of brutish appearance.

---

* Described by L. A. Waddell, M. B., M. R. A. S., in the *Journal of the Royal Asiatic Society*, April, 1894. Luxuriously reproduced in colors on Plate 8, Vol. I, of *The Paintings in the Buddhist Cave Temples of Ajanta*, by John Griffiths. London, Griggs, 1896.

† The Tibetan and Japanese pictures are explained by Professor Bastian in his *Ethnologisches Bilderbuch*.

‡ We must remember that in some parts of India the serpent is the symbol of perfection and wisdom,—a belief which was adopted by the Ophites, a gnostic sect that revered the snake of the Garden of Eden as the instructor in the knowledge of good and evil and the originator of science.

The second nidana (in Pali *Sankhara*, Sanskrit *Samskara*), which is commonly but badly translated in English by "confection," represents the ultimate constitutions of life or primary forms of organisation, meaning a disposition of structures that possess the tendency to repeat the function once performed. It is represented as a potter's wheel on which vessels are manufactured. The word should not be confused with *samsara*, which is the whole wheel of life, or the eternal round of transmigration.

The third nidana is vinnyana, or awareness, being the sentiency that originates by the repetition of function in the dispositions or organised structures previously formed. It is animal sense-perception, represented as a monkey.

The fourth nidana is "nama-rupa," i.e., name and form, which expression denotes what we call personality, the name of a person and his personal appearance. It is represented by a pilot steering a boat.

The fifth nidana is called the six fields or "shadayatana," which are what we call the five senses and mind, or thinking, which is considered by Buddhists as a sixth sense. It is pictured as a human organism.

The sixth nidana is "phasso" or "sparsa," i.e., the contact of the six fields, with their objects, represented as a lover's embrace.

Rising from a contact of the six fields with their objects, the seventh nidana is produced as "vedana," i.e., sensation or sentiment, illustrated by a sighing lover. If the sixth nidana is enacted in the garden scene of Goethe's "Faust," the seventh is characterised by Margaret's song, "My peace is gone, my heart is sore." (Scene xv.)

From sentiment, as the eighth nidana, "tanha," i.e., thirst or desire, rises. The picture exhibits the flirtation of two separated lovers.

The ninth nidana is "upadana," i.e., the clinging to existence. The picture shows us the lover following the footsteps of his love.

The tenth nidana is "bhava" (bridal embrace), or existence in its continuation, finding its artistic expression in the union of the lovers, who, seated on the back of an elephant, are celebrating their marriage feast.

The eleventh nidana is birth, "jati," in the picture represented as a woman in her throes.

The remaining groups represent the twelfth nidana and its various sufferings, which consist of old age, disease, death, lamentation, complaints, punishments, and all kinds of tribulations.

The twelve pictures on the Hindu wheel are less distinct, but there is no question about their meaning being exactly the same. Beginning at the top on the righthand side, we find first an angry man, representing ignorance, then a figure which might be a potter forming vessels of clay on the potter's wheel, representing the formation of dispositions or primary soul-forms. The third picture represents a monkey climbing a tree, symbolising animal perception or the individuality of organisms. The fourth picture shows a ship on a stream, representing the origin of mind under the allegory of a pilot. The fifth picture seems to be a house built upon five foundation stones, which we interpret as the five senses, the superstructure representing mind, the sixth sense. Then follows the sixth picture, a woman, kindling desire of contact. The seventh represents sentiment in the shape of two sighing lovers. The eighth picture represents thirst or desire as two separated lovers. The ninth picture, reminding us of Adam and Eve in Paradise, is a man plucking flowers or fruits from a tree; it illustrates the tasting of the apple of sexual love. The tenth picture illustrates pregnancy, the eleventh birth, and the twelfth is the demon of death carrying away the white body of a dead man.

THE WHEEL OF LIFE AS now frequently pictured in Buddhist temples of Japan can, in its wanderings from India through Tibet and China, be traced back to a remote antiquity, for we know positively that this conception of the Evil One in his relation to the world, existed about two thousand years ago, in the days when Buddhism still flourished in India, but it is not improbable that it must be dated back to a time preceding Buddha. We may fairly assume that when Buddha lived, such or similar representations of the significance of evil in life existed and that he utilised the traditional picture for the purposes of spreading his own religion, adding thereto his own interpretation, and thus pouring new wine into old bottles. There is a possibility that the picture must be dated back to the age of demonolatry, when the idea prevailed that the good god need not be worshipped but only the evil god, because he alone is dangerous to mankind.

That the same idea as expressed in the Buddhist wheel of life existed in the remotest antiquity of our earliest civilisations can be seen at a glance by looking at the picture of the Chaldean bronze tablet (on p. 46 of this volume), which represents the three worlds, the realm of the gods, the abode of men, and the domain of the dead, as being held in the clutches of a terrible monster. The similarity of the tablet to the Buddhist wheel of life is too striking to be fortuitous.

Religious symbols, formulas, and rites are, as a rule, punctiliously preserved even after a radical change of the fundamental ideas that are embodied therein. Judging by analogy from the religious evolution of other nations, we must assume that the original form of worship among the Accadians was as much demonolatrous as it is at a certain stage of civilisation among all savage tribes, and this bronze plate appears to preserve the lingering features of a prehistoric world-conception. The simplest explanation that suggests itself is to regard the monster holding the world-picture as the deity of evil, who in the period when religion still consisted merely in the fear of evil, was worshipped as the actual prince of the world whose wrath was propitiated by bloody sacrifices.

If this view should prove to be correct, the Chaldean bronze plate of the monster holding in its claws the world would be the connecting link between the very dawn of religious notions with the foundation of Buddhism, where the worship of the evil deity has disappeared entirely. But the influence of this old mode of expression extends even into the sphere of the origin of Christianity, although here it fades from sight. In the New Testament the Buddhist term "the wheel of life" is used once more, but it is a mere echo of a remote past; its original significance is no longer understood. Speaking of the great damage caused in the world by the tongue, St. James says:

"οὕτως ἡ γλῶσσα καθίσταται ἐν τοῖς μέλεσιν ἡμῶν ἡ σπιλοῦσα ὅλον τὸ σῶμα καὶ φλογίζουσα τὸν τροχὸν τῆς γενέσεως, καὶ φλογιζομένη ὑπὸ τῆς γεέννης."

[Thus the tongue that defileth the whole body standeth among our limbs; and it setteth on fire the wheel of becoming and is set on fire by hell.]

The version of King James translates the term τροχὸς γενέσεως which in the Vulgate reads *rosa nativitatis*, by "course of nature."

Northern Buddhism

THE BUDDHISM OF TIBET IS not yet sufficiently explored on account of the inaccessibility of the country, but it is safe to say that its demonology is highly developed and shows traces of strong Hindu influences. Prominent among the evil spirits is mKha'sGroma, the Tibetan form of the Hindu Goddess Kali (see p. 99), who is represented as a frightful monster with a leonine head, surrounded by a halo of flames and ready to devour everything she sees.

In China Taoism, Confucianism, and Buddhism exist peacefully side by side, and there is scarcely a home in the country where the customary homage would not be paid to Lao-Tsze and Confucius as well as to Buddha. Indeed, there are numerous illustrations in which these three great masters are together represented as dominating the moral life of China.

In Japan the conditions are similar, except that in the place of the popular Taoism we find Shintoism, which is the aboriginal nature-worship of the country, consisting at present in the observation of national festivals, in which form it has of late been declared to be the official state religion of the country.

The folklore of Chinese Taoism and Japanese Shintoism was naturally embodied in the mythology of the Buddhists, and we find therefore in their temples innumerable representations of hell with all their traditional belongings; Emma, the stern judge of Meifu, the dark tribunal; Kongo, the sheriff, and all the terrible staff of bailiffs, torturers, and executioners, among whom the steer-headed Gozu and the horse-headed Mezu are never missing. By the side of the judge's desk stands the most perfect mirror imaginable, for it reflects the entire personality of every being. Since man's personality, according to the Buddhistic soul-conception, is constituted by the deeds done during life, the glass makes apparent all the words, thoughts, and actions of the delinquent who is led before it; whereupon he is dealt with according to his deserts. If good deeds prevail, he is rewarded by being reincarnated in a higher state of existence, be it on earth, or in the Western Paradise, or in one of the heavens of the gods; or, if bad deeds prevail, he sinks into lower spheres, in which case he must go back to life in the shape of that creature which represents his peculiar character; or, if he has been very wicked, he is doomed to hell, whither he is carried in the *ho nokuruma*, the fiery cart, the conveyance of the infernal regions. The sentence is pronounced in these words:

"Thy evil deeds are not the work of thy mother, father, relatives, friends, advisers. Thou alone hast done them all; thou alone must gather the fruit." (Devad. S.)

Dragged to the place of torment, he is fastened to red hot irons, plunged into fiery lakes of blood, raked over burning coals, and "he dies not till the last residue of his guilt has been expiated."

But the Devil is not always taken seriously, and it appears that the Chinese and Japanese exhibit all the humor they are capable of in their devil pictures and statues, among which the Oni-no-Nembutzu, the Devil as a monk, is perhaps the most grotesque figure.

In the later development of Northern Buddhism, all the evils of this world, represented in various devil personalities, are conceived as incarnations of Buddha himself, who, by showing the evil consequences of sin, endeavors to convert mankind to holiness and virtue.

We find in the Buddhist temples of China and Japan so-called Mandaras, which represent the world-conception of Buddhism in its cosmic entirety. The word *Mandara* means "a complete *ensemble*," and it exhibits a systematically arranged group of Buddha-incarnations. The statue of the highest Buddha who dwells in Nirvana always stands in the centre. It is "Bodhi," enlightenment, or "Sambodhi," perfect enlightenment, that is to say, the Truth, eternal rightness, or rather, Verity, the objective reality that is represented in truth, which is the same forever and aye. He is personified under the name Amitabha, which means boundless light, being that something the recognition of which constitutes Buddhahood. He is like God, the Father of the Christians, omnipresent and eternal, the light and life of the world, and the ultimate authority of moral conduct. Another prominent Buddha incarnation is Maitreya, the Buddha to come, who is the Christian holy spirit. He is the comforter whose appearance was promised by Buddha shortly before parting from his disciples.

The catalogue of the Musée Guimet of Paris, the best religious museum in the world, describes a Mandara, in which the highest Buddha in the centre of the group is surrounded by a number of his incarnations of various degrees and dignities. These are the Bodhisattvas, prophets and sages of the world, who have either taught mankind or set them good examples by their virtuous lives. On the right we see a group of personified abstracts,—piety, charity, science, religion, the aspiration for progress. On the left is a third class, consisting of the ugly figures of demons, whose appearance is destined to frighten people away from sensuality, egotism, and evil desires.

The devils of Buddhism, accordingly, are not the enemies of Buddha, and not even his antagonists, but his ministers and co-workers. They partake of Buddha's nature, for they, too, are teachers. They are the rods of punishment, representing the curse of sin, and as such have also been fitly conceived as incarnations of the Bodhi. In this interpretation, the Buddhist devils cease to be torturers and become instruments of education who contribute their share to the general system of working out the final salvation of man.

Christian salvation consists in an atonement of sin through the bloody sacrifice of a sinless redeemer; Buddhist salvation is attained through enlightenment. Hence Christ is the sufferer, the innocent man who dies to pay with his life the debt of others who are guilty. Buddha is the teacher who by example and instruction shows people the path of salvation.

The Dawn of a New Era

Gnostic Societies and Congregations

The transition from the Old to the New Testament is an age of unrest. The Jews had become familiar with the civilisation of Assyria and Babylonia, and enjoyed friendly relations with the Persians. But the intercourse and general exchange of thought among the nations of Western Asia became more extended and grew livelier since Alexander the Great's time, for now Greek as well as Indian views mixed and produced a powerful fermentation in the religious beliefs of the people. We may fairly assume that the doctrines of the Hindu reached Syria in vague and frequently self-contradictory forms, but they were new and attractive, and apt to revolutionise the traditional ethics of the people. Formerly procreation of children was regarded as a duty and the acquisition of wealth as a blessing, now it became known that there were also people who sought salvation in absolute chastity and poverty. The highest morality of the monks of India was no longer the strength of maintaining oneself in the struggle for existence, but the surrender of all strife and a radical renunciation of self.

There are especially three ideas which dominated the whole movement and acted as a leaven in the dough: the idea of the spirituality of the soul, the hope of the soul's escape from bodily existence, and the method of obtaining this liberation by wisdom ($\sigma o\varphi i\alpha$) or enlightenment ($\gamma\nu\tilde{\omega}\sigma\iota\varsigma$).

The realisation of the Gnostic ideal was called $\pi\lambda\eta\rho\tilde{\omega}\mu\alpha$ or fulfilment, which was either expected by the soul's attainment of salvation after the fashion of the Buddhist Nirvâna, or for the whole world through the appearance of a savior—a messiah.

The spirit of the times showed itself in the foundation of various religious societies, which originated somewhat after the fashion of the modern theosophical movements. There were bands of students of the new problems in almost all larger cities, who investigated the doctrines of salvation and immortality, and in addition there were enthusiasts who tried to apply the new principles in practical life. The former called themselves μαθηταί, learners or disciples, the latter holy ones (ἄγιοι), or healers (θεραπευταί, therapeutae).*

With regard to the problem of evil, the most peculiar sect were the Gnostics of Syria whom the Church fathers called serpent-worshippers or Ophites, because on becoming acquainted with the Biblical books they regarded Yahveh, the demiurge or author of this visible and material world, as an evil deity while the serpent with his promise of giving knowledge or gnosis to man, appeared to them as a messenger of the true and good God. This God of goodness, they declared, was unlike Yahveh free of passions and full of love and mercy. He was, as Irenæus informs us, triune, being at once the Father, the Son, and the Spirit. The Father is the prototype of man, an idea which is carried out in the Cabala as the Adam Kadmon; the Son is the eternal reason or comprehension ('Έννοια), and the Spirit is the female principle of spiritual generation.

Similar ideas concerning the triune Godhead and the salvation from evil are reported of other sects and especially of Simon Magus who is mentioned in the Acts as having been baptised by St. Peter and condemned for his opinion that the Holy Ghost could be bought with money.

We know of sects in Judæa, the Nazarenes, the Sabians† or Baptisers, the Essenes, and the Ebionites, which were born of the same seeking spirit of the age. But we must bear in mind that the members of these societies belonged exclusively to the poorer class of society and formed a third party which was quite distinct from the orthodox Pharisees and the liberal Sadducees.‡ They are to us of importance, however, because from their midst proceeded the man who was destined to become the

---

* Philo explains the name "therapeutæ" also as "worshippers." The genuineness of Philo's book *De vita contemplativa* and with it the very existence of the therapeutæ has been doubted by P. E. Lucius, whose views, however, are thoroughly refuted by Fred. C. Conybeare, *Philo About the Contemplative Life* (Clarendon Press, Oxford, 1895)

† St. John the Baptist was a Sabian. The name is derived from צבה (tsabha) to baptise.

‡ The word Essenes, or Essees (in Greek Ἐσσηνοί and Ἐσσαῖοι, in Latin Esseni), is derived by Ewald from סין preserver, guardian, a rabbinical term, because they called themselves "watchers, guardians, servants of God." Others derive the word from אסא (to heal). Both derivations would remind one of the Therapeutæ. The root חסה (to fly, to take refuge) seems to be quite probable, philologically considered, especially as the word is used in the sense in which the Buddhist takes refuge in the Dharma, illustrated in such phrases as חסה ב יהוה (to take refuge in God), Psalms ii. 12; v. 15; vii. 2; xxv. 20; xxxi. 2; xxxvii. 40, etc. A fourth derivation is from חסד (to be pious, to be enthusiastic, to be zealous in love). Philo says they are called "Essenes" on account of their holiness (παρά τὴν ὁσιότητα) and

standard bearer of a new faith and the representative incarnation of the new religion—Jesus of Nazareth.

The Apocrypha of the Old Testament

THE LITERATURE OF THIS PERIOD was no longer received into the canon of the Old Testament and is therefore in spite of many good qualities even to the present day regarded as apocryphal.

The new world-conception which emphasised the contrast between body and soul developed a new moral ideal; and the conception of evil underwent the same subtle changes as the conception of goodness. Since the lower classes began to make their influence felt, it is natural that in the Apocryphal Books of the Old Testament the conception of Satan grew more mythological and at the same time more dualistic. He developed into an independent demon of evil, and now, perhaps under the influence of Persian views, the adversary of man became the adversary of God himself.

In the story of Tobit (150 B.C.) an evil spirit called Asmodi plays an important part. His name which in its original form is *Aeshma Daeva,* indicates a Persian origin. He tries to prevent Sarah's marriage, because he is in love with her himself. In the Talmud, Asmodi develops into the demon of lust.

Very valuable books among the Apocrypha are the book of Daniel and the two books of Esdras; but the noblest thoughts are mixed with Judaistic chauvinism and bitter hatred of the Gentile nations.

Esdras anticipates the general eschatology as well as many smaller details of the Christian doctrines in a more definite shape than any

uses the term δσιοι, i.e., "the saints," or "the holy ones," as a synonym for Essenes. This hint, however, is of little avail, as it would suit almost any one of the various derivations.

The word Ebionites אֶבְיוֹנִים means the poor.

The early Christians seem to have been most closely allied with the Nazarenes, for as early as in the year 54 of our era (see Harnack's *Chronologie,* p. 237) St. Paul was accused by the Jewish authorities of being a ringleader of the sect of the Nazarenes. (Acts, xxiv. 5.)

The name ΝαζωραῖοιName (sometimes Ναζαρηνοί) has nothing to do with the name of the town of Nazareth (Ναζαρξθ), which was presumably written with a צ (*Tsaddi*) or sharp *ts* sound. The name Nazareth is nowhere mentioned in its original Aramaic form, and occurs only in the New Testament whence it made its way into the patristic literature of later Christianity. Neither must the name Nazarene be confounded with Nazarite נָזִיר abstainer, who as a visible sign of his vow let his hair grow, but both words may have been derived from the same root נזר, the former in the sense of "Separatist." The Niphel of the verb means "to separate oneself from others; to abstain, to vow, to devote oneself to."

other author of the period. He even proclaims (2 Esdras, vii. 28) the name of the Saviour whom the Lord calls "my son Jesus."[*]

Esdras mentions two abysmal beings, Enoch and Leviathan, but they do not take any part in the production of evil. He might as well have omitted to mention them. In the name of God, an angel explains to him the origin of evil as follows in a simile which reminds us of both the Buddhist parable of the city of Nirvana and Christ's Sermon on the Mount:

> "'A city is builded, and set upon a broad field, and is full of all good things: The entrance thereof is narrow, and is set in a dangerous place to fall, like as if there were a fire on the right hand, and on the left a deep water: And one only path between them both, even between the fire and the water, so small that there could but one man go there at once. If this city now were given unto man for an inheritance, if he never shall pass the danger set before it, how shall he receive this inheritance?'
>
> "And I said, 'It is so, Lord.'
>
> "Then said he unto me, 'Even so also is Israel's portion. Because for their sakes I made the world: and when Adam transgressed my statutes, then was decreed that now is done. Then were the entrances of this world made narrow, full of sorrow and travail; they are but few and evil, full of peril and very painful. For the entrances of the elder world were wide and sure, and brought immortal fruit. If then they that live labor not to enter these strait and painful things, they can never receive those that are laid up for them.'" (2 Esdras, vii, 6–14.)

A peculiarly interesting apocryphal work is ascribed to the patriarch Enoch.

The book of Enoch undertakes to explain in allegorical form God's plan of the world's history. The book is not yet Christian but shows many traces of doctrines professed by the sects which appeared at the beginning of the Christian era as competitors of Christianity.

While Enoch's demonology smacks of the religious myths of the Gentiles, his ideas of salvation from evil betray Gnostic tendencies.

---

[*] The passage is of course subject to the suspicion of being a later interpolation.

We read, for example, in Chapter 42:

"Wisdom came to live among men and found no dwelling-place. Then she returned home and took her seat among the angels."

We read of the Messiah, commonly designated "the son of a woman," sometimes "the son of man," and once "the son of God," that he existed from the beginning:

"Ere the sun and the signs [in the zodiac] were made, ere the stars of the heavens were created, his name was pronounced before the Lord of the spirits. Before the creation of the world he was chosen and hidden before Him [God], and before Him he will be from eternity to eternity."

"All the secrets of wisdom will flow from the thoughts of his mouth, for the Lord of the spirits has given wisdom unto him and has glorified him. In him liveth the spirit of wisdom, and the spirit of Him who giveth comprehension, and the spirit of the doctrine and of the power, and the spirit of all those who are justified and are now sleeping. And He will judge all hidden things, and no one will speak trifling words before Him, for He is chosen before the Lord of the spirits. He is powerful in all secrets of justification, and injustice has no place before Him."

And God says of the sons of the earth:

"I and my son shall unite ourselves with them for ever and aye in the paths of righteousness for all their lives."

The spiritualistic views in the Book of Enoch, especially the supernatural personality of the Messiah, are not peculiarly Christian, but Essenic or Gnostic, standing even in contradiction to the idea that the Messiah would become flesh and live among men as a real man.

It is a pity that we do not possess the original, but only an Ethiopian version of the Book of Enoch, which has been translated into German by Dr. A. Dillmann, for it is of great interest to the historian. It breathes the spirit of a Judaistic Gnosticism, and it is probable that the original

Book of Enoch was written in the year 110 B.C. by a Jew of the Pharisee party.[*]

The Book of Wisdom and the Gnostic Trinity Idea

THE BOOK OF WISDOM, a product of Alexandrian Judaism, showing traces of both Greek and Eastern influences, speaks of the Devil as having through envy introduced death into the world. We read:

> "God created man to be immortal, and made him to be an image of his own eternity; nevertheless, through envy of the Devil came death into the world, and they that do hold of his side do find it."

The Wisdom literature shows many traces of Indian influence. The very word wisdom, or *sophia,* seems to be a translation of the term *bodhi.* At the same time, the trinity idea begins to take root in the Jewish mind, the oldest form of it being moulded after the pattern of the family, which consists of father, mother, and child. The Wisdom books represent the relation of Sophia to God as his spouse and the Messiah as their son. Many Gnostics used the terms Sophia, Pneuma, and Logos as names for the second person of the Deity, who represented the divine motherhood of the God-man. But during the first period of the development of the Christian Church, the ideal of a God-mother was abandoned, the Logos was identified with God the Son, who now became the second person of the Trinity; and the name Pneuma or spirit was alone retained for the third person. The Gnostic Trinity-conception, however, left its trace in the Christian apocrypha, for in "the Gospel according to the Hebrews" Christ spoke of the Holy Ghost as his mother.[†]

The Trinity idea is of a very ancient origin. We encounter it in the religion of Babylon (see p. 40), in Brahmanism (see p. 75), and in Buddhism. The Buddhists take refuge in the Buddha, the Dharma, and the Sangha, called the three jewels, representing (1) Buddha the teacher, (2) the Buddhist religion or the good law, and (3) the Buddhist brotherhood or Church. The Trinity doctrine is not contained in

---

[*] See Dillmann, *Das Buch Henoch,* p. xliv.
[†] *Hieron. adv. Pelag.* III, 2.

the New Testament, all the passages which seem to involve it being spurious; but it forms an integral part of almost all Gnostic systems, where it either appears as three abstract principles, or as the family relation of Father, Mother, and Child, viewed as one.

The Trinity idea of God as a divine unity of Father, Mother, and Christ-child was retained among the Oriental Christians to the days of the rise of Mohammedanism. The Koran knows as yet nothing of the spiritualised Trinity conception of the Western Church, but represents the Christian Trinity as consisting of God, Christ, and Mary. And this Gnostic Trinity—conception is a natural ideal which in the further development of Christianity proved strong enough to influence the Roman Catholic Church in her devotion to Mary, the mother of Christ, whose personality was sometimes superadded to the Trinity, and sometimes even suffered to replace the Holy Ghost.

The more abstract form of the Trinity, emphasising it as a triunity, found its artistic expression in pictures of God as possessed of three faces. The most striking among these productions is an old oil painting which was discovered by a German artist at Salerno and published for the first time in *Die Gartenlaube* (1882, No. 47). The four eyes in their meditative attitude make a weird impression on the spectator, the three elongated noses show a freedom from sensuality, the brown hair and beard indicate strength, the broad forehead wisdom.

A Modern Gnostic

Jacob Böhme's philosophy is, in this connexion, of interest because it represents a revival of the spirit of Gnosticism in its best and most typical form. It may serve as a substitute to characterise by way of example the modes of thought of the ancient Gnostic systems and their comprehension of the problem of evil.

Jacob Böhme was a German mystic, born in 1575 at Alt-Seidenberg near Görlitz in Silesia. Like David he was in his childhood a shepherd. Having served from his fourteenth year as a shoemaker's apprentice and being affiliated with the shoemaker guild, he established himself as a master shoemaker in Görlitz in 1599. Later on in his life he changed his trade for that of a glover. His books circulated during his life-time in manuscript-form only, but even this sufficed to make his name known beyond the limits of his native town. He died on Sunday, November 17th, 1624, at his home in Görlitz, much admired by his friends and persecuted by some narrow-minded enemies who showed their malice even after his death by defacing the monument of the deceased philosopher. The best evidence, however, of his genius and the recognition which his honest aspirations found among his fellow citizens appears in the fact that the son of the Rev. Gregorius Richter, the pastor primarius of Görlitz and the bitterest antagonist of Jacob Böhme, edited a collection of extracts from his writings, which were afterwards published complete at Amsterdam in the year 1682.

The similarity of Jacob Böhme's speculations to Gnosticism is apparent, but the coincidence is almost spontaneous. His education was very limited, and he was only superficially familiar with the theories of Paracelsus (Theophrastus Bombast von Hohenheim, 1493–1541), Kasper Schwenkfeld (1490–1561), and Valentin Weigel (1533–1588). His own system is original with him. It is mainly due to a reflection on the Bible, which he read with a deeply religious spirit but preserving at the same time great independence of thought.

Jacob Böhme conceives God as the unfathomable ground of existence, as the *Ungrund*. His biographer in the Encyclopædia Britannica says of his philosophy:

"Nature rises out of Him, we sink into Him. . . The same view when offered in the colder logic of Spinoza, is sometimes set aside as atheistical.

"Translating Böhme's thought out of the uncouth dialect of material symbols (as to which one doubts sometimes whether he means them as concrete instances, or as pictorial illustrations, or as a mere *memoria technica*) we find that Böhme conceives of the correlation of two triads of forces. Each triad consists of a thesis, an antithesis, and a synthesis; and the two are connected by an important link. In the hidden life of the Godhead, which is at once *Nichts* and *Alles*, exists the original triad, viz., Attraction, Diffusion, and their resultant, the Agony of the unmanifested Godhead. The transition is made; by an act of will the divine Spirit comes to Light; and immediately the manifested life appears in the triad of Love, Expression, and their resultant Visible Variety. As the action of contraries and their resultant are explained the relations of soul, body, and spirit; of good, evil, and free will; of the spheres of the angels, of Lucifer, and of this world.

"It is a more difficult problem to account on this philosophy for the introduction of evil. . . Evil is a direct outcome of the primary principle of divine manifestation—it is the wrath side of God."

The problem of the idea of evil is very prominent in Jacob Böhme's philosophy, and has found a monistic solution. Without identifying good and evil, he arrives at the conclusion that the existence of evil is intrinsically necessary and unavoidable; it is ultimately rooted in the nature of God himself. The yearning for self-realisation constitutes a suffering in God himself, and in the act of revealing himself his will manifests both the bright and the dark aspect of life.

Jacob Böhme anticipates Schopenhauer. He says, in his book on "The Threefold Life of Man," p. 56:*

"For all things stand in the will, and in the will they are conducted. If I do not conceive a will to walk, my body remaineth at a stand-still. Therefore my will beareth me, and if I have no desire for [moving to] some place, there is no will in me. But if I desire something else, it is of the essence the will.

"The eternal word is the eternal will."

Ibid., p. 17

Materiality and sensuality are identified with sin, and sin begins not with the actual fall but with lusting, sleep being a symptom of this condition.

"Before his sleep Adam was in the form of an angel, but after his sleep he had flesh and blood, and there was a clod of the ground in his flesh."

Die drey Principien, p. 221

With all his gnostic tendencies Jacob Böhme is not a dualist but a monist. The duality of life viewed under the aspect of a higher unity

---

* *Hohe und tiefe Gründe von dem Dreyfachen Leben des Menschen nach dem Geheimnüss der drey Principien göttlicher Offenbahrung. Geschrieben nach göttlicher Erleuchtung.* Amsterdam, 1682.

constitutes a trinity whose three principles are represented in the frontispiece of Jacob Böhme's book on the subject* as two overlapping spheres which by meeting produce a third domain. There is an eternal goodness, and there is an eternal badness, and there is an eternal mixture of both. The eternal goodness contains the divine spirit and all the angels. But the sphere of badness is no less eternal. It is in its ultimate constitution the materiality of the world. The original Adam (a kind of Platonic prototype of man) was spiritual: his fall begins with his falling to sleep (p. 124), the result of carnal desire which changes his nature and leads to the creation of the woman to tempt him.

But Jacob Böhme is not a dualist, for he conceives of the three spheres as being one. He says in his book on *The Threefold Life of Man*, p. 16:

"We remind the God-loving and seeking reader to recognise this of God. He should not concentrate his mind and senses to seek the pure Godhead in loneliness, high above the stars, as living solely in the heavens. . . No, the pure Godhead is everywhere, entirely present in all places and ends. There is everywhere the birth of the Holy Trinity in one Being, and the angelic world reaches unto all the ends wherever thou mayest think; even into the middle of the earth, stones, and rocks; consequently also into Hell; briefly, the empire of the wrath of God is also everywhere."

Jacob Böhme does not believe in the letter but in the spirit of the Bible; and although he is counted a mystic, the illumination which he seeks is as sober as you can expect of a man of his culture. He freely utilises the Scriptures, but urges good Christians to seek the key to the problems of existence deeper. He says: "No one can come to God except through the Holy Ghost," and by the "Holy Ghost" he understands this spiritual illumination of heart and mind. He says (*ibid.*, 15–16):

"Search for the ground of nature. Thus you will comprehend all things. And do not madly go for the mere letter of the histories, nor make any blind laws according to your own imaginings

---

* *Beschreibung der drey Principien göttlichen Wesens.* Amsterdam, 1682.

wherewith you persecute one another. In this you are blinder than the heathen. Search for the heart and spirit of the Scriptures that the spirit may be born in you, and that the center of the Divine Love may be unlocked in you. Thus you may recognise God and speak of him rightly. For out of the histories merely, no one shall call himself a master, cogniser, and knower of the Divine essence, but out of the Holy Ghost which appeareth in another principium in the center of man's life, and only to him who searches rightly and seriously."

Jacob Böhme condenses his philosophy in his explanation of the frontispiece of his *Threefold Life*, where he says:

"Every work indicates by its form, essence, and character, the wisdom and virtue of its maker. Now if we contemplate the grandly marvellous edifice of the visible heaven and earth, consider their motions, inquire into their efficiencies and forces, and judge of the differences of the bodies of the creature, how they are hard and soft, gross and subtile, dark and radiant, opaque and pellucid, heavy and light: we shall at once discover the twofold mother of the revelation of God, viz., darkness and light which have breathed themselves out of all their forces and sealed miracles and form themselves together with the firmament, the stars, the elements, and all the visible conceivable creatures, where life and death, goodness and evil are at once in each thing. That is the third of the two hidden lives and it is called time contending with vanity. . .

"Thus this world standeth in the mixed life of time between light and darkness as a genuine mirror of the two, in which the marvels of eternity are revealed in the form of time through the Word, as John announces. All things were made by it, and without it was not anything made that was made."

The Gnostic movement and especially its Jewish phase, manifesting itself in sectarian life and in the postcanonical literature, is of greater importance than is generally admitted, for it prepared the way for Christianity. Many Christian dogmas, such as the bodily resurrection of the dead, the Messiah as the son of man, the approach of the day of judgment, are in the Old Testament Apocrypha, as it were, tentatively pronounced. A comprehensive formulation of the new religious ideals begins to be needed; and the people find at last in Jesus of Nazareth a leader whose powerful personality affords a centre around which the fermenting innovations can crystallise into an organised institution, the Christian Church, destined to become a new and most influential factor in the history of the world.

Early Christianity

Jesus and the New Testament

The Evil One played an important part in the imagination of the people in the time of Christ. Satan is mentioned repeatedly by the scribes and the people of Israel in the synoptic gospels, by the Apostles, especially by St. Paul, and very often in the revelation of St. John. Jesus follows the common belief of the time in attributing mental diseases to the possession of demons, and we may assume that he shared the popular view. Nevertheless, he speaks, upon the whole, less of the Devil than do his contemporaries.

The Jesus of the Gospels is said to have been tempted by the Devil in much the same way that Buddha was tempted by Mâra, the Evil One. Even the details of the two stories of temptation possess many features of resemblance.

Christ is very impressive in depicting the evil consequences of sin. He compares the last judgment to the selection made by fishermen who gather the good fishes into vessels, but cast the bad away (Math. xiii, 47). He speaks of the reward of "the good and faithful" while "the unprofitable servant" will be cast "into outer darkness where there shall be weeping and gnashing of teeth." Hell is described as "the fire that shall never be quenched" and "the worm that dieth not." And the wicked people are compared to goats to whom the Son of Man will say: "Depart from me ye cursed ones, into everlasting fire prepared for the Devil and his angels."

Christ represents the Devil as the enemy that sows tares among the wheat, and once addresses as Satan one of his favorite disciples who speaks words that might lead him into temptation. We read in Mark, viii, 33, and Matth., xvi, 23:

> "He rebuked Peter, saying: 'Get thee behind me, Satan, for thou savorest not the things that be of God, but the things that be of men.'"

This fact alone appears sufficient to prove that, while it is natural that Christ used the traditional idea of Satan as a personification of the evil powers to furnish him with materials for his parables, Satan to him was mainly a symbol of things wicked or morally evil.

If the Gospel stories actually reflect the real views of the historical Jesus, it appears that his idea of justice was based on the notion that the future life would be an exact inversion of the present order of things. According to the literal meaning of the language of the parable, Dives is not punished for his sins, and Lazarus is not rewarded for his good deeds: the future fate of the former in Hell and the latter in Heaven is the result of an equalisation, as we read in Luke xvi. 25:

> "But Abraham said, 'Son, remember that thou in thy lifetime receivedst thy good things, and likewise Lazarus evil things: but now he is comforted, and thou art tormented.'"

And as on earth Dives had the distress of Lazarus before his eyes, so now Lazarus, seated in the bosom of Abraham, sees with complacency the pains of Dives.

The keynote of the Christian sentiment of the apostolic age is expressed in the second epistle to the Thessalonians, where St. Paul says:

> "Now we beseech you, brethren, by the coming of our Lord Jesus Christ, and by our gathering together unto him,
> "That ye be not soon shaken in mind, or be troubled, neither by spirit, nor by word, nor by letter as from us, that the day of Christ is at hand."

St. Paul's belief "that the day of Christ is at hand" is based upon Christ's own utterances. We read in Mark ix. 1:

> "And he (Jesus) said unto them: 'Verily I say unto you that there be some of them that stand here which shall not taste of death till they have seen the kingdom of God come with power.'"

That in this passage the second advent of Christ is referred to there can be no doubt, especially as there are parallel passages which are written in the same spirit. In Matt. x. 23, Christ declares that his disciples preaching the Gospel in Palestine and fleeing from one city to another when persecuted for his name's sake, "shall not have gone over the cities of Israel till the Son of Man be come."

St. Paul confidently expected that he himself would see the day of the Lord, and in consideration of its nearness he deemed all worldly care unnecessary. Having explained in his epistle to the Corinthians the significance of the events in Jewish history and the punishments of sinners, he adds:

> "Now all these things happened unto them for ensamples, and they are written for our admonition upon whom the ends of the world are come."* (1 Cor. x. ii.)

When some of the Thessalonian Christians died, St. Paul comforted them by declaring that those who sleep will be resurrected and taken together up to heaven with those who survive. And the words of Paul expressly implied that he himself, together with the Thessalonians whom he addresses, will remain, of which fact he is so sure as to pronounce his opinion as being "the word of the Lord." He says:

> "But I would not have you to be ignorant, brethren, concerning them which are asleep, that ye sorrow not, even as others which have no hope.
>
> "For if we believe that Jesus died and rose again, even so them also which sleep in Jesus will God bring with him.
>
> "For this we say unto you by the word of the Lord, that we which are alive and remain unto the coming of the Lord shall not prevent them which are asleep.
>
> "For the Lord himself shall descend from heaven with a shout, with the voice of the archangel, and with the trump of God; and the dead in Christ shall rise first.
>
> "Then we which are alive and remain shall be caught up together with them in the clouds to meet the Lord in the air: and so shall we ever be with the Lord.
>
> "Wherefore comfort one another with these words."

When the early disciples became more and more disappointed at the non-appearance of the Lord in the clouds of heaven, a prominent leader of the Christian Church wrote an epistle to revive their faith, which was apt to suffer by the ridicule of those who did not share this belief. We read in the second epistle of St. Peter:

---

* τὰ τέλη τῶν αἰώνων. See also Hebr. ix. 26, where the appearance of Christ is said to have taken place at the consummation of the time (ἐπὶ συντελείᾳ τῶν αἰώνων).

"This second epistle, beloved, I now write unto you; in both which I stir up your pure minds by way of remembrance:

"That ye may be mindful of the words which were spoken before by the holy prophets, and of the commandment of us, the apostles of the Lord and Savior:

"Knowing this first, that there shall come in the last days scoffers, walking after their own lusts,

"And saying, 'Where is the promise of his coming? for since the fathers fell asleep, all things continue as they were from the beginning of the creation.'

". . . The Lord is not slack concerning his promise, as some men count slackness; but is longsuffering to us-ward, not willing that any should perish, but that all should come to repentance.

"But the day of the Lord will come as a thief in the night; in the which the heavens shall pass away with a great noise, and the elements shall melt with fervent heat, the earth also and the works that are therein shall be burnt up.

"Seeing then that all these things shall be dissolved, what manner of persons ought ye to be in all holy conversation and godliness,

"Looking for and hasting unto the coming of the day of God, wherein the heavens being on fire shall be dissolved, and the elements shall melt with fervent heat?

"Nevertheless, we, according to his promise, look for new heavens and a new earth, wherein dwelleth righteousness."

The present world remains in the power of Satan until the prophecy of the second advent of Christ be fulfilled, and we had better be prepared for meeting his onslaughts; as says the author of the first epistle of St. Peter:

"Be sober, be vigilant; because your adversary, the Devil, as a roaring lion walketh about, seeking whom he may devour."

In addition to his old names of Satan, Beelzebub, and Devil (which latter appears first in Jesus Sirach), the Evil One is called in the New Testament the prince of this world, the great dragon, the old serpent, the prince of the devils, the prince of the power of the air, the spirit that now worketh in the children of disbelief, the Antichrist. Satan is represented as the founder of an empire that struggles with and counteracts the kingdom of God upon earth. He is powerful, but less powerful than Christ and his angels. He is conquered and doomed through Christ, but he is still unfettered.

The newly discovered fourth book of Daniel* contains a story which characterises the expectations of the early Church. We read of a certain man, holding the office of president (προεστώς) in a Christian congregation of Syria:

> "He persuaded many of the brethren, with their wives and children, to go out into the wilderness to meet the Christ, and they went wandering in the mountains and wastes, there losing their way; and the end was that all but a few were apprehended as robbers and would have been executed by the mayor of the city (ἡγεμών) had it not been that his wife was a believer and that in response to her entreaties he put a stop to the proceedings to prevent a persecution arising because of them."

Cases of this kind happened frequently. We read of another Christian officer (also a προεστώς) in Pontus that he also preached the approaching day of judgment:

> "He brought the brethren to such a pitch of fear and trembling that they abandoned their lands and fields, letting them become waste, and sold, the most of them, their possessions."

The belief in the imminent approach of the day of judgment waned during the third century, but was temporarily revived in the year 1000, which was commonly believed to be the end of the millennium prophesied by St. John the Divine in the Revelation. The disorder and misery which resulted from the foolish acts that people committed in anticipation of the approaching day of judgment all over Christendom are beyond description. Some squandered their property in order to enjoy the last days of their lives; some sold all they had and gave to the poor; some invested all their possessions in masses and Church donations; and thus almost all who were filled with the belief in the coming of the Lord fell a prey to the most wretched poverty and distress.

---

* Edited by Dr Ed. Bratke. Bonn, 1891.

THE REVELATION OF ST. JOHN, WRITTEN between 68 and 70 A.D., after Nero's death and before the destruction of Jerusalem, propounds the eschatology of early Christianity, which closely follows such traditions of the Jews as are preserved in the prophetic books of the Old Testament Apocrypha.

The author of the Revelation is a Jew-Christian, who in the name of the son of man informs the seven churches of Asia Minor that God hates the Nicolaitanes (i., 6 and 15), an antinomistic sect among the Gnostics who according to Irenaeus (I, Chap. 26) regarded the Mosaic law, the nomos, as unessential to salvation. The warning given out against "those who say that they are Apostles and are not" seems to be directed against St. Paul, who, like the Nicolaitanes, is also known for his strong antinomistic principles and finding no sin in eating with pagans, even though the meat might have been offered as a sacrifice to idols.*

An unpleasant denunciation of a follower of antinomistic, i.e., Pauline Christianity in the city of Thyatira, is mentioned in chapter ii, verses 20–29, which probably has reference to Lydia, a seller of purple, who was baptised by Paul (Acts xvi. 14–15). The great promises of the Lord offered to the faithful through John the Divine, are strictly limited to the Jew Christian, to him who keeps the law and holds fast to it till Christ's second advent (ii. 25). As a reward Christ, according to John the Divine's vision, allows him the great pleasure of destroying the Gentiles, saying:

"And he that overcometh and keepeth my works (i.e., the law) unto the end, to him will I give the power over the nations; and he shall rule them with a rod of iron: as the vessels of a potter shall they be broken to shivers; even as I received from my Father."

St. John believes that the judgment of the world is near at hand. The Lamb opens the seven seals, and four men on horseback, one with a crown, one with a sword, one with a pair of balances, and the last one Death, followed by Hell, are let loose. The martyrs of

---

* Rom. 14 and 1 Cor. 8.

God receive white robes, the sun becomes black as sackcloth, and the moon becomes as blood. Then an angel pronounces a triple woe upon the inhabitants of the earth. The pit is opened and four angels who had been bound are loosed to slay the third part of men. A struggle ensues between a women that travaileth and the dragon, but the dragon is cast down. A beast with seven heads and ten horns appears; another beast follows and makes an image of the first beast that should be worshipped by men. "The number of the beast" is "six hundred and three score and six," which according to cabalistic symbolism means "Nero." The Roman Emperor is thus regarded as an incarnation of Satan, and for a short time power is given to the pagan government over the world. But the victorious Lamb stands on Mount Zion; the Gospel is preached, and the sickle of the harvest is ready for gathering in the clusters of the vine. Then the seven vials of wrath are poured out upon mankind. The city "which reigneth over the kings of the earth" (i.e., Rome), the old Babylon, the mother of abominations, shall fall, and the fowls of the air are called to fill themselves with the flesh of the slain. Satan is bound for a thousand years, but let loose again. In a final struggle, Gog and Magog are conquered, whereupon a new heaven and a new earth are created. A heavenly Jerusalem descends upon earth and the twelve tribes inhabit the city, which needs no sun because God is its light. The pagan Christians remain outside: "The nations of them which are saved shall walk in the light of it, and the kings of the earth bring their glory and honor into it."

Such is briefly the contents of the Revelation of St. John the Divine, which is a very important book, as it embodies the views of the early Jew-Christians concerning God's plan in the history of the world, and the powers of evil play in it a most important part.

The main prophecy of the Jewish Christian author of the revelation remained unfulfilled. By a strange irony of fate Judaic Christianity disappeared from the face of the earth, while Rome became the centre of the Gentile Christianity, in which capacity she rose almost to more glorious power than pagan Rome ever possessed through her political superiority. Christianity was thoroughly Romanised and remained under the sway of Rome until the Reformation split the Church in twain and opened new possibilities for a progressive development of Christianity, no longer subject to the dictates of a conclave of Italian cardinals and a Roman pope.

The Descent Into Hell

THE BELIEF IN SATAN AND Hell form an essential part of early Christianity, and Christ was believed immediately after his death on the cross to have battled with and to have conquered the prince of hell. Although the oldest manuscripts of the so-called Apostle's Creed do not contain the passage "descended into hell," which is an addition of the seventh century, there can be no doubt that the idea actually prevailed as early as the second century. The Gospel of Nicodemus, which is commonly regarded as a product of the third century, dwells on this part of the Christian belief and offers a detailed account of Christ's descent into Hell, which in Chapters xv–xvi reads as follows:

"Satan, the prince and captain of death, said to the prince of hell, Prepare to receive Jesus of Nazareth himself, who boasted that he was the Son of God, and yet was a man afraid of death, and said, My soul is exceeding sorrowful even unto death.* Besides he did many injuries to me and to many others; for those whom I made blind and lame and those also whom I tormented with several devils, he cured by his word; yea, and those whom I brought dead to thee, he by force takes away from thee.

"To this the prince of hell replied to Satan, Who is that so powerful prince, and yet a man who is afraid of death? For all the potentates of the earth are subject to my power, whom thou broughtest to subjection by thy power. But if he be so powerful in his nature, I affirm to thee for truth, that he is almighty in his divine nature, and no man can resist his power. When, therefore, he said he was afraid of death, he designed to ensnare thee, and unhappy it will be to thee for everlasting ages.

"Then Satan, replying, said to the prince of hell, Why didst thou express a doubt, and wast afraid to receive Jesus of Nazareth, both thy adversary and mine? As for me, I tempted him and stirred up my old people, the Jews, with zeal and anger against him. I sharpened the spear for his suffering; I mixed the gall and vinegar, and commanded that he should drink it; I prepared the cross to crucify him, and the nails to pierce through his hands

---

* See Matth., xxvi. 38.

and feet; and now his death is near at hand, I will bring him hither, subject both to thee and me.

"Then the prince of hell answering said, Thou saidst to me just now, that he took away the dead from me by force. They who have been kept here till they should live again upon earth were taken away hence, not by their own power, but by prayers made to God, and their almighty God took them from me. Who, then, is that Jesus of Nazareth that by his word hath taken away the dead from me without prayer to God? Perhaps it is the same who took away from me Lazarus, after he had been four days dead, and did both stink and was rotten, and of whom I had possession as a dead person, yet he brought him to life again by his power.

"Satan, answering, said to the prince of hell, It is the very same person, Jesus of Nazareth, which, when the prince of hell heard, he said to him, I adjure thee by the powers which belong to thee and me, that thou bring him not to me. For when I heard of the power of his word, I trembled for fear, and all my impious company were at the same time disturbed; and we were not able to detain Lazarus, but he gave himself a shake, and with all the signs of malice he immediately went away from us; and the very earth in which the dead body of Lazarus was lodged, presently turned him out alive. And I know now that he is Almighty God who could perform such things, who is mighty in his dominion, and mighty in his human nature, who is the Saviour of mankind. Bring not, therefore, his person hither, for he will set at liberty all those whom I hold in prison under unbelief, and bound with the fetters of their sins, and will conduct them to everlasting life.

"And while Satan and the prince of hell were discoursing thus to each other, on a sudden there was a voice as of thunder and the rushing of winds, saying, Lift up your gates, O ye princes; and be ye lift up, O everlasting gates, and the King of Glory shall come in.

"When the prince of hell heard this, he said to Satan, Depart from me and begone out of my habitations; if thou art a powerful warrior, fight with the King of Glory. But what hast thou to do with him? And then he cast him forth from his habitations. And the prince said to his impious officers, Shut the brass gates of cruelty and make them fast with iron bars, and fight courageously, lest we be taken captives.

"But when all the company of the saints heard this they spake with a loud voice of anger to the prince of hell, Open thy gates that the King of Glory may come in.

"And the divine prophet David cried out, saying, Did not I when on earth truly prophesy and say, O that men would praise the Lord for his goodness and for his wonderful works to the children of men. For he hath broken the gates of brass, and cut the bars of iron in sunder. He hath taken them because of their iniquity, and because of their unrighteousness they are afflicted.

"After this another prophet, namely, holy Isaiah, spake in like manner to all the saints, Did not I rightly prophesy to you when I was alive on earth? The dead men shall live, and they shall rise again who are in their graves, and they shall rejoice who are in earth; for the dew which is from the Lord shall bring deliverance to them. And I said in another place, O death, where is thy victory? O death, where is thy sting?

"When all the saints heard these things spoken by Isaiah, they said to the prince of hell, Open now thy gates, and take away thine iron bars, for thou wilt now be bound, and have no power.

"Then there was a great voice, as of the sound of thunder, saying, Lift up your gates, O princes; and be ye lifted up, ye gates of hell, and the King of Glory will enter in.

"The prince of hell perceiving the same voice repeated, cried out as though he had been ignorant, Who is that King of Glory? David replied to the prince of hell, and said, I understand the words of that voice, because I spake them by his spirit. And now, as I have above said, I say unto thee, the Lord strong and powerful, the Lord mighty in battle: he is the King of Glory, and he is the Lord in heaven and in earth. He hath looked down to hear the groans of the prisoners, and to set loose those that are appointed to death. And now, thou filthy and stinking prince of hell, open thy gates, that the King of Glory may enter in; for he is the Lord of heaven and earth.

"While David was saying this, the mighty Lord appeared in the Form of a man, and enlightened those places which had ever before been in darkness, and broke asunder the fetters which before could not be broken; and with his invincible power visited those who sate in the deep darkness by iniquity, and the shadow of death by sin. Impious Death and her cruel officers hearing these things, were seized with fear in their several kingdoms, when they saw the clearness of the light, and Christ himself on a sudden appearing in their habitations; they cried out therefore, and said, We are bound by thee; thou seemest to intend our confusion before the Lord. Who art thou, who hast no sign of corruption but that bright appearance which is a full proof of thy greatness, of which yet thou seemest to take no notice? Who art thou, so powerful and so weak, so great and so little, a mean and yet a soldier of the first rank, who can command in the form of a servant as a common soldier? The King of Glory, dead and alive, though once slain upon the cross? Who layest dead in the grave, and art come down alive to us, and in thy death all the creatures trembled, and all the stars were moved, and now hast thou thy liberty among the dead, and givest disturbance to our legions? Who art thou, who dost release the captives that were held in chains by original sin, and bringest them into their former liberty? Who art thou, who dost spread so glorious and divine a light over those who were made blind by the darkness of sin?

"In like manner all the legions of devils were seized with the like horror, and with the most submissive fear cried out, and said, Whence comes it, O thou Jesus Christ, that thou art a man so powerful and glorious in majesty, so bright as to have no spot, and so pure as to have no crime? Then the King of Glory trampling upon death, seized the prince of hell, deprived him of all his power, and took our earthly father Adam with him to his glory.

"Then the prince of hell took Satan, and with great indignation said to him, O thou prince of destruction, author of Beelzebub's defeat and banishment, the scorn of God's angels and loathed by all righteous persons! What inclined thee to act thus? Why didst thou venture without either reason or justice, to crucify him, and hast brought down to our regions a person innocent and righteous, and thereby hast lost all the sinners, impious and unrighteous persons in the whole world?

"While the prince of hell was thus speaking to Satan, the King of Glory said to Beelzebub, the prince of hell, Satan the prince shall be subject to thy dominion forever, in the room of Adam and his righteous sons, who are mine. Then Jesus stretched forth his hand, and said, Come to me, all ye saints, who are created in my image, who were condemned by the tree of the forbidden fruit, and by the devil and death; live now by the wood of my cross: the devil, the prince of this world, is overcome, and death is conquered."

Hell

THE IDEA OF HELL AMONG the early Christians has found a detailed description in the revelation of St. Peter, which was counted as canonical by Clement of Alexandria who annotated it together with the Catholic Epistles, while the Muratorian Fragment mentions it as a book of the New Testament. According to the testimony of Sozomenos it was read in some of the churches of Palestine annually, as a preparation for the celebration of Easter in about 440 A.D.[*] It was used in Rome and Alexandria at the end of the second century, together with the revelation of St. John, where, according to Eusebius, both writings belonged to the contested canonical books, that is to say, they were received as canonical but not without protest in some quarters.

According to the revelation of St. Peter, Heaven and Hell are places. Heaven is described by St. Peter as follows:[†]

"And I spake to him (the Lord): 'And where are the just, and what is their æon in which they that possess this glory live?' And the Lord showed me a large space outside of this world overflowed with light, and the air there was illuminated all through by the rays of the sun. And the earth itself was blooming with unfading flowers, and filled with sweet odors, and grandly blossoming and imperishable and blessed fruit-bearing plants. Such was the fulness of flowers that the sweet odor thence penetrated even unto us. The inhabitants of that space were clothed with the robes of radiant angels; and similar were their robes to their surroundings. Angels were hovering about them. The glory of all who lived there was the same, and with one voice they sang in gladness responsive hymns of praise to God the Lord in that place. Said the Lord to us: 'That is the place of your high priests, of the just people.'"

---

[*] See Harnack, *Bruchstücke des Evangeliums und der Apokalypse des Petrus*, p. 5–6.
[†] Translated into English from Harnack's edition.

Hell is described in the following words:

"And I saw another place right opposite, rough and being the place of punishment. And those who are punished there and the punishing angels had their robes dark; as the color of the air of the place is also dark: and some people were hung up by their tongues: they were those who had blasphemed the path of righteousness; and underneath them a bright baneful fire was lit. And there was a pit large and filled with burning dirt (βόρβορος), in which several people stuck who had perverted justice, and the avenging angels assaulted them. There were others there: women hung up by their braids above the seething dirt. They were those who had adorned themselves for adultery; but those who had soiled themselves with the miasma of the adultery of those women were hung up by their feet and had their heads in the dirt, and I said, 'I did not believe that I should enter into this place.' I saw murderers and their accomplices thrown into a narrow place filled with evil vermin and tormented by those animals and squirming under this punishment. Worms like dark clouds assaulted them. The souls of the murdered people, however, stood by and gazed at the punishment of their murderers and said: 'O God, just is thy judgment.' But near unto that place I saw a place of torment in which the blood and the stench of the punished flowed down so as to make a pool, and there were women to whom the blood reached up to the neck; opposite them many infants sat who had been brought into the world before their season, and they were weeping. And fiery rays proceeded from the children and bit the eyes of the women. For they were the cursed ones who had conceived and made abortions. And there were men and women standing in flames with half their bodies, and they were thrown into a dark place and were scourged by evil spirits. And they were devoured in their bowels by worms which do not die. They were those who had persecuted the righteous and surrendered them; and near by to those again were women and men who bit their lips and were punished and received hot irons on their eyes. They were those who had blasphemed and betrayed the path of righteousness. Opposite them were other men and women who bit their tongues and had burning fire in their mouths. They were those who bore false witness. In another place were flints sharper than swords and lances, rendered burning hot, and women and men in dirty rags were wallowing on them in torment. They were the rich and those who relying on their riches had not taken compassion on orphans and widows, who had a contempt for the commands of God. In another large field with matter and blood and seething dirt were those who take interest and interest on interest. Other men and women were thrown from a high precipice, and having reached the bottom were urged up again by their assaulters to climb the precipice, and were then again thrown down, and they were given no respite from this torment. They were those who had polluted their own bodies.* . . . And by the side of this precipice was a place which was filled entirely with fire, and there stood the people who had made with their own hands carved images and worshipped them instead of God, and near them were men and women with switches who beat them and did not cease from this castigation. And again other women and men stood near by, burning, and wriggling, and roasting. They were those who had left the path of God."

Another description of Hell according to the views of the Christian Gnostics of the third century is contained in the *Pistis Sophia*, where all the places of torment are described at considerable length in all details. "It is remarkable," says Professor Harnack,† "that the *Pistis Sophia* anticipates on this subject as well as in many other respects the development of the Catholic Church. It insists on the power of salvation of the sacraments, of the mysteries, of penance, and ascetic practices. At the same time it recognises Apostolic authority, and attempts in every respect to base its doctrines on the canon of the Old and New Testament." Its date has been fixed with great accuracy on the second part of the third century.‡ This strange book contains questions of Mary and of some of the apostles, which Christ after his resurrection answers on the Mount of Olives, and it is probably identical with a gnostic book mentiond by Epiphanius under the title *The Minor Questions of Mary*. Harnack calls attention to the fact that the book is an evidence of the astonishing agreement of this later Gnosticism with

---

* We prefer to omit further details.

† See Harnack, *Texte und Untersuchungen,* etc., p. 98.

‡ *Ibid.,* pp. 94 et seq.

later Catholic Christianity. The author of the *Pistis Sophia* is apparently imbued with the spirit of Syrian Gnosticism or Ophitism; but he wrote in Egypt where the Syrian Gnostics exercised quite a powerful influence. The revelation of mysteries culminates in the doctrine of Christ's identity with his disciples, which is uttered repeatedly and with emphasis.* The peculiarly Gnostic features of the book consist in the idea of reincarnation. So, for instance, St. John is directly said to be a reincarnation of Elias, and the Apostles are, as much as Christ, regarded as being possessed of a mystical pre-existence.

The *Pistis Sophia* reveals all the mysteries of the world, among them the mysteries of Hell, or, as the Egyptians called it, Amenti, which is described as follows:

"And Mary continued further and said unto Jesus: 'Again, Master, of what type is the outer darkness? How many regions of punishment are there therein?'

"And Jesus answered and said unto Mary: 'The outer darkness is a huge dragon, with its tail in its mouth; it is outside the world and surroundeth it completely.† There are many regions of punishment therein, for there are in it twelve [main] dungeons of horrible torment.

"'In each dungeon there is a ruler; and the faces of the rulers are all different from one another.

"'The first ruler, in the first dungeon, is crocodile faced, and it hath its tail in its mouth. From the jaws of this dragon there come forth cold of every kind and freezing, and all diseases of every kind: it is called by its authentic name, in its region, Enchthonin.

"'And the ruler in the second dungeon; its authentic face is a cat's: it is called, in its region, Charachar.

"'And the ruler in the third dungeon; its authentic face is a dog's: it is called, in its region, Acharôch.

---

* "Qui acceperit μυστήριον Ineffabilis, ille est ego."—"Ego sum isti, isti sum ego."—"Ego sum mysterium illud."—"Vis quae est in vobis, e me est." Harnack says (p. 30): "These brief significant sentences are not invented by the author who makes his Christ express himself in quite different sermons: they point, in my opinion, to an older gnostic book, or a gnostic gospel."

† This reminds us of the myths of the Midgard-serpent and anticipates the innumerable mediæval representations of Hell as a big-mouthed dragon.

"'And the ruler in the fourth dungeon; its authentic face is a serpent's: it is called, in its region, Achrôchar.

"'And the ruler in the fifth dungeon; its authentic face is a black bull's: it is called, in its region, Marchour.

"'And the ruler in the sixth dungeon; its authentic face is a boar's: it is called, in its region, Lamchamôr.

"'And the ruler in the seventh dungeon; its authentic face is a bear's: it is called, in its region, by its authentic name, Louchar.

"'And the ruler in the eighth dungeon; its authentic face is a vulture's: it is called, in its region, Laraôch.

"'And the ruler in the ninth dungeon; its authentic face is a basilisk's: it is called, in its region, Archeôch.

"'And in the tenth dungeon are many rulers; each of them, in its authentic face, hath seven dragons' heads: and that which is above them all, in their region, is called Xarmarôch.

"'And in the eleventh dungeon, in this region also, are many rulers; each of them, with authentic faces, hath seven cats' heads: and the great one that is over them, is called, in their region, Rhôchar.

"'And in the twelfth dungeon there are also many rulers exceedingly numerous, each of them in its authentic face, hath seven dogs' heads: and the great one that is over them, is called in their region, Chrêmaôr.

"'These rulers, then, of these twelve dungeons, which are in the inside of the dragon of outer darkness, each hath a name for every hour, and each of them changeth its face every hour.

"'And each of these dungeons hath a door which openeth to the height, so that the dragon of outer darkness containeth twelve dungeons of darkness, each of which hath a door that openeth to the height; and an angel of the height watched at each of the doors of the dungeons.

"'These Ieou,* the first man, the overseer of the light, the ancient of the first statute, hath set to watch over the dragon, lest the dragon and its rulers should turn the dungeons that are in it, upside down.'

---

* The idea of "Ieou, the first man, the overseer of the light, the ancient of the first statue," reminds us of the archetypal man of Simon Magus and other Gnostics and also of the Adam of the Cabala.

"And when the saviour had thus spoken, Mary Magdalene answered and said: 'Master, are the souls, then, that are brought into that region, led into it by these twelve doors, by each according to the judgment they have merited?'

"The saviour answered and said unto Mary: 'No soul is brought into the dragon by these doors; but the souls of blasphemers, and of them that remain in the doctrines of error, and of those who teach such doctrines, and also of them that have intercourse with males, of the polluted and impious, atheists, murderers, adulterers, sorcerers, all souls, then, of this kind, if they have not repented while still in life, and have remained persistently in their sin, and all the other souls which have remained without [the light-world], that is to say, who have exhausted the number of the cycles apportioned to them in the sphere without repenting,—they take hold of these souls, in their last cycle, them and all the souls which I have just enumerated to you, and carry them through the opening in the tail of the dragon into the dungeons of the outer darkness. And when they have finished bringing those souls into the outer darkness by the opening in its tail, it putteth back its tail again into its mouth and shutteth them in. This is the way in which souls are brought into the outer darkness.'"*

"'And the dragon of the outer darkness hath twelve authentic names which are written on its doors, a name for the door of every dungeon; and these twelve names are all different from one another, but all twelve are contained one in the other, so that he who uttereth one name will utter all. And these will I tell you, when I explain the emanation of the pleroma. This, then, is the way in which is the outer darkness, which is also the dragon.'

"When the saviour had spoken these things, Mary answered and said unto the saviour: 'Master, are the torments of this dragon terrible beyond the punishment of all the judgments?'

"The saviour answered and said unto Mary: 'Not only are they more painful than all the chastisements of the judgments, but every soul that shall be carried into that region shall be

---

* In mediæval Hell-representations, which rarely are lacking in coarse humor, the souls are thrown with pitchforks into the open jaws of the dragon. The coarseness of the description of Hell in the *Pistis Sophia* is apparently serious.

imprisoned in relentless ice,* in the hail and scorching fire which are therein. And in the dissolution of the world, that is to say, in the ascension of the pleroma, these souls shall perish in the relentless ice and scorching fire, and shall be non-existent for the eternity.'

"Mary answered and said: 'Woe for the souls of sinners! Now, therefore, O Master, whether is the fire in the world of human kind or the fire in Amenti the fiercer?'

"The saviour answered and said unto Mary: 'Amen, I say unto thee, the fire in Amenti scorcheth far more than the fire among men, nine times more.

"'And the fire which is in the punishments of the great chaos is nine times fiercer than the fire in Amenti.

"'And the fire which is in the judgments of the rulers who are in the way of the midst, is nine times fiercer than the fire of the punishments which are in the great chaos.

"'And the fire which is in the dragon of outer darkness, and all the torments which it containeth, are fiercer far than the fire which is in the chastisements and judgments of the rulers who are in the way of the midst,—this fire is fiercer than they seventy times.'

"And when the saviour had said this unto Mary, she smote her breast, she cried out aloud, with tears, and all the disciples with her, saying: 'Woe for the sinners, for their torments are exceedingly great.'"

The Gnostic Christian view of Doomsday and Hell embodies many ancient traditions of Egyptian, Indian, and Persian mythology and foreshadows at the same time the later Roman Catholic view as represented in mediæval art, finding its poetical consummation in Dante's *Divina Comedia.*

Satan was regarded by the early Christians as the Prince of this World, and this belief dominated in the Church as long as pagan authorities remained in power. As soon as they were replaced by Christian rulers, and when Christianity became established as the state religion of the Roman Empire, Satan was gradually dethroned and God reinstated in the government of the world.

---

* An anticipation of Dante's ice hell.

The empire of the Caesars broke to pieces under the repeated assaults of Vandals, Huns, and Goths, but Charlemagne founded a new empire on its ruins, which, being based upon the rising power of the Teutonic tribes, the Franconians and the Germans, was called the "Holy Roman Empire of German nationality," lasting about a thousand years, from 800 until 1806. This period (by Stahl actually regarded as the realisation of the millennium of Revelation) is the age in which Christianity was officially recognised and the attempt was made to apply its ethics by all means to the private and public affairs of the people. It is natural that the Trinity was now conceived after the pattern of the Imperial government of the age; God was represented as the emperor, Christ as the king, vicegerent and heir, while the Holy Ghost hovered above them as the spirit of order and authority.

The most essential and at any rate practically most important dogma of the early Christian Church, the doctrine of the imminent approach of the day of judgment, faded away when the Church rose to power, but it reappeared from time to time, sometimes not unlike an acute attack of a frightful alienation of men's minds rendering them forgetful of the duties of the living present for the sake of trying to escape the imaginary evils of the doom to come. The scenes of the last judgment, however, have always remained a favorite subject of Christian artists and poets, the keynote of which vibrates through the old Church hymn:

"Dies irae, dies illa,
Solvet sæclum in favila,
Teste David cum Sibylla."

The Idea of Salvation in Greece and Italy

ἀλλὰ ῥῦσαι ἡμᾶς ἀπὸ τοῦ πονηροῦ.

—Matt. vi. 14

T he first century of our era is a time in which the fear of evil leads to the organisation of religious institutions having in view the atonement of sin and the redemption of the soul from the terrors of hell. The ideas evil, sin, hell, salvation, and immortal life were familiar to the Greek mind even before the days of Plato, but were still mixed up with the traditional mythology. When philosophers began to wage war against the gross idolatry of Greek polytheism, a fermentation set in which prepared the Greek nation for the reception of Christianity. We say "prepared," but we might just as well say that it resulted in the formation of the Christian Church as an institution to deliver mankind from evil. The fear of punishment in the life to come led in the days of savagery to human sacrifices as a vicarious atonement. This barbarous practice was abandoned in the progress of civilisation by a substitution of animal victims. But the idea lingered in the minds of the people and was retained in Christianity, where, however, it received a new significance when restated under the influence of Paul's message of the crucified, and therefore glorified, Saviour. Christ's death was now declared to be a sacrifice that would be sufficient for all the ages to come.[*]

The Greeks, equally with other nations, feared punishment after death as the greatest evil, and their belief in hell can be traced back to the dawn of the history of Greece.

The most ancient description of the Greek conception of the land of the dead, which is found in Homer, resembles the Jewish Sheol in so far as Hades is the abode of the shades of the dead, both good and evil. It is a gloomy place; there is a grove of willow and poplar trees, and a large lawn covered with asphodels. The shade of Achilles declares that

---

[*] The Christian Church never lost sight of the idea that a human sacrifice is indispensable for the expiation of sin, the atonement being procured by the mystic effects of faith. Hence the constant reference of Christ's death on the cross to both Abraham's offering of Isaac and the miraculous healing power of the brazen serpent in the desert.

he would rather be upon earth a day laborer in a poor man's employ than ruler in the land of the dead. While the oldest reports do not as yet contain any reference to a reward of the good (for even Achilles shares the sad fate of all mortals), we learn of the tortures to which the wicked are subjected,—Tantalus, the Danaides, Sisyphos, Ixion, Oknos.

Homer represents the dead as unsubstantial forms, like dream images. However, an exception is made in the case of Hercules, whose shadow is in Hades, while Hercules himself, who is an Immortal, lives among the gods in Olympus (*Odyssey,* XI, 601–626). Another hero whose fate after death is more cheerful than that of common people is Menelaos. Being a son-in-law of Zeus, the husband of Helen, who is apparently conceived as the goddess of the moon, he lives in Elysion where Rhadamanthys rules. There the people live in ease. There is no snow, no winter, no storm, but only gentle and refreshing zephyrs blow from the ocean.

The Egyptian origin of the belief in Elysion is guaranteed by the name Rhadamanthys which is the god Ra Amenthes, the Lord of the Hidden World, Amenti.

When the spread of gnostic views prepared the Greek nation for Christianity, the ancient pagan myths were not abandoned but transformed. Hesiod tells us in the Theogony of the terrible struggle between Zeus and the Titans; and St. Peter,[*] when speaking in his second letter of the revolution of the angels that sinned, says that "God hurled them down to Tartarus." The expression, however, is obliterated in the version of King James, for the word ταρώταρσας (having hurled them to Tartarus) is translated "sent them down to hell."

We read in the Theogony of the battle between Zeus and the monster Typhon (also called Typhoeus):

"When Zeus had driven the Titans out from heaven, huge Earth bare her youngest born son, Typhoeus, . . . whose hands, indeed, are fit for deeds on account of their strength. . . On his shoulders there were one hundred heads of a serpent, of a fierce dragon, playing with dusky tongues. From the eyes in his wondrous heads fire struggled beneath the brows. From his terrible mouths voices were sending forth every kind of sound ineffable,—the bellowing of a bull, the roar of a lion, the barking of whelps,

---

[*] Or rather the author of the second epistle of St. Peter, so called.

and the hiss of a serpent. The huge monster would have reigned over mortals unless the sire of gods and men quickly observed him. Harshly he thundered, and heavily and terribly the earth re-echoed around. Beneath Jove's immortal feet vast Olympus trembled, and the earth groaned. Heaven and sea were boiling. Pluto trembled, monarch of the dead. The Titans in Tartarus trembled also, but Jove smote Typhoeus and scorched all the wondrous heads of the terrible monster. When at last the monster was quelled, smitten with blows, it fell down lame, and Zeus hurled him into wide Tartarus."

This description reminds us not only of the Second Epistle of St. Peter, but also of Revelation, xii. 7–9:

"And there was war in heaven. Michael and his angels fought against the dragon; and the dragon fought and his angels; and prevailed not; neither was their place found any more in heaven. And the great dragon was cast out, that old serpent called the Devil and Satan, which deceiveth the whole world; he was cast out into the earth, and his angels were cast out with him."

Thus the old Greek demons merely changed names and reappeared in new personalities. In this shape they were embodied into the canonical books of the New Testament and became the integral part of the new religion, which at that time began to conquer the world.

The Greek idea of salvation is mirrored in the legends of Hercules, Bellerophon, Theseus, Dionysus, and other myths, which had become dear to the Greek mind through the tales of poets and the works of artists.

The powers of evil which Hercules overcomes are represented as a lion, a dragon, a wild boar, harpy-like birds, and a bull. In addition he captures the swift hind of Arcadia, he cleanses the stables of Augeas, tames the man-eating mares of Diomedes, conquers Hypolyte, the queen of the Amazons, brings the oxen of Geryon from the far West, and carries Cerberus to the upper world.

The poet Peisander (who lived about 650 B.C.) wrote an apotheosis of Hercules, called the *Heracley,* which contributed much toward idealising the hero. Later Greek philosophers, such men as Xenophon and the sophist Prodicus,* regarded him as the realisation of divine perfection, and now it became customary to look upon the old legends as perversions of a deeper religious truth. Epictetus, who speaks of Hercules as the saviour, and as the son of Zeus, says (iii. 24): "Do you believe all the fables of Homer?"

Hercules is called repeller of evil (ἀλεξίκακος), leader in the fray (πρόμαχος), the brightly victorious (καλλίνικος),† the celestial (ὀλύμπιος), destroyer of flies, vermin, and grasshoppers (μυίαργος, ἱπόκτονος, κορνοπίων). He, the solar hero, is identified with Apollo, the sun-god, in the names prophet (μάντις), and leader of the Muses (μουσαγέτης).

The legends of Perseus are in many respects similar to the tales of Hercules. Perseus, too, the Greek prototype of the Christian St. George, is a divine saviour. Assisted by Athene, he liberates Andromeda, the bride of Death, held captive by the horrible Medusa, a symbol of deadly fright.‡

As a symbol which destroys evil influences, the Medusa-head frequently appears on shields and coins.

Bellerophon is another solar hero. He rides on Pegasus, a mythological representation of the thundercloud,§ and slays the Chimæra, a monster half lion, half goat, representing barbarism and savagery, or some similar evils.

Some of the tales of divine saviours may be ultimately founded upon local Greek traditions, but many features of these religious myths indicate that they were introduced early from the Orient whose religions began to influence the occidental nations at the very dawn of their civilisation. Thus Hercules is the Tyrian Baal Melkarth, probably identical with the Babylonian Bel,—the conqueror of Tiamat; and his twelve labors are the deeds of the sun-god in the twelve months of the year. Phœnix-like, he dies by self-combustion and rises in a transfigured shape from the flames of the pyre. The Jews also appropriated the figure

---

* Xen., *Mem.*, ii. 1. Plato, *Symp.*, 177 B.

† The Greek καλός is not limited to the definition of beautiful as we use the word.

‡ The Medusa is mentioned by Homer, λ 634, as a terrible monster of the Nether World; it was used as an amulet to avert evil, and became therefore a favorite device on shields. The original of the upper illustration on p. 207 is colored,—which adds to the frightful appearance of this picture found on the Acropolis at Athens.

§ The statue reproduced on p. 208 belongs to an older period of Greek art, and the horse Pegasus is not as yet endowed with wings, which became very soon its never-missing attributes. The modern notion that Pegasus is the symbol of poetical enthusiasm only dates back to the fifteenth century of our era, and was foreign to the Greek.

of this solar hero in the shape of Sampson whose strength is conditioned by his hair, as the power of the sun lies in his rays.

In spite of the strong admixture of foreign mythology, Hercules has become the national hero of Greece, and the Greek idea of salvation has found in him the most typical expression, which has been most beautifully worked out by Æschylus in a grand tragedy which represents Prometheus (the fore-thinker) as struggling and suffering mankind, tied to the pole of misery by Zeus as a punishment for the sin of having brought the bliss of light and fire down to the earth. But at last the divine saviour, Hercules, arrives, and, killing the eagle that lacerates the liver of the bold hero, sets him free.

Prometheus and Hercules are combined into one person in the Christian Saviour, Jesus Christ. The similarity of the story of Golgotha with the myth of Prometheus is not purely accidental. For observe that in some of the older pictures, as for instance in the vase of Chiusi (see illustration on p. 210), Prometheus is not chained to a rock but tied to a pole, i.e., to a σταυρός or cross, and Greek authors frequently use expressions such as the verb άιασκολοπίζεσθαι (Æschylus) and άνασταυ ροῦσθαι (Lucian) which mean "to be crucified."*

Seneca speaks of Hercules as the ideal of the good man who lives exclusively for the welfare of mankind. Contrasting him to Alexander the Great, the conqueror of Asia, he says (*De Benef.,* I, 14):

"Hercules never gained victories for himself. He wandered through the circle of the earth, not as a conqueror, but as a protector. What, indeed, should the enemy of the wicked, the defensor of the good, the peace-bringer, conquer for himself either on land or sea!"

Epictetus praises Hercules frequently and declares that the evils which he combated served to elicit his virtues, and were intended to try him (I, 6). Zeus, who is identified with God, is called his father and Hercules is said to be his son (III, 26). Hercules, when obliged to leave his children, knew them to be in the care of God. Epictetus says (III, 24):

---

* In the beautiful sarcophagus (see illustration on p. 212) which represents the Prometheus myth, the first design is apparently incomplete; for we should expect to see Prometheus represented as stealing the fire and offering it to Deukalion.

PAUL CARUS

"He knew that no man is an orphan, but that there is a father always and constantly for all of them. He had not only heard the words that Zeus was the father of men, for he regarded him as *his* father and called him such; and looking up to him he did what Zeus did. Therefore he could live happily everywhere."

In Christianity the struggles of the saviour receive a dualistic interpretation and are spiritualised into a victory over the temptations of the flesh and other worldly passions.

THE CONCEPTION OF EVIL AS hell received a philosophical foundation in the dualism of Plato who did not shrink from depicting its minutest details; and his views of the future state of the soul, its rewards in heaven and hell, are in close agreement with Christian doctrines, even in most of their details, with the exception of the doctrine of the transmigration of the soul.

Plato concludes his book on the Republic (X, 614–621) with the tale of Er, the son of Armenius, a man who had died and come back to life for the purpose of giving information to mankind concerning the other world which might serve to warn people as to what they had to expect in the life to come. Plato says that this Er, a Pamphylian by birth, was slain in battle, but when the dead were taken up his body was found unaffected by decay, and, on the twelfth day, as he was lying on the funeral pile, he returned to life. Plato continues:

"He [Er, the son of Armenius] said that when his soul left the body he went on a journey with a great company, and that they came to a mysterious place at which there were two openings in the earth; they were near together, and over against them were two other openings in the heaven above. In the intermediate space there were judges seated, who commanded the just, after they had given judgment on them and had bound their sentences in front of them, to ascend by the heavenly way on the right hand; and in like manner the unjust were bidden by them to descend by the lower way on the left hand; these also bore the symbols of their deeds, but fastened on their backs.

"Er said that for every wrong which they had done to any one they suffered tenfold."

Hell is described as follows:

"'And this,' said Er, 'was one of the dreadful sights which we ourselves witnessed. We were at the mouth of the cavern, and, having completed all our experiences, were about to reascend, when of a sudden Ardiaeus [the tyrant] appeared and several others, most of whom were tyrants; and there were also, besides the tyrants, private individuals who had been great criminals: they were, as they fancied, about to return into the upper world, but the mouth, instead of admitting them, gave a roar, whenever any of these incurable sinners or some one who had not been sufficiently punished, tried to ascend; and then wild men of fiery aspect, who were standing by and heard the sound, seized and carried them off; and Ardiaeus and others they bound head and foot and hand, and threw them down and flayed them with scourges, and dragged them along the road at the side, carding them on thorns like wool, and declaring to passers-by what were their crimes, and that they were being taken away to be cast into hell.' And of all the many terrors which they had endured, he said that there was none like the terror which each of them felt at that moment, lest they should hear the voice; and when there was silence, one by one they ascended with exceeding joy. These, said Er, were the penalties and retributions, yet there were blessings as great."

The idea of the rising and sinking of the wicked in hell is similar to the Buddhist view of Buddhagosha who in his parables (translated by Capt. T. Rogers, R. E., pp. 128–129) tells us how the condemned go up and down like grains of rice in a boiling cauldron. The conceptions of the mouth of hell, of the fierce tormentors and the various punishments are probably older than Plato; they reappear in the gnostic doctrines and were retained by Christianity down to the age of the Reformation.

The belief in hell and the anxiety to escape its terrors produced conditions which are drastically described by Plato, who says, speaking of the desire of the wicked to ransom their souls from a deserved punishment:

"Mendicant prophets go to rich men's doors and persuade them that they have a power committed to them by the gods of making an atonement for a man's own or his ancestor's sins by sacrifices or charms, with rejoicings and feasts. . . And they produce a host of books written by Musaeus and Orpheus, who were children of the Moon and the Muses—that is what they say—according to which they perform their ritual, and persuade not only individuals, but whole cities, that expiations and atonements for sin may be made by sacrifices and amusements which fill a vacant hour, and are equally at the service of the living and the dead; the latter sort they call mysteries, and they redeem us from the pain of hell, but if we neglect them no one knows what awaits us."

The dualism that underlies Plato's views began to be taken more seriously by his disciples, the Neo-Platonists, and reached an extraordinary intensity in the beginning of the Christian era. The philosopher longed for death, and the common people feared the terrors of the next life.

The philosophical longing for death is satirically described in one of the epigrams of Callimachus, who says (No. XXIV):

"Cleombrot,* he of Ambracia, took leave of the sun in the heavens:
    Leapt from a wall in the hope Sooner to reach the Beyond;
Not that he e'er had encountered an ill that made life to him hateful;
    Merely because he had read Plato's grand book on the soul."

The idea of immortality became more and more accepted by the masses of the people; but there were many to whom it was no welcome news, for it served only to enhance the fears of man's fate after death. Acquaintance with other religions revealed new terrors everywhere. The Egyptians' dread of judgment in the nether world, the Jews' horror of Gehenna, the Hindus' longing for an escape from future sufferings, were now added to the Greek notions of Hades, and rendered them more terrible than before. The Christian conception of hell is more fearful and at the same time drastic than any one of the older beliefs in future punishment.

---

* Cleombrotus may have been the same disciple of Socrates who is mentioned in Phaedo II, p. 59, c. This strange case of suicide is alluded to by St. Augustine in *de Civ. Dei*, I, 22.—The verses are translated in the original metre.

Lucian tells the story of Peregrinus, surnamed Proteus, who after various adventures became a convert to Christianity. He would have been forgotten and his name would never have been mentioned in history but for the fact that in the presence of a great crowd at the Olympian festivals he burned himself to death on a big pile of wood.

All these strange facts were symptoms which illustrated the religious zeal of the people and characterised the unrest of the times. Further, Plutarch tells us in his *Morals* that the superstitious are chastised by "their own imagination of an anguish that will never cease." He says:

"Wide open stand the deep gates of the Hades that they fable, and there stretches a vista of rivers of fire and Stygian cliffs; and all is canopied with a darkness full of fantasms, of spectres threatening us with terrible faces and uttering pitiful cries."

Mr. F. C. Conybeare, in his *Monuments of Early Christianity*, says, concerning the belief in hell:

"We make a mistake if we think that this awful shadow was not cast across the human mind long before the birth of Christianity. On the contrary, it is a survival from the most primitive stage of our intellectual and moral development. The mysteries of the old Greek and Roman worlds were intended as modes of propitiation and atonement, by which to escape from these all-besetting terrors, and Jesus the Messiah, was the last and best of the λυτήριοι θεοί, of the redeeming gods. In the dread of death and in the belief in the eternal fire of hell, which pervaded men's minds, a few philosophers excepted, Christianity had a *point d'appui*, without availing itself of which it would not have made a single step towards the conquest of men's minds."

And why was Christ a better Saviour than the gods and heroes of Greece? Simply because he was human and realistic, not mythological and symbolical; he was a sufferer and a man,—the son of man, and not a slayer, not a conqueror, not a hero of the ferocious type, ruthless and bloodstained; he fulfilled the moral ideal which had been set up by Plato, who, perhaps under the impression of Æschylus's conception of the tragic fate of Prometheus,* says of the perfect man who would rather be than appear just:

> "They will tell you that the just man who is thought unjust will be scourged, racked, bound; will have his eyes burnt out; and, at last, after suffering every kind of evil, he will be hung up at the pale."

The strangest thing about this passage is that the word ἀνασχινδυλευθήσεται, which means "he will be hung up at the stake," or "fixed on a pale," is an older synonym of the New Testament term σταυρόειν, commonly translated "to crucify."

Alluding to Plato, Apollonius, a Christian martyr, declares:

> "One of the Greek Philosophers said: The just man shall be tortured, he shall be spat upon, and last of all he shall be crucified. Just as the Athenians passed an unjust sentence of death, and charged him falsely, because they yielded to the mob, so also our Saviour was at last sentenced to death by the lawless."†

In the days of Augustus and his successors the people were taught to expect salvation, the dispensation of justice, protection, peace, and prosperity from the emperor; and just as we have today monarchies where the king regards himself as the Anointed One by the grace of God and a representative of God on earth, so the Roman emperor arrogated to himself divine honors, and even philosophers such as Seneca did not hesitate to acknowledge the claim. The practical significance of this view is that the government should be regarded with religious awe, and its officers, as such, are divine. The Christians who refused to worship before the emperor's images must have appeared to the Romans of those days as anarchists and rebels. But when Nero committed matricide and other most outrageous crimes, the belief in the emperor's divinity dwindled away, and the idea of the suffering God, the man who died on the cross because he would rather be than appear just, gained ground among the people.

---

* See above, p. 210.
† The Apology and Acts of Apollonius, 40–41. Translated by F. C. Conybeare in *Monuments of Early Christianity,* p. 47.

CHRISTIANITY WAS NOT THE ONLY religion which promised deliverance from evil through the saving power of blood and by means of a vicarious atonement, for we know of the immortality-promising mysteries, and especially of the cult of Mithras, which had embodied many ideas and ceremonies that are also met with in Christianity.

The early Christians belonged exclusively to the lower walks of life, and the earliest Church authorities, with few exceptions, were by no means cultured or highly educated persons. Some Christian writers were quite talented men; but few of the Church fathers can be said to have enjoyed more than a mediocre education. Platonic philosophy, for instance, did not enter into Christian minds directly, but only through the channels of Philo's books. Thus it is natural that Christians were lacking both in knowledge as to the origin of many of their rites and also in critique, and when they were confronted with the same practices and conceptions among non-Christians, they were puzzled and found no other explanation for such remarkable coincidences, than the guiles of Satan. Even the most peculiarly Christian sacrament, the Lord's Supper, was, according to the testimony of Justin Martyr, celebrated by the Persians in the same way as by the Christians;[*] and Justin is ingenuous enough to attribute this coincidence without the slightest hesitation to the influence of evil spirits. Tertullian is also aware of many similarities between Church institutions and the pagan modes of Mithras worship, which observation prompted him to declare that "Satan imitates the sacraments of God."[†] The Devil appears to have been very cunning in those days, for if he had not daring spies in heaven, he must himself have anticipated the Lord's plans; for the pagan institutions spoken of as Satanic imitations, such as the Persian haoma sacrifice, the eating of consecrated cakes in commemoration of the dead for the sake of obtaining life immortal are older than Christianity.[‡]

The competitors of Christianity which endeavored to embody the religious ideals of the age, for various reasons failed to be satisfactory, leaving the field to Christianity, which in its main doctrines was simple

---

[*] *Apol.*, 86.

[†] Dei sacramenta Satanas affectat. *De exh. cast.*, 13.

[‡] After Chiflet, reproduced from C. W. King. Two erect serpents stand like supporters, on both sides. Mithras, between the stars of the twins (the Dioscuri), holds the horses of the rising and of the setting sun, or of life and death. Above his head, the raven; in the sky, the emblems of sun and moon. Underneath. the table with the consecrated bread and the cup of the Eucharist.

PAUL CARUS

and in its morality direct and practical. But it is to be regretted that the fanaticism of Christian monks has almost totally wiped out the traces of other religious aspirations, leaving only scattered fragments, which are, however, very interesting to the historian, partly on account of their similarity to Christianity, partly through their dissimilarities.

We know of several Oriental gods who became fashionable at Rome, among whom Mithras, the Egyptian Serapis, and Iao-Abraxas were the most celebrated.

The influence of Mithras worship on Christianity is well established.* We mention especially the rites of baptism, the Eucharist, facing the Orient in prayer, the sanctification of the day of the sun, and the celebration of the winter solstice as the birthday of the Saviour. Concerning this latter institution, the Rev. Robert Sinker says in William Smith's *Dictionary of Christian Antiquities* (pp. 357–8):

> "As Mithraicism gradually blended with Christianity, changing its name but not altogether its substance, many of its ancient notions and rites passed over too, and the Birthday of the Sun, the visible manifestation of Mithras himself, was transferred to the commemoration of the Birth of Christ.
>
> "Numerous illustrations of the above remarks may be found in ancient inscriptions, *e.g.,* SOLI INVICTO ET LUNAE AETERNAE C. VETTI GERMANI LIB. DUO PARATUS ET HERMES DEDERUNT,[†] or ΗαιΩ ΜιΘΡα ΑΝΙΚΗΤΩ[‡] (Gruter, *Inscriptiones Antiquae,* p. xxxiii). In the legend on the reverse of the copper coins of Constantine, SOLI INVICTO COMITI,[§] retained long after his conversion, there is at once an idea of the ancient Sun-God, and of the new Sun of Righteousness.
>
> "The supporters of this theory cite various passages from early Christian writers indicating a recognition of this view. The sermon of Ambrose, quoted by Jablonsky, is certainly spurious, and is so

---

* The mysteries of Mithras were introduced into Greece at the time of Alexander. They gained more and more influence until they reached a climax in the second century of the Christian era. Most of the many monuments which the Mithras worship left all over the Roman empire, especially in Gallia and Germany, date from this period when it had almost become a rival of Christianity.

† "To the unconquerable sun and the eternal moon this is given by P. and H., the two children of C. V. G."

‡ I.e., Helios (or the sun) Mithras the invincible.

§ "To the invincible Sun, the protector."

marked in the best editions of his works; it furnishes, however, an interesting illustration of an early date. The passage runs thus: 'Bene quodammodo sanctum hunc diem Natalis Domini *So-'lem novum* vulgus appellat, et tanta sui auctoritate id confirmat, 'ut Judaei etiam atque Gentiles in hanc vocem consentiant. Quod 'libenter amplectandum nobis est, quia oriente Salvatore, non so-'lum humani generis salus, sed etiam solis ipsius claritas innova-'tur.'* (Serm. 6, *in Appendice,* p. 397, ed. Bened.)

"In the Latin editions of Chrysostom is a homily, wrongly ascribed to him, but probably written not long after his time, in which we read: 'Sed et *Invicti Natalem* appellant. Quis utique 'tam invictus nisi Dominus noster, qui mortem subactam devicit? 'Vel quod dicunt Solis esse Natalem, ipse est Sol Justitiae, de quo 'Malachias propheta dixit, Orietur vobis timentibus nomen ipsius 'Sol Justitiae et sanitas est in pennis ejus.'† (*Sermo de Nativitate S. Joannis Baptistae;* vol. ii. 1113, ed. Paris, 1570.

"Leo the Great finds fault with the baneful persuasion of some 'quibus haec dies solemnitatis nostrae, non tam de Nativitate 'Christi, *quam de novi ut dicunt solis ortu, honorabilis videtur.'‡* (Serm. 22,§ 6, vol. i. p. 72, ed. Ballerini.) Again, the same father observes: 'Sed hanc adorandam in caelo et in terra Nativitatem nul'lus nobis dies magis quam hodiernus insinuat, et nova etiam

---

* "Well do the common people call this somehow sacred day of the birth of the Lord 'a new sun,' and confirm it with so great an authority of theirs that Jews and Gentiles concur in this mode of speech. And this should willingly be accepted by us, because with the birth of the Saviour there comes not only the salvation of mankind, but the brightness of the sun itself is renewed."

† "But they call it the birthday of the Invincible (i.e., Mithras). Who, however, is invincible if not our Lord, who has conquered death? Further, if they say 'it is the birthday of the sun,' He is the sun of righteousness, about whom the prophet Malachi says, 'Unto you that fear my name shall the sun of righteousness arise with healing in his wings.'" Observe in this passage that the prophet thinks of the sun of God after the Babylonian and Egyptian fashion, as having wings which are of a wholesome or healing influence.

The preceding lines of this quotation from Chrysostom (Hom. 31) plainly state that Christ's birthday has been fixed upon the day of the birth of Mithras: "On this day (the birthday of Mithras) also the birthday of Christ was lately fixed at Rome in order that whilst the heathen were busied with their profane ceremonies, the Christians might perform their holy rites undisturbed."

‡ Some to whom this day of our celebration is worthy of honor not so much on account of the birth of Christ as for the sake of the renewal of the sun."

in 'elementis luce radiante, coram (al. totam) sensibus nostris mira'bilis sacramenti ingerit claritatem.'* (Serm. 26, § 1, p. 87.)

"We may further cite one or two instances from ancient Christian poets:. Prudentius, in his hymn *Ad Natalem Domini,* thus speaks (*Cathemerinon*, xi. init., p. 364, ed. Arevalus):

> '*Quid est, quod arctum circulum sol jam recurrens deserit?*
> *Christusne terris nascitur qui lucis auget tramitem?*'[†]

Paulinus of Nola also (*Poema* xiv. 15–19, p. 382, ed. Muratori):

> '*Nam post solstitium, quo Christus corpore natus*
> *Sole novo gelidae mutavit tempora brumae,*
> *Atque salutiferum praestans mortalibus ortum,*
> *Procedente die, secum decrescere noctes*
> *Jussit.*'[‡]

Reference may also be made to an extract in Assemani (*Bibl. Or. i.* 163) from Dionysius Bar-Salibi, bishop of Amida, which shows traces of a similar feeling in the East; also to a passage from an anonymous Syrian writer, who distinctly refers the fixing of the day to the above cause; we are not disposed, however, to attach much weight to this last passage. More important for our purpose is the injunction of a council of Rome (743 A.D.): 'Ut nullus Kalendas Januarias et broma (= brumalia) colere praesumpserit'[§] (can. 9, Labbé vi. 1548), which shows at any rate that for a long time after the fall of heathenism, many traces of heathen rites still remained."

---

* "But no other day appears to us more appropriate than today for worshipping in heaven and earth the Feast of the Nativity, and while even in the material world (in the elements) a new light shines, He confers on us before our very senses, the brightness of His wonderful sacrament."

† "Why does the sun already leave the circle of the arctic north?

  Is not Christ born upon the earth who will the path of light increase?"

‡ "Truly, after the solstice, when Christ is born in the body,

  With a new sun he will change the frigid days of the north wind.

  While he is offering to mortals the birth that will bring them salvation,

  Christ with the progress of days gives command that the nights be declining."

§ "No one shall celebrate the 1st of January and the Brumalia."

Æon, the lion faced, with key, torch, and measuring staff is a divinity of considerable importance in the religion of Mithras. He is the Zrvan Akarana (Time unlimited) of the *Zendavesta*, not so much a personality as a personified abstraction, representing the primordial state of existence from which Ahura Mazda is born. The serpent's coils that surround his body represent the revolutions of time, his wings the four seasons. His relation to the deities of the Greek pantheon, Hephæstus, Æsculapius, Hermes, and Dionysius, is indicated by the presence of their emblems.

Mr. W. C. King quotes from Flaminius Vacca (No. 117) the interesting story of the discovery of an Æon statue as follows:

"I remember there was found in the vineyard of Sig. Orazio Muti (where the treasure was discovered), opposite S. Vitale, an idol in marble, about 5 palms high (3½ feet), standing erect upon a pedestal in an empty chamber, with the door walled up. Around him were many little lamps in terra cotta, set with their nozzles towards the idol. This had a lion's head, and the rest of the body that of a man. Under his feet was a globe, whence sprang a serpent which encompassed all the idol, and its head entered into his mouth. He had his hands crossed upon the breast: a key in each, four wings fastened upon the shoulders, two pointing upwards, two downwards. I do not consider it a very antique work, being done in a rude manner; or perhaps it is so ancient that at the time it was made the good style was not yet known. Sig. Orazio, however, told me that a theologian, a Jesuit Father, explained its meaning, saying it signified the Devil, who in the time of heathenism ruled over the world; hence the globe under his feet; the serpent which begirt him and entered into his mouth, his foretelling the future with ambiguous responses; the keys in his hands, his sovereignty over the world; the lion's head, the ruler of all beasts. The wings signified his presence everywhere. Such was the version given by the aforesaid Father. I have done everything to see the idol, but Sig. Orazio being now dead, his heirs do not know what has become of it. It is not unlikely that by the advice of the theologian, Sig. Orazio may have sent it to some *lime-kiln to cure its dampness*, for it had been buried many and many a year."

Iao, the god with the adorable name (i.e., Abraxas),* bears the cock's head, which is the emblem of Æsculapius, the god of healing. When Socrates died he requested his friends to sacrifice a cock to Æsculapius because his soul had recovered from the disease of bodily existence. The serpent (the emblem of mystery, of eternity, of wisdom, the prophet of the gnosis) walks without feet, and therefore Iao is serpent-legged.

The God of Goodness, or Agathodæmon, exercised a great charm upon the minds of the people. He is represented on gems in the shape of a serpent whose head is surrounded with solar rays, hovering about the sacred cista, the cylindrical box, from which the priest emerged at the celebration of the mystery.

The design of the Agathodæmon is as common as the Iao design and that it was used as an amulet appears from a passage of Galen, who says:

"Some, indeed, assert that a virtue of this kind is inherent in certain stones, such as is in reality possessed by the green jasper, which benefits the chest and mouth of the stomach, if tied upon them. Some, indeed, set the stone in a ring and engrave upon it a serpent with his head crowned with rays, according as is prescribed by King Nechepsos in his thirteenth book."

How excusable these gnostic superstitions were in those days appears from the strange fact that such a sober man as Galen believed in the efficiency of these amulets. He continues:

"Of this I have had ample experience, having made a necklace of such stones and hung it round the patient's neck, descending low enough for the stones to touch the mouth of the stomach, and they proved to be of no less benefit thus than if they had been engraved in the manner laid down by King Nechepsos." (De Simp. Med., IX)

To us who have grown up under the influence of Christian traditions, the idea of representing the Good God under the allegory of a serpent

---

* Abrak is Egyptian, and means "bow down" or "adore." The word occurs in the Bible, Gen. 41, 43. Sas (standing for *Sadshi*) means "name." Abraxas is the name to be adored. (See King, *The Gnostics*, p. 36.)

seems strange, but we must bear in mind that other people and other ages had different ideas associated with the serpent. To the people of the Orient the limbless serpent was a symbol of mystery, and represented health and immortality. Eusebius (I, 7) informs us:

> "The serpent never dies naturally, but only when injured by violence, whence the Phœnicians have named it the good genius (Agathodaemon). Similarly the Egyptians have called him Cneph and given him a hawk's head on account of the special swiftness of that bird."

Serapis, which is a Hellenised form of Osiris-Apis, was a religion which in many respects resembled Christianity. Their sacred symbol was the cross, as we know through Christian authors,[*] and Emperor Adrian (no mean authority in such matters) speaks of Serapis worshippers as Christians, saying that those who consecrated themselves to Serapis called themselves "bishops of Christ." Even if a local blending of Christianity with the Serapis cult in Egypt had not taken place we must recognise that the monkish institutions of the Serapean temples were an exact prototype of the Christian monasteries which originated in Egypt and flourished there better than anywhere else.

The Serapis cult was a reformation of the old Egyptian Osiris worship, introduced by Ptolemy Soter for the purpose of adapting the old traditions of Egypt to the Hellenic culture of Alexandria.

Akin in spirit but independent in its development, is the worship of the Egyptian Tot, the ibis-headed scribe of the gods. Originally a personification of the moon, Tot, or Tehuti, was the deity of all measure, and thus his importance grew to signify the divine cosmic order. He is called "Ibis the Glorious," and "the Ibis who proceeded from Ptah." Osiris, the dying and resurrected God, is identified with him as "Osiris the Ibis, the Blessed One." Together with the moon god, Xunsu and Máut, he is worshipped in the trinity Xunsu-Máut-Tehuti as the "child ever being born again."[†]

Among the Greeks, Tot was identified with Hermes, who now begins to play a very prominent rôle as Hermes Trismegistos, the thrice great, the saviour of souls. Hermes is now adored as the first-born

---

[*] See Socrates, *Eccl. Hist.*, 5, 17, which report is repeated by Sozomenes.
[†] R. Pietschmann. *Hermes Trismegistos,* p. 7.

son of Zeus, and is even identified with the father of the gods as his representative and plenipotentiary.

The philosophers of the time bear the stamp of their age. Thus Seneca, Epictetus, Marcus Aurelius, and other pagan sages are kindred in spirit to the Christian religion; they are under the influence of Platonism; they object to the idolatry of polytheism and demand a pure theism; they speak of the fatherhood of God; they insist upon morality and are inclined to conceive the soul as distinct from, and superior to, the body which is regarded as its temporal tabernacle, and as the seat, if not cause, of all evil. Yet they are philosophers, not pastors. They are too aristocratic to appreciate their kinship to Christianity. They even show a contempt for the religion of the vulgar, and they themselves appeal to the thinkers, not to the toilers, not to the multitudes, not to the poor in spirit.

Græco-Egyptians developed a religious philosophy upon the basis of ancient Egyptian traditions, compiled in a book called the *Divine Pymander*,* which contains many beautiful sayings that remind us of Christian views; but the *Divine Pymander* (like other philosophical books) is addressed to the few not to the many, and its mysticism rendered it unfit to become the religion of mankind.

Apollonius of Tyana is a figure in many respects similar, but by no means superior, to Jesus Christ. For in him the philosophy of the age becomes a religion. His followers, however, were neither better nor wiser than the early Christians; they shared with them the same superstitions, cherishing the same trust in miracles, yet for all we know, they had only few of their redeeming features.

Julian, surnamed by Christian authors the Apostate, is in spite of his idealism a reactionary man who set his face against Christianity because he recognised in the latter the most powerful representative of the coming faith. This last pagan emperor, it is true, was a noble-minded and thoughtful man who opposed Christianity mainly on account of its shortcomings, its Jewish affiliations, and the narrowness of its devotees, but he was enamored with the past, and his highest ambition was to revive the barbarism of pagan institutions, which tendency appears most plainly in his retention of bloody sacrifices, his esteem for oracles and a general indulgence in the mysteries of Neo-Platonism.

---

* The term "Pymander" is commonly explained to mean ποιμὴν ἀνδρῶν, i.e., "shepherd of man."

The various schools of post-Christian gnosticism were in all probability the most dangerous competitors of Christianity, which explains the bitterness with which the Church-fathers revile gnostic doctrines. But the gnostics were after all so similar to the Christians that some Church-fathers use the name "Gnostic" as a synonym for Christians. Gnostic teachers are looked upon less as strangers than as heretics, and their speculations have been an important factor in the development of Christian dogmas.

The gnostics, as a rule, represent the demiurge, i.e., the architect of the world, whom they identify with the Jewish Yahveh, as the father of all evil. They describe him as irascible, jealous, and revengeful, and contrast him with the highest God who had nothing to do with the creation. As the demiurge created the world, he has a right to it, but he was overcome through the death of Jesus. The demiurge thought to conquer Jesus when he let him die on the cross, but his triumph was preposterous, for through the passion and death of the innocent Jesus the victory of God was won and the salvation of mankind became established.

One peculiarly interesting sect of gnostics is called the Ophites, or serpent worshippers. The demiurge (so they hold), on recognising the danger that might result from the emancipation of man through gnosis (i.e., knowledge or enlightenment), forbade him to eat from the fruit of the tree of knowledge. But the God, the highest Lord, the all-good and all-wise Deity, took compassion on man and sent the serpent to induce him to eat of the tree of knowledge so that he might escape the bondage of ignorance in which Yahveh, the demiurge, tried to hold him.

The serpent appears on many gnostic gems and is never missing in the Mithras monuments. Frequently it is found on Christian devices where it is sometimes difficult to interpret it as the representative of evil.

Irenæus, an adversary of the gnostic view, replaced the demiurge by the Devil, whom he regards as a rebel angel, having fallen by pride and arrogance, envying God's creation (*Adv. hær.*, No. 40). He agrees, however, with the gnostics, in that he maintains that the Devil had claims upon man because of man's sin. Jesus, however, having paid the debt of mankind, has the power to redeem the souls of men from the clutches of the Devil who, by having treated a sinless man as a sinner, became now himself a debtor of mankind.

This juridical theory of the death of Jesus and his relation to the Devil was further elaborated by Origen. According to Origen the sacrifice of

Jesus is not rendered to make an atonement to God or satisfy his feeling of justice (which is the Protestant conception), but to pay off the Devil. Jesus is, as it were, a bait for the Devil. Satan imagines he must destroy Jesus, but having succeeded in killing him, finds out to his unspeakable regret that he has been outwitted by the Lord. God had set a trap, and the Devil was foolish enough to allow himself to be caught.

Manes, a man educated in the Zoroastrian faith, endeavored to found a universal religion through the synthesis of all the religions he knew; and because Manicheism, as this view is called, contains many Christian elements, it is commonly regarded as a Christian or a gnostic sect, but it was strongly denounced as heretical by St. Augustine. Manes taught the Persian dualism, but St. Augustine, who formulated the orthodox Christian doctrine denying the independent existence of evil, explains the presence of sin in the world by the free will with which Adam was endowed at creation, and regards evil as a means to an end in God's plan of education.

CHRISTIANITY TRIUMPHED OVER PAGANISM, AND it did so by embodying in its fabric everything that in those days was regarded as true and good and elevating. Thus the adoration of statues and images, at first so vehemently denounced by Christians as heathenish, was reintroduced with all the pagan methods of worship, the burning of incense, processions, sprinkling with holy water, and other rituals. The old symbol of the labarum was interpreted as the monogram of Christ; and the sacred mark of two intersecting lines, a religious emblem of great antiquity, was identified with the cross of Golgotha. The figure of two intersecting lines was a mark of salvation among the Syrians and other nations, and the probability is that it represented the four quarters of the compass;* but now since is was called a cross, it recovered in a higher degree its traditional reputation as a powerful magic charm and was extensively used for exorcisms.† There is no doctrine on which the

---

* The equilateral cross of Paganism is frequently, though not always, ornamented with four dots, one in each corner. We believe we are not mistaken when we interpret the dots as emblems of the sun in its four resepective positions, in the east, south, west and north. Egyptian wall-pictures show the Apis covered with this sacred symbol, (see e.g. Lenormant, *L'Hist. Anc. de l'Orient,* V, 183.) and it serves as a not uncommon pattern on the dresses of various Greek deities.

† For further details see the author's articles on *The Cross, Its History and Significance in The Open Court,* 1899 and 1900. Their publication in book form is contemplated by The Open Court Publishing Co.

Christian fathers so thoroughly agree as on the belief that the Devil is afraid of the cross.

The Greek gods were regarded as demons by the early Christians, but the ideas which found expression in the mythology of Greece, in the tales of Greek deities and heroes, were retained and Christianised. The old Greek saviours simply changed names and became Christian saints, or at least contributed important features to the legends of their lives.

Christianity is a religion of peace, but the Western nations are warlike, and at the very beginning of the Christian era the need was felt to have the spirit of belligerency consecrated by religious sentiment and represented in struggling saints and angels.

The Christian patron saint of fighters is St. George, and it is natural that the English, who among the Christian nations are not the least pious and at the same time not the least belligerent, have chosen the name of St. George for their battle-cry.

The legend and pictures of St. George remind us strongly of the myths of Perseus. In its Christian form the tale appears first in the *Legendæ Sanctorum* of Jacobus de Voragine, who tells us of a pagan city, the neighborhood of which was infested by a dragon that had to be appeased by human sacrifices. The monster was finally slain by St. George, a chivalrous Christian knight, who arrived at the moment the king's daughter was offered as a victim. The princess, at the request of the knight, tied her girdle round the dragon's neck, who now, although the beast had been reported dead, rises and follows the virgin like a tame lamb to the city. The people are frightened by the sight, but St. George kills him once more, this time for good. St. George is richly rewarded, but he distributes his wealth among the poor, converts the King and his subjects to Christianity, and goes to another land, where he dies a martyr's death.

The historical St. George, an archbishop of Alexandria and a follower of Arius, possesses no features whatever of the heroic dragon-slayer of the legend. According to the unanimous report of Christian and pagan historians, he was an abject, cringing fellow, and when he had attained the high position of archbishop, proved a cruel and extortionate tyrant who was greatly hated by the people. He was deposed by the worldly authorities and put in jail on Christmas eve, 361. But his enemies, mostly poor people belonging to his diocese, grew tired of the delay of the law; a mob broke open the prison doors and lynched the deposed archbishop on January 17, 362. His violent death was later on regarded as a sufficient title to the glory of the martyr's crown. The most important service he rendered the Church consisted in the fact, that the official recognition of an Arian saint helped to reconcile the followers of Arius.

Gelarius seems to be the first Roman Catholic Pope who mentions St. George, and he knows nothing of his life, but counts him among those saints "who are better known to God than to mankind."* It is difficult to say whether His Holiness was conscious of the irony of this passage.

It is an unsolved problem how St. George could have been identified with the dragon-slaying deities of ancient pagan mythologies. The connecting links are missing, but it is probable that there is no deeper reason than a similarity in the sound of names. Perhaps a solar deity was somewhere worshipped under the name γεωργός, i.e., tiller of the ground, because the civilisation of agriculture overcame the dragon of savage barbarism.

The final conqueror of the dragon, however, is not St. George, but the Archangel Michael, who, on the day of judgment, plays the part of Zeus defeating the giants and Typhaeus, or the Teuton God Thor, slaying the Midgard serpent; and when the victory is gained Michael will hold the balances in which the souls are weighed.

The belligerent spirit did not remain limited to Michael and St. George, but was also imputed to other saints who proved their prowess in various ways in their encounters with the Evil One. St. Anthony, of Egypt (251–356), the founder of the Christian monastery system, is reported to have battled with evil spirits in the desert near Thebes, whither he withdrew from the world to practise severe penances. His heroic deeds, which consist of frightful struggles with the demons of his imagination, have been recorded by the good Bishop Athanasius, whose book on the subject is of special interest because it contains an essay written by St. Anthony himself, containing the gist of his wisdom and experience in struggling with evil spirits.†
The artistic genius of Salvator Rosa gave a concrete plausibility to the story in a highly dramatic picture illustrating the combat in a critical moment when only the cross saved the undaunted saint from defeat

---

* Qui *Deo magis quam hominibus noti sunt.*

† See the *Acta Sanctorum* of the Bolandists for January 17, which is observed as St. Anthony's day. In addition there are several Latin translations of St. Anthony's letters extant in the *Biblioticia Patrum.*

during a daring onslaught of the fiend in his most horrible shape. (See the illustration on p. 236.)

There can scarcely be any doubt that the original doctrine of Jesus of Nazareth was an ethics of peace; not only peacefulness and gentleness of mind in general, but peace at any price, and a non-resistance to evil. The warlike spirit among later Christians and the worship of belligerent archangels and saints were introduced into the writings of the early Church from pagan sources and the importance of this phase of Christianity grew with its expanse among the energetic races of the North. The Teutonic nations, the Norsemen, the Germans, the Anglo-Saxons and their kin, whose conversion is the greatest conquest Christianity ever made, proved no less belligerent than the Greek and Roman, but they were their superiors in strength, in generosity, in fairness toward their enemies, and in purity of morals.

The Demonology of Northern Europe

The religion of the Teutons was in the main a religion of fighters, and we do not hesitate to say that they, more than any other people on earth, developed the ethics of struggle. War, strife, and competition, are frequently regarded as in themselves detestable and immoral, but the Teutons discovered that life means strife, and that therefore courage is the root of all virtue. Their highest ideal was not to shrink from the unavoidable, but to face it squarely and unflinchingly. Their chief god was the god of war, and their noblest consummation of life was death on the battlefield. They despised the coward who was afraid of wounds and death. They respected and even honored their enemies if they were but brave. They scorned deceit and falsity and would rather be honestly defeated than gain a victory by trickery. And this view did not remain a mere theory with them, but was practised in life. The Teutons were repeatedly defeated by the Romans, by Marius, Cæsar, and others who were less scrupulous in their methods of fighting, but in the long run they remained victorious and built a Teutonic empire upon the débris of Rome.

The idea of evil played an important part in the religion of the Teutons.

Loki, the god of fire, the cunning mischief-maker among the Asas, is believed to have brought sin and evil into the world. In the younger Edda, Loki takes part in the creation of man, whom he endows with the senses, passions, and evil desires. Loki's children are (1) the Fenris wolf, (2) the Jormungander, i.e., the Midgard serpent, and (3) Hel, the queen of Nifelheim, the world of the dead.

Loki induced the gods to build fortifications, for which the architect, who was one of the giants and an enemy of the gods, should, if he finished his work in a stipulated time, receive as remuneration Freyja, the goddess of beauty and love. But when it became apparent that the walls would be soon completed, Loki, true to his treacherous character, assisted the gods in cheating the architect. He further helped the giant Thjasse to steal Idun with her immortality-giving golden apples. Only when the gods threatened to punish him did he become accessory in bringing Idun back again. The worst deed which Loki accomplished was the death of Baldur, the god of light and purity. After that he was outlawed and resided no longer in Asgard. But he came back and mocked the gods when they were assembled at Ægir's banquet. At last he was captured and in punishment for his crimes tied upon three pointed rocks right beneath the mouth of a serpent. Sigyn, Loki's wife, remains with him to catch the dripping venom in a bowl, which from time to time she empties. Whenever the bowl is withdrawn the venom drops into Loki's face and he writhes with pain, which makes the world tremble in what men call earthquakes.

The most remarkable feature of Teutonic mythology is the conception of doomsday or Ragnarok (the twilight of the gods), boding a final destruction of the world, including all the gods. At present the powers of evil are fettered and subdued, but the time will come when they will be set loose. Loki, the Fenris wolf, the Midgard serpent, and Hel, with their army of frost giants and other evil beings, will approach; Heimdall, the watchman of the gods, will blow his horn, and the Asas prepare for battle. The combat on the field Vigrid will be internecine, for the Asas are to die while killing the monsters of wickedness whom they encounter, and the flames of Muspil will devour the wrecks of the universe.

The world had a beginning, it therefore must come to an end; but when the world is destroyed a new heaven and a new earth will rise from the wreck of the old one, and the new world will be better than the old one. Leif-thraser and his wife Lif (representing the desire for Life and potential Life) remained concealed during the catastrophe in Hodmimer's grove and were not harmed by the flames. They now become the parents of a new race that will inhabit the new abode, called *Gimel* (the German *Himmel*), and among them will be found Odhin with his sons, Thor, Baldur, Fro, and all the other Asas.

Christianity Teutonised

WHEN CHRISTIANITY SPREAD OVER NORTHERN Europe it came into contact with the Teutonic and Celtic nations, who added new ideas to its system and transformed several characteristic features of its world-view. Christianity today is essentially a Teutonic religion. The ethics of Christianity, which formerly was expressed in the sentence "Resist not evil," began, in agreement with the combative spirit of the Teuton race, more and more to emphasise the necessity of struggle. Not only was the figure of Christ conceived after the model of a Teutonic war-king, the son of the emperor, while his disciples became his faithful vassals; not only did the archangels assume the features of the Asas, the great northern gods, Wodan, Donar, Fro, and others; not only were the old pagan feasts changed into Christian festivals; the Yuletide became Christmas and the Ostara feast in the spring was celebrated in commemoration of Christ's resurrection; but the individual features of the evil powers of the North were also transferred to Satan and his host.

Teutonic legends and fairy tales frequently mention the Devil, and there he possesses many features that remind us of Loki. In addition, the ice giants of the Norsemen, the Nifelheim of the Saxons, the Nether-world of the Irish, all contributed their share to the popular notions of the Christian demonology of the Middle Ages. The very name "hell" is a Teutonic word which originally signified a hollow space or a cave underground, and denotes the realm of Hel, Loki's daughter. The weird and terrible appearances of the gods, too, were retained for the adornment of demoniacal legends; and Odhin as storm-god became "the wild hunter."

Dr. Ernst Krause, who is best known under his *nom de plume* of Carus Sterne, has undertaken the work of proving the Northern influence upon Southern fairy tales and legends.* He finds that all the myths which symbolise the death and resurrection of the sun, giving rise to the idea of immortality, doomsday, and the final restoration of the world, have originated in Northern countries where on Christmas day the sun that seemed lost returns spreading again light and life. Our philologists believe that the Nibelungenlied contains features of Homer's great epics; but, according to Dr. Krause, it would seem that the original source of the Nibelungenlied is older than Homer, and that the theme of the Völuspa, the first song of the Edda, being a vision that proclaims the final destruction and degeneration of heaven and earth, antedates Christ's prophecies of the coming judgment. (Matt., 24.) Christianity comes to us from the Orient, but the idea that a God will die and be resurrected is of Northern origin.

Dr. Krause proceeds to prove that the conception of hell as depicted in Dante's *Divina Comedia,* which may be regarded as the classical conception of Roman Catholic Christianity, is in all its essential elements the product of a Northern imagination.† Dante followed closely Teutonic traditions, which in his time had become

---

* *Die Trojaburgen Nord-Europas.* Glogau, Carl Flemming, 1893.
† *Vossische Zeitung,* 1896, Feb. 2, 9, 10; Sonntagsbeilagen.

a common possession in the Christian world through the writings of Saxo Grammaticus, Beda Venerabilis, Albericus, Caedmon, Caesarius of Heisterbach, and others. It is specially noteworthy that the deepest hell of Dante's Inferno is not, as Southern people are accustomed to describe the place of torture, a burning sulphur lake, but the wintry desolation of an ice-palace. That this ice hell can be traced back to the days of Gnosticism would only prove that this Northern influence may, in many of its most characteristic features, date back to a prehistoric age.

Dante's vision is by no means the product of his own imagination. It embodies a great number of old traditions. Dante reproduced in his description of Satan and hell the mythological views of the North so popular in his days. His cantos not only remind us of Ulysses's and Virgil's journey to the Nether-world, but also and mainly of Knight Owain's descent into St. Patrick's Purgatory in Ireland, and of the vision of hell as described by Beda, Albericus, and Chevalier Tundalus. In the last song of the Inferno, Dante describes the residence of the sovereign of hell, which is surrounded by a thick fog, so as to make it necessary for the poet to be led by the hand of his guide. There the ice-palace stands almost inaccessible through the cold blizzards that blow about it; and there the ruler of hell and his most cursed fellows stand with their bodies partly frozen in the transparent ice.

Dante's portraiture of the evil demon whom he calls "Dis" agrees exactly with the appearance of the principal Northern deity of evil, as he was commonly revered among the Celts, the Teutons, and the Slavs. Dis has three faces: one in front, and one on each side. The middle face is red, that on the right side whitish-yellow, that on the left side, black. Thus the trinity idea was transferred to Satan on account of the ill-shaped idols of the crude art of Northern civilisation. Dante's description of Dis reminds us not only of the three-headed hoar-giant of the Edda, Hrim-Grimnir, who lives at the door of death, but also of the trinity of various pagan gods, especially of Triglaf, the triune deity of the Slavs.

When Bishop Otto of Bamberg converted the Pomeranians to Christianity, he broke, in 1124, the three-headed Triglaf idol in the temple of Stettin and sent its head to Pope Honorius II. at Rome. Dr. Krause suggests that since Dante, who as an ambassador of Florence visited Rome in 1301, must have seen with his own eyes the head of the Pomeranian Triglaf, it is by no means impossible that he used it as a prototype for the description of his trinitarian Satan.

The Giants

IT IS INTERESTING TO OBSERVE the transformation of the old Teutonic giants who were plain personifications of the crude forces of nature, into Christian devils. Northern mythology represents the giants, be they mountain giants, storm-giants, frost-giants, fog-giants, or what not, as stupid, and they are frequently conquered by the wisdom of the gods, or by human cunning and invention. There are innumerable legends which preserve the old conception and simply replace the names of giants by devils; and we can observe that all the conquests of man over nature are, in the old sense of the Teutonic mythology, described as instances in which giants or devils are outwitted in one way or another.

The giants, as representatives of mountains, forests, rivers, lakes, and the soil of the earth, are always bent on collecting the rent that is due to the owner of the land, for men are merely tenants of the earth, which by right belongs to the giants. The giants envy men their comfort and try to destroy their work. Thus the fog-giant Grendel appears at night-time in the hall of King Hrodhgar and devours at each visit thirty men. Beowulf, the sun-hero, fights with him and cuts off his arm; he then encounters Grendel's mother, the giantess of the marsh whence the fog rises, and finally succeeds in killing both Grendel and his mother.

The parades of giant families which form an important feature of Dutch and Flemish carnivals may be a relic of older customs representing visits of the lords of the ground collecting their rents, which is given in refreshments while the people sing the giant-song* with the refrain:

> *"Keer u eens om, reuzjen, reuzjen!"*
> [Return once more little giant, little giant.]

Burying Alive

THE PRIVILEGE OF COLLECTING RENT which the forces of nature, be they gods, demons, or giants, and later on in their stead, the Devil, were supposed to possess, led to the idea of offering sacrifices in payment of the debt due to the powerful and evil-minded landlords, the owners of the soil. And this notion resulted in the superstition of burying alive

---

* *Floegel's Geschichte des Grotesk-Komischen,* by Ebeling, p. 286, quotes the giant-song as sung in Ypern.

either human beings or animals, a practice which at a certain stage of civilisation probably was all but universal and received even the sanction of the God of Israel.*

Grimm says (*Mythology*, p. 109):

"Frequently it was regarded as necessary to entomb within the foundation of a building living creatures and even men, an act which was regarded as a sacrifice to the soil which had to endure the weight of the structure. By this cruel custom people hoped to attain permanence and stability for great buildings."

There are innumerable stories which preserve records of this barbaric custom, and there can be no doubt that many of them are historical and that the practice continued until a comparatively recent time. We read in Thiele (*Dänische Volkssagen*, I, 3) that the walls of Copenhagen always sank down again and again, although they were constantly rebuilt, until the people took an innocent little girl, placed her on a chair before a table, gave her toys and sweets, and while she merrily played, twelve masons covered the vault and finished the wall, which since that time remained stable. Scutari is said to have been built in a similar way. A ghost appeared while the fortress was in the process of building, and demanded that the wife of one of the three kings who should bring the food to the masons on the next day should be entombed in the foundation. Being a young mother, she was permitted to nurse her baby, and a hole was left for that purpose which was closed as soon as the child was weaned.

We read in F. Nork's *Sitten und Gebräuche* (*Das Kloster*, Vol. XII) that when in 1813 the ice broke the dam of the river Elbe and the engineers had great trouble in repairing it, an old man addressed the dike-inspector, saying: "You will never repair the dike unless you bury in it an innocent little child," and Grimm adduces even a more modern instance (*Sagen*, p. 1095) which dates from the year 1843. "When the new bridge in Halle was built," Grimm tells us, "the people talked of a child which should be buried in its foundations."

So long did these superstitions continue after the cruel rite had been abandoned; and they were held, not only in spite of the higher morality which Christianity taught, but even in the name of Christianity. In

* 1 Book of Kings, xvi. 34.

Tommaseo's *Canti Populari* an instance is quoted of the voice of an archangel from heaven bidding the builders of a wall entomb the wife of the architect in its foundation. The practice is here regarded as Christian and it is apparent that there are instances in which Christian authorities were sufficiently ignorant to sanction it, for even the erection of churches was supposed to require the same cruel sacrifice; and there were cases in which, according to the special sanctity of the place, it was deemed necessary to bury a priest, because children or women were not regarded as sufficient. In Günther's *Sagenbuch des Deutschen Volkes* (Vol. I, p. 33 ff.) we read that the Strassburg cathedral required the sacrifice of two human lives, and that two brothers lie buried in its foundation.

The Power of Evil Outwitted

THE PRESENCE OF ALL THE big bowlders that lie scattered in the low lands of Germany is attributed either to giants or to the devils; they are sometimes said to be sand grains which giants removed from their shoes, or they were thrown down in anger when they found themselves cheated out of their own by the wit of mortals.

There is a *Märchen* of a farmer who undertook to till heretofore uncultivated ground and the Devil (that is to say, the giant who owned the land and had seen nothing except sterile rocks and desolate deserts) gazed with astonishment at the green plants that sprang from the earth. He demanded half the crop, and the farmer left him his choice whether he would take the upper or the lower half. When the Devil chose the lower half, the farmer planted wheat, and when the upper half, he planted turnips, leaving him now the stubble and now the useless turnip tops. Whichever way the Devil turned he was outwitted.[*]

The story came in its migration south to Arabia, where it was discovered by Friedrich Rückert, who retold it in his poem "The Devil Outwitted,"[†] which Mr. E. F. L. Gauss, of Chicago, has kindly translated for the special purpose of quotation in this connection:

> *"The Arabs tilled their fields align,*
> *Then came the Devil in a flare*

---

[*] Grimm, *Märchen,* No. 189. *Deutsche Mythologie,* No. 981. Müllenhoff. No. 377. Thiele, *Dänische Sagen,* No. 122.

[†] *Der betrogene Teufel.*

Protesting: 'Half the world is mine,
Of your crops, too, I want my share.'

"The Arabs said, for they are sly,
'The lower half we'll give to thee,'
But the Devil, always aiming high,
Replied: 'It shall the upper be!'

"They turnips sowed all o'er their field,
And when he came to share the crops,
The Arabs took the subsoil yield,
And the Devil got the turnip tops.

"And when another year came round
The Devil spoke in wrathful scorn:
'To have the lower half I'm bound!'
The Arabs then sowed wheat and corn,

"When came the time again to share,
The Arabs took the sheaves pell-mell,
The Devil took the stubbles bare
And fed with them the fire of hell."

There are innumerable other legends of stupid devils. A miller of the Devil-mill in Kleinbautzen tied the Devil to the water-wheel.* A smith who for his hospitality once had a wish granted by Christ, bewitched the Devil and placed Lucifer, the chief of devils, on his anvil, which frightened him so much that the smith, when he died, was not admitted to hell.† And there is a humorous German folk-song of a tailor, which begins:

A tailor went to wander,
On Monday, in the morn,
And there he met the Devil,
His clothes and shoes all torn.
Hey, tailor, follow me!

---

* Preusker, *Blicke in die vaterländische Vorzeit*, I, p. 182.
† Mentioned in Grimm's *Märchen*.

In hell the boys need thee;
For thou must clothe the devils
Whatever the cost may be.

The tailor, on arriving in hell, maltreated all the devils with his tailor utensils in the attempt at dressing them, and they swore that they would never again allow a tailor to come near them, even though he might have stolen ever so much cloth.*

Another comical story is told of Dunstan, abbot of Glaston, later archbishop of Canterbury. While busily engaged in the fabrication of a Eucharist cup, the Devil suddenly appeared to him. But the saint was not afraid; he took the pincers out of the fire and seized the nose of Satan, who ran off with a howl and never again dared to molest him. The event is commemorated in an old rhyme, thus:

"St. Dunstan, as the story goes,
Once pulled the Devil by the nose
With red-hot tongs, which made him roar
That he was heard three miles or more."

An act of bravery is told of St. Cuthbert. Sir Guy Le Scoope (as Thomas Ingoldsby tells us, closely following the chronicle of Bolton) expected company, but finding at the appointed hour the banquet hall empty, because the guests had been kept away through a bad joke of the inviting messenger, he called on the Devil and ten thousand fiends to eat the dinner and take all that was there with them to the infernal regions. The Devil came with his devilish company and all the folk of Sir Guy fled, leaving the little heir behind, who was at once seized by Black Jim, the leader of the fiendish company. In his anxiety Sir Guy cried to St. Cuthbert of Bolton, who actually made his appearance in the shape of an old palmer and forced the demoniac crowd to surrender

---

* Translated by the author. The song may be found in various collections of German folk-songs. Its first verse runs:

"Es wollt ein Schneider wandern.   *Es koste was es wöll."*
Des Montags in der Fruh.   *Du sollst die Teufel kleiden,*
Begegnet ihm der Teufel,   *Du musst mit mir zur Höll,*
Hat weder Kleider noch Schuh.   *"He, he, du Schneidergesöll,*

the child, but he generously allowed them to remain as the guests of Sir Guy, adding:

> *"But be moderate, pray,—and remember thus much,*
> *Since you're treated as Gentlemen, shew yourselves such,*
> *And don't make it late, But mind and go straight*
> *Home to bed when you've finished—and don't steal the plate*
> *Nor wrench off the knocker—or bell from the gate.*
> *Walk away, like respectable Devils, in peace,*
> *And don't "lark" with the watch or annoy the police!'*
> *Having thus said his say, That Palmer grey*
> *Took up little Le Scoope and walk'd coolly away,*
> *While the Demons all set up a 'Hip! hip! hurray!'*
> *Then fell tooth and claw on the victuals, as they*
> *Had been guests at Guildhall upon Lord Mayor's day,*
> *All scrambling and scuffling for what was before 'em,*
> *No care for precedence or common decorum."*

Still another story of saintly courage is told of St. Medard, who while once promenading on the shore of the Red Sea in Egypt, saw Old Nick carrying in a bag a number of lost sinners. The saint took compassion on the poor souls and slit Satan's bag open, whereupon Old Nick's prisoners escaped.

> *"Away went the Quaker,—away went the Baker,*
> *Away went the Friar—that fine fat Ghost,*
> *Whose marrow Old Nick Had intended to pick,*
> *Dressed like a Woodcock, and served on toast!*
>
> *"Away went the nice little Cardinal's Niece,*
> *And the pretty Grisettes, and the Dons from Spain,*
> *And the Corsair's crew, And the coin-clipping Jew,*
> *And they scamper'd, like lamplighters, over the plain!*
> *"Old Nick is a black-looking fellow at best,*
>
> *Ay, e'en when he's pleased; but never before*
> *Had he looked so black As on seeing his sack*
> *Thus cut into slits on the Red Sea shore."*

Old Nick took up a stone and threw it at the saint.

> *"But Saint Medard Was remarkably hard*
> *And solid about the parietal bone."*

The stone recoiled.

> *"And it curl'd, and it twirl'd, and it whirl'd in the air,*
> *As this great big stone at a tangent flew!*
> *Just missing his crown, It at last came down*
> *Plump upon Nick's Orthopedical shoe!*
>
> *"It smashed his shin, and it smash'd his hoof,*
> *Notwithstanding his stout Orthopedical shoe;*
> *And this is the way That, from that same day,*
> *Old Nick became what the French call* Boiteux!*"*

One of the oldest triumphs of human skill in bridge building gave rise to the *Märchen* of the Devil's Bridge which boldly overspans the yawning gorge of the Reuss where the mountain road passes up to the furca of the St. Gotthard. A new bridge has been built by engineers of the nineteenth century right above the old one; but the old one remained for a long time in its place, until it broke down in recent years. The legend goes that a shepherd-lad engaged the Devil to build the bridge on the condition that the soul of the first living creature that crossed it should be forfeited. When the work was finished the lad drove a chamois over the bridge, which, seeing that he was cheated out of the price he had expected, the Devil wrathfully tore into pieces.[*]

All these stories are Christianised pagan notions of evil conquered either through cleverness and wit or by divine assistance; and even the church doctrines of sin and salvation are based upon pre-Christian conceptions ultimately dating back to human sacrifices and the mystic rites of cannibalism in which man hoped to partake of divinity and immortality by eating the flesh and drinking the blood of his incarnated God or his representative.

---

[*] Grimm, *Deutsche Sagen*, 336, and Tobler, *Appenzeller Sprachschatz*, 214.

The Christian scheme of salvation may be briefly called the vicarious atonement of man's sin through the blood of Christ. God's wrath upon the guilty human race is purified through the sufferings and death of the innocent god-man. Divine Justice is satisfied by the sacrifice of Divine Love.

The mystery of this doctrine and also of the doctrine of original sin, which in its literal sense can hardly be regarded as commendable, has a deep sense which appears when we consider the organic unity of the human race. We not only inherit the evil consequences of our ancestors' evil deeds, but we actually consist of their evil dispositions themselves. Thus the sin of our fathers is our curse because it is our own, and, in the same way, the merit of our brothers becomes, or may become, our own blessing. We can easily share in the benefit that will accrue from inventions or other advances made by one man if we are only willing to accept the lesson which his example teaches.

The idea of a salvation through vicarious atonement has grown dimmer of late. The old interpretation reminding us of the bloody sacrifices of savages is beginning to wane, although it can scarcely be regarded as entirely abandoned; it is not surrendered but merely transformed, and may now be called the idea of salvation through sacrifice.

THE DEVIL'S PRIME

Miracles and Magic

A LATIN PROVERB SAYS: "*SI duo faciunt idem, non est idem*" (if two do the same thing, it is not the same thing); and this is true not only of individuals, but also of nations and of religions. It is a habit common among all classes of people to condone the faults of their own kind but to be severe with those of others. The oracles of Delphi were divine to a Greek mind, but they were of diabolical origin according to the judgment of Christians. Jesus was a magician in the eyes of the pagans, while the Christians worshipped him as the son of God, and a man who performed miracles.

The priests of Pharaoh and Moses perform the same tricks still performed by the snake charmers of Egypt and India, but the deeds of Moses alone are regarded as miracles, and the Israelites claim that he could accomplish more than the Egyptians. Father Juan Bautista (of about 1600) tells us that among the natives of Mexico there are magicians who "conjure the clouds, and can make a stick look like a serpent, a mat like a centipede, a stone like a scorpion, and similar deceptions."[*]

Simon Magus and his disciples were believed by the early Christians to possess power over demons;[†] but Simon was a competitor of the Apostles, and therefore his deeds were not regarded as divine. Before an impartial tribunal the methods and aspirations of both parties would resemble one another more than the one-sided statements of Christian authors at first sight seem to warrant. The accusation made against Simon by Luke, of having offered money to the Apostles for communicating to him the Holy Ghost, does not prove a depravity of heart, as the later Christians thought; for Simon took the rebuke in the proper spirit and apparently remained on good terms with the Apostles. The reports of the church fathers which make Peter and Simon rivals in working miracles, develop the story in the spirit of the age; they characterise the superstitions of the time; yet, although they probably

---

[*] Cf. *Fourteenth Annual Report of the B. of Eth.*, 1892–1893, p. 150.

[†] *Iren. adv. haer.*, I, 20–21; *Justin Martyr.*, App. II, pp. 69–70; *Epiphan, ad. haer.*, XXII, 1; Euseb., *H. E.*, II, p. 13.

reflect historical facts, they are as unreliable as are the charges of pagan authors hurled against the Christians.

The early Christians practised healing the sick by the laying on of hands and by praying; so did the Therapeutæ and other Gnostics; yet faithcure and Christian science are not countenanced by the churches today.

Minucius Felix* puts the common notions, which in his days prevailed in Greece and Italy concerning the practices of the Christians, into the mouth of Cæcilius who describes them as a desperate class of vulgar men and credulous women threatening the welfare of mankind. He states that they are atheists, for they cherish a contempt for temples, spit at the gods, and ridicule religious ceremonies; that their own cult is a mixture of superstition and depravity; that they possess secret symbols by which they recognise one another; they call themselves brothers and sisters, and degrade these sacred words by sensuality. Further, it is said that they adore a donkey's head, and that their worship is obscene. The libel culminates in the assertion that the reception of new members is celebrated by slaughtering and devouring a child covered all over with flour, which is an obvious perversion of the Communion, but Cæcilius declares that it is done because partnership in guilt is the best means of securing secrecy. Lastly, he adds, that on festival days they celebrate love feasts which after the extinction of the lights end with sexual excesses.

Similar accusations are found in various authors, and even the noble-hearted and high-minded Tacitus speaks of the Christians with contempt; while on the other hand the Christians do not shrink from ridiculing the holiest and noblest of paganism. For instance, Minucius Felix, a Christian of the highest type and best education, speaks of Socrates as "the Athenian buffoon."†

Justinus Martyr in his *Apologia* makes the asseveration that the Christians are innocent, but leaves the question open whether the heretics, such as the Gnostics, might not be guilty of these abominations (App. II, p. 70), and Eusebius directly claims that the practices that prevailed among the heretics were the direct cause of the evil rumors concerning the life of the Christians.

---

* *Octavius, ein Dialog des M. Minucius Felix.* Edited by B. Dombart. Second edition. Erlangen, 1881. *Ante Nicene Chr. Libr.,* Vol. XIII, p, 451 ff.

† *Octavius,* Chap. 38. "Socrates scurra Atticus."

While we must bear in mind that the moral rigidity of the Gnostics leaves upon the whole no doubt about the purity of their life, we may grant the probability of the presence of black sheep among them. But the same is true of the Christians, as we know for certain on the good authority of St. Paul who in his First Epistle to the Corinthians, after an enumeration of such sinners as will not inherit the kingdom (v. 8–11,— the passage had better remain unquoted) says, "and such were some of you." Accordingly, there can be no doubt that there were abuses in the Church of Corinth. St. Paul believes the rumor of a sin, "that is not so much as named among the Gentiles," and the Second Epistle is the best evidence that the Corinthians did not deny the facts. They repent, whereupon St. Paul recommends charity toward the main offender (2 Cor. ii. 6–11), saying: "To whom ye forgive anything, I forgive also."

The various aberrations among the Christians which were very apparent in many of their most prominent leaders, such as Constantine the Great, must not astonish us, because Christianity originated in an age of unrest, and the new movement was the centre of attraction for all kinds of eccentricity. In spite of various excrescences, we cannot but say that Christianity opened to the world new vistas of truth. Represented by such men as St. Paul, it tended toward purity of heart; but the same is true of the Gnostics and the Manichees. The accusations on both sides rest mainly upon partisan statements and cannot be trusted, or at least must be used with due reserve. But it is natural that here as always, the same things are no longer the same when reported of people of another faith. Thus the virtues of the pagans are to St. Augustine only "polished vices," and the heroism of Christian martyrs is mere obstinacy in the opinion of Roman prætors.

We look with contempt upon the Indian prophet who poses as a rain-maker, but read the story of Elijah with great edification, and while we justify the holy zeal of the latter, we would make no allowance for the severity of Indian reformers who fail to spare the lives of their rivals. One instance will suffice: Tenskwatawa, the Shawano prophet, preached in the beginning of the nineteenth century a nobler religion and a purer morality to the tribes of the prairie, and was revered by his followers as an incarnation of Manabozho (i.e., first doer). Drunkenness, the besetting sin of the Indians since their acquaintance with the whites, and the traditional superstition practised by the medicinemen ceased. But reform was coupled with persecution. Tenskwatawa "inaugurated a crusade against all who were suspected of dealing in witchcraft or magic arts," and he took advantage of the faith of his followers "to effectually rid himself of all who opposed his sacred claims." All his rivals were successively marked by the prophet, and doomed to be burned alive.*

All these facts are so many instances which prove the truth of the proverb, that if two do the same thing it will not be regarded as the same thing: and thus the miracle of our own religion is mere magic and witchcraft in other religions.

ONE OF THE MOST CHARACTERISTIC features of the pre-scientific age is man's yearning for the realisation of that which is unattainable by natural means. The belief in magic will inevitably prevail so long as the dualistic world-conception dominates the minds of the people, and in that period of civilisation supernatural deeds are expected as the indispensable credentials of all religious prophets. It is the age of miracles and witchcraft.

Now we know that wherever contra-natural things are believed, there the strangest events will be experienced by those who are under the suggestion of the belief; and then at once a competition will originate between those who represent the established religion and others who perform, or pretend to perform, similar deeds. The former are prophets and saints, and they work miracles; the latter are wizards and witches, and their art is called witchcraft.

Miracles and witchcraft possess this in common that both are supposed to supersede the laws of nature, but there is this difference that the miracle is believed to be the supernatural power of one's own religion, while witchcraft is the miracle of heretics. Miracle is anything contra-natural that is legitimate; and witchcraft is the same thing, but illegitimate; the former is supposed to be done with the help of God, the latter with the help of Satan; the former is boasted of as the highest glory of the Church, the latter is denounced as the greatest abomination possible.

It is natural that wizards and witches are always represented as obnoxious, and it is said that their art is practised to injure the welfare of mankind. Nevertheless, some very mean deeds are counted as miracles,† while good deeds if only performed by believers in other

---

* For details see the *Fourteenth Annual Report of the Bureau of Ethnology,* Part 2, p. 673 ff., and Drake, *Tecumseh,* 2.

† There are miracles attributed in the Christian Apocrypha even to Jesus himself, which would be criminal.

gods are branded as witchcraft. Moreover, all priests are unanimous in condemning the application of charms and spells, except those of their own religion, even though they be used for the best and purest ends. A faith-cure by heretics, and even a successful operation through the unusual skill of a surgeon, would be set down as deeds of darkness by those who believe in a religion of miracles,[*] but official processions with prayers and sprinkling of holy water are still employed, as could be observed during a late small-pox epidemic in French Canada.

The belief in magic is a natural phase in the evolution of mankind, producing the medicine-man who dispels diseases by charms, the prophet who by an appeal to his Deity (be it the sun-god of the American Indians, or the Baal of the Phœnicians, or El or Yahveh of the Israelites) undertakes to make rain, and the medium who vaticinates or foretells fortunes and calls the dead from Spirit-Land.

The rain-priests play a most important part in the life of all the American Indians. The snake-dance among the Pueblo Indians of Mexico is a prayer for rain.[†] Frequently the sun is invoked for rain. Dreams, visions, and ecstasies are regarded as the best means of divine revelation, and the medicine-bag possesses magic powers. The devotional spirit is not less intense among the pagans of the prairie than it was among the ancient Israelites and the early Christians.[‡]

All attempt to practise magic, and a religion that promises success in life and proposes to accomplish the salvation of man by miracles, be it the miracles of their founders or the continued miracles of Church institutions, such as sacraments, pilgrimages, sprinkling of holy water, mass-reading, or other rites supposed to possess other than a purely symbolical significance, is a religion of magic. In brief, a religion of magic is based on a belief in the contra-natural, and as soon as a religion of magic becomes an established institution, it will develop the notion of witchcraft by a discrimination between its own miracles and those of other people who are unbelievers.

---

[*] In 1521, a surgeon of Hamburg was executed for witchcraft because he had saved the life of a babe which the midwife had given up as lost. (See Soldan, *Hexenprocesse*, p. 326.)

[†] See, e.g., *Fourteenth Annual Report of the Bureau of Ethnology*, 1892–1893, p. 561.

[‡] Notice, for instance, the deeply religious spirit of the ghost dance taught the North American Indian by the prophet Wovoka. The devotion of Wovoka's followers is well illustrated in the accompanying illustrations of some characteristic attitudes in the ghost dance. Cf. *Annual Report of the American Bureau of Ethnology*, 1892–1893.

How similar the notions of legitimate and illegitimate miracles are, may be learned from the writings of Agrippa of Nettesheim (1486–1535), one of the greatest sages and philosophers of the age of the Reformation, who proclaimed that the perfection of philosophy could be attained by magic, which in distinction to black magic* he called "natural" or "celestial" magic, and which, he assumed, leads to a perfect union with God. His book, *De Occulta Philosophia*, written in 1510 but published only in 1531, exhibits his belief in the possibility of creating hatred and love by spells, of discovering thieves, confounding armies, making thunderstorms and rain, all of which he expects to accomplish by magic through a mystical union with God. It is difficult for us to understand how a man of his caliber could believe in the efficacy of spells and mystic keys; but grant the reality of magic, and such aberrations become legitimate experiments. Witches have been frequently accused of the very same feats, only they were said to have performed them through the assistance of the Devil. In spite of the resemblance which Agrippa unconsciously had discovered between witchcraft and miracles, he remained unmolested, for his views were at the time commonly accepted. Nor would he ever have excited the hostility of the Papal party had he not lectured with fervor, at the University of Dôle, Burgundy (1509), on Reuchlin's book, *De Verbo Mirifico*, and had he not, in 1519, when syndic at Metz, ventured to save the life of a witch that had fallen into the hands of the Inquisitor Nicolas Savini.[†]

What a strange mixture of occultism with exact observation, based upon anatomical measurements, is contained in the chapter on "The Proportions of the Human Body." Mathematics, natural science, and mysticism are all combined in Agrippa's *Occulta Philosophia*, and the learned author is unable to discriminate between facts and fancy.[‡]

Agrippa's celestial magic is not different from black magic; for both kinds of magic consist in the hope of contra-natural accomplishments. When after years of varied disappointments Agrippa discovered that there was no magic, be it black or white, he came to the conclusion that there was no science. As the agnostic who, after having wrongly

---

* The idea and name of black magic originated from a corruption of the word necromancy into nigromancy.

[†] *De Vanitate Scientiarum*, Chap. 96; *Epist. libr.*, II, pp. 38–40, quoted by Soldan, *Hexenprocesse*, p. 325.

[‡] The accompanying illustrations are reproduced from the original edition of *Occulta Philosophia*, Chap. XXVII.

formulated the problems of philosophy, and finding his mind hopelessly entangled in confusion, pronounces the dreary doctrine of the impossibility of knowledge, so Agrippa of Nettesheim began to despair not only of magic, but also of science; and he wrote, in 1526, his "Proposition about the Incertitude and Vanity of the Sciences and Arts; and about the excellence of the word of God."*

All in all, we find that a religion of magic involves a belief in witchcraft. Where sacraments are employed as exorcisms, every attempt at exercising extraordinary powers is regarded not as impossible but as a lack of loyalty. Hence heresy and witchcraft are always declared to be closely allied, for witchcraft is nothing but the performance of miracles without the licence of an established Church, which claims to have a monopoly in supernaturalism.

The belief in and the prosecution of witchcraft are the necessary result of a firmly established religion of magic. All the religions of magic are naturally intolerant. As soon as one of them triumphs over its rivals, as soon as it is worked out into a systematic creed and organised in an institution such as the Church, it will, like all combinations or trusts, with all means at its command, insure and perpetuate its supremacy. Considering that the mediæval Church was practically a religion of magic, witch prosecution was the inevitable result of the Pope's ascendancy, and it continued in Protestant countries as an heirloom of the Dark Ages so long as the belief in magic was retained.

Exorcism

THE BELIEF IN SATAN AS held by many Christians today is harmless and tame in comparison with the old conception, which was taken seriously. Satan, it is true, was regarded as the foe of mankind, but there was no doubt about his power, and the idea prevailed that his services could easily be procured by those ready to surrender to him their souls.

As soon as the Church became possessed of power, it was at once bent on the suppression of magic and witchcraft. Constantine began the policy of threatening the severest punishment on all kinds of black art, allowing its application only for curing diseases and preventing hail

---

* *De Incertitudine et Vanitate Scientiarum et Artium, atque Excellentia Verbi Dei Declamatio.* Published in 1530.

and rain storms during the harvest. And Constantine's successors did not fail to preserve the tradition.

A prohibition to fish implies that there is good fishing, which tempts many to try. In the same way, the policy of the Christian authorities was tantamount to an official recognition of witchcraft as a mighty and powerful weapon that could be wielded by the initiated both for good and for evil; and thus it could not fail to strengthen the Devil's credit, as well as to develop most exuberantly a peculiar mediæval demonology. Belief in witchcraft rapidly became so common that almost all countries were in possession of laws against magicians, soothsayers, and witches. One remarkable exception only is found in the law-code of the Lombards, which contains the declaration that witches cannot perform any such feats as devouring people alive, and therefore the burning of a woman on the pretext of her being a witch is prohibited.

There is a remarkable Latin book of "Dialogues on the Life and Miracles of the Italian Fathers,"* which characterises the superstitious spirit that prevailed among both the laity and the clergy. It is replete with all kinds of ridiculous tales which are taken in good earnest. We are told, for instance, that Gregory the Great, when consecrating an Arian church for Roman Catholic worship, successfully exorcised the Devil with the help of sacred relics; Satan flew before him in the shape of a huge pig and vacated the place completely the following night with great noise.

The Devil came more and more into prominence in the eighth and ninth centuries. Baptism was regarded as an expulsion of the evil spirit. The convert had, according to Dionysius, to exhale three times, and according to the Greek euchologion, also to spit at him upon the floor. The Synod of Leptinæ in the year 743 added to the confession of faith an "abrenunciation" of the Devil.

A Low-German formula which renounces the three foremost German deities with all their hosts† consists of questions and answers, which read as follows:

"*Q.* Forsakest thou the Devil?
"*A.* I forsake the Devil!

---

* *De vita et miraculis patr, Italic. libri,* IV. See Roskoff, *Geschichte des Teufels,* p. 292.
† Massmann, "Die deutschen Abschwörungs-, Glaubens-, Beicht- und Betformeln." *Bibliographie der Geschichte der Nationalliteratur.* Vol. VII. Roskoff, *Geschichte des Teufels,* p. 292; Otto Henne am Rhyn, *Kulturgeschichte des deutschen Volkes.*

"*Q.* And all Devil guilds?

"*A.* And I forsake all Devil guilds.

"*Q.* And all Devil works?

"*A.* And I forsake all Devil works, and words, Thonar (Thor) and Wodan and Saxnot (Fro) and all the evil ones that are his companions."*

The fact is that Christianity itself was regarded as a kind of magic which in distinction to the black magic or necromancy would have to be classed together with white magic. The sacraments were supposed to be miraculous methods of performing supernatural feats quite analogous to exorcisms, and the church itself was, in the minds of the people, an institution of sacred sorcery.

Belief in Witchcraft

WITH THE BELIEF IN WITCHCRAFT a new period begins in the evolution of mankind. The Devil becomes greater and more respected than ever; indeed, this is the classical period of his history and the prime of his life. Contracts were made with the Devil in which men surrendered their souls for all kinds of services on his part.

In the thirteenth century the Devil reached the acme of his influence, and it is only possible to give a meagre sketch of the Devil's activity during this period. Nothing extraordinary could happen without its being attributed to him, and to the people of the Middle Ages many things, ordinary to us, were very extraordinary.

Gervasius Tilberiensis composed a collection of stupid fables which he published in 1211 under the title *Otia Imperialia*, dedicating them to Emperor Otto IV. He repeats some spook stories of Apuleius as events that happened in France and England and invents new tales which surpass the old ones only in crudity. He accepts the medical explanation of nightmares as due to an overheated imagination, but proves even then the presence of demoniacal influence, on the authority of St. Augustine.

---

* The original, which is Old Low-German, reads as follows:

Q. "Forsachistu diabolæ?" *A.* "Ec forsacho diabolæ!"—*Q.* "End allum diabol gelde?" *A.* "End ec forsacho allum diabol gelde."—*Q.* "End allum diaboles uuercum?" *A.* "End ec forsacho allum diaboles uuercum, end uuordum, Thunaer, ende Uuoden, ende Saxnote, ende allem dem unholdum the hira genotas sint."

In the *Dialogus Miraculorum*,[*] by Cæsarius von Heisterbach (who died about 1245), we find that not only thunder-storms, hail-storms, inundations, diseases, but also unexpected noises, the rustling of leaves, the howling of the wind, were attributed to Old Nick. He appears as a bear, a monkey, a toad, a raven, a vulture, as a gentleman, a soldier, a hunter, a peasant, a dragon, and a negro.

Cæsarius's book has become famous, and rightly so, not on account of any peculiar merit of its author but because it is a true picture of the average conception of the times.[†]

The book is written mainly for the instruction of young monks. The initials of the original editions are emblazoned with pious pictures, and the tendency of all stories is that there is no surer salvation than in the brotherhood of the Cistercian monks, the order to which the author belongs. He declares that "there is no safer road than the order of the Cistercians; nor do fewer people go down to the lower regions than the members of that religion."[‡] Cæsarius makes the Lord appear as a sovereign who regards it as his duty to protect his faithful servants and takes an interest in concealing their crimes. He works a special miracle, lest the slander of a clergyman become public (Book I, p. 23). The Devil having caused a man to sin against the sixth commandment, is unable to accuse and punish the sinner, or make his guilt known, because the latter escapes all evil effects through the confessional (Book III, p. 4). The Devil once went to a confessor and confessed. Having enumerated his sins, the confessor declared that a thousand years would not have sufficed to commit them all, and the Devil answered that indeed he was much older than a thousand years, for he was one of the demons who fell with Lucifer. The priest considered his sins unpardonable, and asked him whether he wanted to do penance. "Yes," he said, "if the penance is not too heavy for me." "Well," replied the confessor, "bow down thrice a day, saying: 'God, my Lord and Creator, I have sinned against thee; forgive me.'" "No," said the Devil, "that would be too humiliating for me" (III, 26, and IV, 5).

---

[*] *Illustrium miraculorum et historiarum memorabilium libri XII, ante annos fere Cccc a Cæsario Heisterbacensi, ordinis Cisterniensis, . . . Colon.* 1599. A new edition was made by Josephus Strange, published by J. M. Heberle.

[†] For a brief summary see Wolfgang Menzel, *Deutsche Literaturgeschichte*, pp. 310–312. See also Roskoff, *Geschichte des Teufels,* pp. 317–326.

[‡] "Non est via securior quam ordo Cisterniencis neque inter omne genus hominum pauciones descendunt ad inferos quam personæ illius religionis." I, Chap. 33.

Arrogance and self-conceit are the main-springs of Satan's character. A curious parallel to Peregrinus is the story of a woman who, for the sake of clearing her soul of sin, burns herself to death (Book VI, p. 35). Imps are seen playing with cupids upon the train of a gentlewoman (Book V, p. 7). A man gambles with the Devil and loses his soul (V, 34).

The theory of incubi and succubi is presented in all its indecency on the authority of St. Thomas Aquinas, who in his commentary on Job (Chap. 40) interprets Behemoth (a large animal, probably the elephant) as the Devil, and derives from the mention of the animal's sexual strength (verse 16) the theory that evil demons can have intercourse with human beings. Satan is supposed to serve first as a succubus (or female devil) to men, and then as an incubus (or male devil) to women; and St. Thomas declares that children begotten in this way ought to be regarded as the children of the men whom Satan served as succubus. They would, however, be more cunning than normal children on account of the demoniacal influence to which they were exposed in their pre-natal condition. Matthæus Paris mentions that within six months one such incubus-baby developed all its teeth and attained the size of a boy of seven years, while his mother became consumptive and died.

The superstitions of the belief in the personal interference of the Devil with human affairs passed away, but they left us an extensive and interesting literature which for all time to come will remain a rich mine for the anthropologist, the antiquarian, the historian, the psychologist, the poet, and the philosopher. There are innumerable miracles and tales of St. Mary, the mother of Jesus, but few of them are endurable, while the general tone of the narration is unworthy of any woman,—let alone the highest woman-ideal of Christianity. A dog has been baptised by rascals, and he turns mad (X, 145). In the hour of death, pious people see the heavens open, while infidels are tortured by black men, ravens and vultures (XI); and for the edification of the faithful the damned are thrown into the crater of a volcano (XII).

The Abbot Richalmus, who wrote about 1270 a book of revelations about the intrigues and persecutions of demons, recognises the Devil's hand in every little inconvenience he might happen to experience. It is devils that make him feel qualmish when he has eaten too much; they make him fall asleep over his breviary. When he exposes his hand, they make it feel chilly; when he hides it under his cloak, they tickle and bite it like fleas. "Once, he says, "when we were gathering stones for building a wall, I heard a devil exclaim, 'What tiresome work!' He only did it to tempt us and make us rebellious." There is no noise but some devil speaks out of it. "While I pull my sleeve," he says, "a rustling is heard, and devils speak through this sound. When I scratch myself, the scratching is their voice. . . Lowly people are mostly seduced by anger and sadness, but the rich and powerful by arrogance and pride."[*]

Another favorite conception of Christianity originated in the Roman idea of looking upon religion as a legal affair. It must have been a lawyer who made that happy hit of presenting the case of Satan *versus* mankind or *versus* Christ juridically, in the form of a regular lawsuit, in which, of course, Satan in the end is worsted. The booklet, which bears the title *Processus Sathanæ*, became so popular that it was repeatedly edited by various authors and is still extant in various redactions, one of the best and oldest being by Bartolus, a lawyer who lived 1313–1355.[†]

The Devil played the rôle of a joker in the Passion plays, and his part became more and more prominent. In France the idea prevailed that the great mysteries should always have not less than four devils, a usage which is mentioned in Rabelais. Hence the proverb, "*Faire le diable à quatre.*" In Mediæval mysteries God the Father, God the Son, and Satan appear on the stage, and the last one is practically the main actor in the whole drama. He was the intriguer who, after his successful revolution against the Lord, set up an empire of his own in Hell; and without the Devil's intrigues the whole plot of man's fall and Christ's salvation would be impossible.[‡]

The works of Cæsarius, of Heisterbach, Richalmus, Bartolus, and others are by no means the only ones that treat on devil-lore; they are typical of a large class of similar literary productions.

While the Church in her struggles for supremacy, aspiring for worldly power, began to neglect her spiritual duties, people sought comfort in sects. The Manichees increased, Catharism spread rapidly and many new sects, such as the Albigenses, were founded. Almost all sectarians were morally earnest and sincere, yet the general character of these sects was similar to the Manichees, an openly avowed dualism. The tendencies of the time were dualistic, and the

---

[*] Roskoff, pp. 535–545.

[†] Concerning the *Processus Sathanæ*, see Dr. R. Stintzing, *Geschichte der populären Litteratur des röm. can. Rechts in Deutschland*, Leipsic, 1867. Roskoff's book on the Devil contains on pp. 349–355 extracts from Stintzing.

[‡] *Floegel's Geschichte des Grotesk-Komischen*, bearbeitet von Fr. W. Ebeling. pp. 70–71, 119–120.

Church also was under the influence of dualistic views. Nevertheless, orthodox Christianity, at least in her noblest expositors, such as Thomas Aquinas and other Christian philosophers, never lost sight of the monistic ideal, in spite of all its demonological errors. The demonology of the Middle Ages was at bottom a mythical excrescence, for the Devil's power was all the time regarded as a mere sham, as *Blendwerk*. He still served the higher purposes of the omnipotent God, who used him for his wise and well-calculated ends. Thus it was a natural consequence that the Devil appeared in spite of his smartness as the dupe of God; his fate was always to be defeated and ridiculed. As such he figures in the mysteries, the Easter and Christmas plays, in which he acts one of the most important parts, that of intriguer, harlequin, and fool.

Kindred Superstitions

BELIEF IN WITCHCRAFT WAS ONLY the main result of the established authority of a religion of magic, involving the belief in a personal Devil. There are other consequences which, though less important, are sometimes bad enough in themselves. We mention a few of them: (1) There were persons who actually tried to make contracts with the Devil. (2) People possessed of a lively imagination began to dream that they stood in all kinds of relations to the Evil One. There are cases in which imaginary witches surrendered themselves voluntarily to the Inquisition. (3) Soldiers entertained the hope of rendering themselves bullet-proof. (4) Many methods were devised to predict the future. (5) There were plenty of fools who tried to become rich by magic; and (6) worst of all, men who knew better than the self-constituted guardians of the right faith, were relentlessly persecuted even unto death.

The Devil was believed to hold court and to celebrate witches' sabbaths, on which occasions homage was paid him and the Christian sacraments were travestied with diabolical malice.

The most remarkable case of bestial demonolatry with all its incidental crimes, is recorded in the annals of France where Giles De Rais (also spelled Raiz and Retz), one of the greatest dignitaries of the State, a descendant of the highest noble families of Brittany, and a marshal of France, was charged with kidnapping about one hundred and fifty women and children, who, after being subjected to all kinds of outrages, were solemnly sacrificed to Satan.* The facts seem impossible but the complete records of the case are still extant, according to which Rais was convicted and executed in 1440. The history of his life has apparently contributed to the formation of the legend of Bluebeard.

Among the persons who gave themselves up to the Inquisition we mention Katharine Jung of Amdorf, Hessia, who confessed to her own father that she was a witch. The poor man regarded it as his duty to denounce her, and after ten days, on May, 11, 1631, the girl was executed.

Another case of comparatively recent date happened in Alvebrode, Hanover. An old spinster, daughter of the widow Steingrob, had a brother who suffered from attacks of asthma. Her mother was blind and lame, and her sister had died of consumption. Some people in the village suggested that the attacks which came upon her brother were due to witchcraft, and at last the old spinster herself declared she was a witch and described her relations with the Devil in the minutest terms. She was convinced herself that she had bewitched her mother and sister and could injure people by a mere glance. Anxious about the welfare of the villagers, she warned them to avoid her, and tried to drown herself during an attack of melancholy, but she was rescued and imprisoned. The physician, a sensible and humane man, declared, judging from bodily symptoms, that she suffered from a disease which had confused her mind, but she could not be prevailed upon to submit to treatment. She insisted that she was as healthy as a fish and that the Devil could not be driven out by medicine. She said: "It is in vain to try to cure a witch. I deserve death and shall gladly die, but please do not burn me, have me dispatched with the sword. Everything will be well when I am dead." Thereupon the physician resorted to a stratagem. He persuaded her that her neck was sword-proof, and succeeded in inducing her to take medicine to make her neck soft again for decapitation. She was then treated according to the prescriptions of her physician, with bodily exercise and regular diet and sleep until her mind improved, and she forgot all about witchcraft and her sword-proof neck.

Christian Elsenreiter, a student of Passau, palmed off upon credulous soldiers for making them bullet-proof a slip of paper upon which he

* See *Encyclo. Brit.*, Vol. XX, p. 258.

wrote, "Devil help me, body and soul I give to thee!" The paper had to be swallowed, and Elsenreiter claimed that he who would die of it within twenty-four hours would go to hell, but he who survived would be bullet-proof all his life.

A Saxon Colonel had been hit twice during his military career by a bullet, but in each case a Mansfeld-Thaler had protected him. This incident gave rise to the notion that Mansfeld-Thalers make one bullet-proof, and there was no officer in the imperial army during the Turkish wars who did not carry at least one of them about his person. The price of Mansfeld-Thalers at that time was fifteen times their face value.

Various kinds of magic wands and divining-rods which were supposed to indicate the place where treasures lay hidden, were made in great quantities. There are innumerable magic formulas and exorcisms, most of them invoking God or the Trinity, or Jesus Christ, in Hebrew or Latin; especially the words Yahveh (יהוה) and Adonai (ארני) play an important part and were believed to be very effective. Among the magic symbols which are met with in old documents, the triangle, the cross, the pentagram, and the signs of the planets are preferred; but other figures, such as squares, hexagrams, circles, and fantastic combinations of irregular lines are also quite frequent. Conjurations were made according to various prescriptions; a circle was drawn at midnight where two roads cross; it was lit with wax candles made after specific recipes. The conjurer had to prepare himself by fasts and prayers, sometimes by partaking of the holy communion at church, and when at last he failed to find the treasure or to accomplish his purpose, whatever it may have been, he had reason to believe that he made some trifling mistake in his preparations.

The most fashionable method of predicting the future was the casting of horoscopes, which still served astronomers in the seventeenth century as a means of making a living. Kepler, who enjoyed the confidence of the superstitious Emperor Rudolf II, felt the deep humiliation of his position, but he bore it with good humor, as we know from himself. He writes:

"Astrology is indeed a foolish child, but, good gracious, where would her mother, the wise astronomy, be if she had not this foolish child! Is not the world more foolish still, so foolish, indeed, that the old sensible mother (i.e., astronomy) must be introduced to the people. . . through her daughter's foolishness. . .

But when guesses are limited to yes and no, one has always about half the chances in one's favor. . . Right guesses are remembered, failures forgotten, and so the astrologer remains in honor."[*]

One reason why there were always so many fools who in spite of their fear of eternal damnation tried to make contracts with the Prince of Darkness was the prevalent idea illustrated in many old legends that it was quite possible to shirk one's obligations; indeed God and all the saints were supposed to be always ready to assist people in cheating the Devil out of his own. As an instance that characterises this belief, quite common in the Middle Ages, we quote the legend of St. Gertrude, an Old-German poem of unknown authorship.[†]

"A knight was stricken by poverty great,
His goods he all had wasted,
And gone from him was his whole estate;
Such bitter want he'd tasted
That to take his life he intended.

"He rode to the forest dark and dim,
But there, the Devil awaited
The knight and said to him:
'Thou shalt be reinstated
If thou wilt assist me in secret.'

"'I'll give thee chests full of glittering gold
In exchange for thy loving maiden,
Then canst thou live well and free and bold,
Until thou diest. Well laden
With joys shalt thou be while living.'

"And happy was the maiden fair,
The new wealth her heart delighted;
'But say, my Lord,' she asked, 'from where

---

[*] Translated from Carus Sterné, *Die allgemeine Weltanschauung*, p. 56.
[†] Translated by E. F. L. Gauss from *Deutscher Liederhort*, (Erk & Böhme) Vol. III. See also *Das Kloster*, Stuttgart, 1846, Vol. II, Part I, p. 176. The original Ms. of the poem is preserved in the Heidelberg Library.

Do the riches come?' Then affrighted
Was the knight at her look and her query.

"'O, lady dear wilt thou ride with me
Through a forest green and pleasant?
The birds of the forest there play in glee,
And the songs are now heard incessant
Which gaily the birds are singing.'

"Together a green forest they reached;
And near the road was standing
A little chapel, where men beseeched
Mary, whose arms were expanding
To all: our worthy mother, our lady.

"To the knight the maiden said: 'Let me
Here stop in pious feeling
In the chapel to pray an Ave Marie.'
At the altar she was kneeling
With her arms acrosswise folded.

"She there fell asleep, forgetting her care,
And Mary stepped forth from the altar
And to the knight she came blooming fair,
In her hand bearing rosary and psalter,
And mounted, as if 'twere the maiden.

"They both reached soon, in the forest dense,
The cross-road where the Devil was standing,
His rage on seeing them was intense.
'Thou hast cheated me!' he was demanding,
'Thou treacherous liar, thou trickster!

"'Thou hast promised to bring here thy lady fair,
And thou bringest the Queen of Heaven!
With her I cannot my conquests share,
From her presence I must be driven
Yea, driven from her forever.'

"Said Mary:

"'Thou evil spirit, away with thee,
To thy fellows thou shalt be given,
The lady thou must leave with me!
My Son's kingdom she shall live in,
Now and forever! Amen.'"

What charms the idea of magic exercises upon a man's mind may be learned from the fact that even Goethe, one of the clearest-headed men of modern times, passed through a period of his life (as we know from his *Wahrheit und Dichtung*) in which he pondered upon the possibility of occultism. Reminiscences of this kind found classical expression in his ballad "The Treasure-Digger," which on account of its practical beauty and sound moral lesson deserves to be translated and quoted.[*] The treasure-digger speaks:

"Sick at heart, poor in possession
Dragged my days unto the latest,
Poverty is of curses greatest,
Riches are the highest good!
And to end my sore depression
I went forth to dig for treasure,
'Thine my soul be at thy pleasure!'
I wrote down with my own blood.

"Circle within circle drawing,
Wondrous flames I then collected
Unto herbs and bones, selected,
And conjured a spell of might,
Then in manner overawing,
As I'd learned, I dug for treasure
On the spot I found by measure.
Black and stormy was the night.

"And I saw a light's formation
Brightening to a star's consistence,

---

[*] Translation by E. F. L. Gauss, of Chicago, Ill.

Coming from the farthest distance
Just as struck the midnight hour.
Vain was further preparation,
And a beauteous youth, with glowing
Splendor from a cup o'erflowing
Spread a flash with searching power.

"Yet his eyes my soul delighted;
'Neath a wealth of flowers tender,
With that cup of heavenly splendor
Stepped he in the magic ring;
Friendly me to drink invited,
And I thought: this youth so purely
Off'ring gifts of heaven, surely
Cannot be the evil king.

"'Courage drink, and life's pure pleasure,'
Quoth he. 'Learn from this occasion,
That by anxious conjuration
No boon can this place afford.
Dig no longer for vain treasure!
Work by day, and guests at leisure,
Toilsome weeks and feastdays' pleasure,
*Be thy future magic word!'"**

The height of folly that the belief in a religion of magic is capable of, was actually attained in the persecution of men of science whose doctrines came in conflict with tradition. Not only religious reformers, like Savonarola and Huss, were condemned to be burned alive and to die a heretic's death, but also thinkers like Giordano Bruno. Galileo at the age of seventy was imprisoned and surrendered to the Inquisition at the

---

* This is most likely the poem of which Schiller writes to Goethe in a letter dated May 23, 1797: "It is so exemplary, beautiful, and round and perfect, that I felt very forcibly, while reading it, how even a small whole, a simple idea, can give us the enjoyment of the highest, by perfect presentation."

demand of Pope Urban. Threatened with torture, he was forced to recant publicly the heresy of the motion of the earth.[*]

The religion of miracles had in the natural course of evolution become the religion of magic. The religion of magic had proved to be a belief in witchcraft, and the belief in witchcraft had brought forth the terrible fruit of witch-prosecution with all kindred superstitions, among which the hatred of science was not the least injurious to true religion and the highest interests of mankind.

The belief in witchcraft ceased naturally with the ascendancy of science. The more Christianity became imbued with the scientific spirit of the eighteenth century, the rarer became the fagot, and the fires were at last extinguished forever. So long as Christianity was interpreted as a religion of magic, nothing could stop the terrible mania for burning witches, neither the fear of future punishments for the tortures inflicted upon many innocent victims, nor the pangs of conscience that were now and then felt by the judges, nor Christian charity and love. There was only one remedy, viz., a clear insight into the nature of things revealing the impossibility of witchcraft; but that one remedy afforded an unfailing cure.

---

[*] The most thorough exposition of this sad chapter in the history of civilisation is found in President Andrew Dickson White's two volumed work *A History of the Warfare of Science with Theology in Christendom.* New York. 1896.

PAUL CARUS

THE INQUISITION

Heretics Outlawed

THE SADDEST SIDE OF THE Devil's history appears in the persecution of those who were supposed to be adherents of the Devil; namely, sectarians, heretics, and witches. The most ridiculous accusations were made and believed of the Manichees, the Montanists, the Novatian Puritans or Cathari (καθαροί), the Albigenses, and other dissenters. They were said to worship the Devil by most obscene ceremonies, and their intercourse with him was described most minutely as indecent and outrageous. In times of a general belief in witchcraft and the Devil's power, nobody was safe against the accusation of being in the service of Satan. Thus the Stedingers, having effectually resisted the Bishop of Bremen when he tried to take their tithes from them by force of arms, were vanquished and cruelly slaughtered after having been denounced as Devil-worshippers. The order of the Templars, the richest and most powerful and even the most orthodox order of Christianity, was accused of the meanest and most bestial idolatry, simply because an avaricious king of France was anxious to deprive them of their wealth and valuable possessions; and innumerable private citizens, poor people as a rule recklessly and rich people deliberately, were made in some way or other victims of this most shameful superstition, sometimes to benefit ecclesiasticism, sometimes to serve the interests of the powerful, sometimes out of sheer ignorance, and sometimes even with the purest and sincerest intentions of doing the right thing for the best of mankind, and with the pious desire of obeying the word of the Lord, "Thou shalt not suffer a witch to live" (Exodus xxii. 18).

The witch-prosecution mania was a general and a common disease of the age. On the one hand, it cannot (as is often supposed) be attributed to the influence of the Church alone, and it would, on the other hand, be a grave mistake to absolve the ecclesiastical institutions of the fearful crimes of this superstition; for the highest authorities of both Catholic and Protestant Christianity not only upheld the idea of witch-prosecution, but enforced it in the execution of the law in all its most terrible consequences.

It was natural that heretics should always be regarded as belonging to the same category as witches and wizards, for they, too, were according to the logic of ecclesiastical reasoning "worshippers of Satan." Deuteronomy commands that prophets and dreamers of dreams, who by signs or wonders that come to pass would persuade Israelites to obey other gods, "shall be put to death" (xiii. 5–11). We read:

> "If thy brother, the son of thy mother, or thy son, or thy daughter, or the wife of thy bosom, or thy friend, which is as thine own soul, entice thee secretly, saying, Let us go and serve other gods, which thou hast not known, thou, nor thy fathers;
>
> "Namely, of the gods of the people which are round about you, nigh unto thee, or far off from thee, from the one end of the earth even unto the other end of the earth;
>
> "Thou shalt not consent unto him, nor hearken unto him; neither shall thine eye pity him, neither shalt thou spare, neither shalt thou conceal him:
>
> "But thou shalt surely kill him; thine hand shall be first upon him to put him to death, and afterwards the hand of all the people.
>
> "And thou shalt stone him with stones, that he die; because he hath sought to thrust thee away from the Lord thy God, which brought thee out of the land of Egypt, from the house of bondage.
>
> "And all Israel shall hear, and fear, and shall do no more any such wickedness as this is among you."

Relying on this passage, St. Jerome (340–420 A.D.) did not hesitate to advise the infliction of capital punishment upon heretics; and Leo the Great (Pope, 440–461 A.D.) takes the same view.[*]

Priscillian, a bishop of Spain, a man of learning and pure morals, was the first heretic who was put to torture and together with some of his adherents decapitated at Treves in the year 385. The followers of Priscillian revered the memory of their teacher as that of a martyr, and formed a sect which continued to exist for a long time in spite of the excommunication of the Church. Pope Leo the Great justified and praised the condemnation of Priscillian.

Under Pope Alexander III, the title "Inquisitor," in the sense of judge in matters of faith, was used for the first time at the council of Tours (in

---

[*] See Epist. xv, *ad Turribium.*

1163). The synod of Verona (in 1184) cursed all heretics, and ordered them, in case they relapsed, to be handed over to the secular authorities for capital punishment. Pope Innocent III. (1198–1216) for the sake of crushing the Albigenses gave power to papal emissaries to sue the heretics, and enjoined all bishops on penalty of deposition to assist in the discovery and prosecution of unbelievers. Following in the footsteps of Gregory VII, he vindicated the supremacy of the Church over the State; he humiliated Philip Augustus of France, deposed Emperor Otto IV, compelled John of England to acknowledge the feudal sovereignty of the Pope and pay tribute. He instigated the fourth crusade (1202–1204) and exterminated the Albigenses. Under his papacy, at the suggestion of Castilian Dominic and the Bishop of Toulouse, the new order of Dominicans was instituted, which was destined to become the working force of the Inquisition. Pope Gregory IX. pursued the traditional policy with great vigor, establishing a regular inquisitorial office for Italy under the name of the "Holy Office," in 1224.

Gregory's policy was codified in an instrument of forty-five articles by the Council of Toulouse, in 1229, and thus the Inquisition became an established Church institution, the appointment and superintendence of which formed an important prerogative of the Pope. It was not until this period that the Pope became the absolute ruler of the Church, for now even bishops could be cited before the papal tribunal of the Inquisition. Gregory IX. appointed (in 1232) the Dominicans as papal inquisitors, who performed the terrible duties of their office so faithfully that they truly earned the title of *Domini canes,* "the sleuth-hounds of the Lord," which originated in a word-play on their name.

A famous fresco in the Santa Maria Novella at Florence entitled *Domini canes*, painted by Simone Memmi, represents the inquisitorial idea under the allegory of a pack of hounds chasing off the wolves from the sheepfold.

Gregory IX. (1227–1241) sent Conrad of Marburg to Germany and gave him unlimited power of citing before his tribunal all people suspected of witchcraft, commanding him to bring the guilty to the fagot. And this fiendish man obeyed with joy his master, whom he revered as the Vicar of Christ on earth. He encountered much opposition, for the people became rebellious, and even the Archbishops of Cologne, Treves, and Mayence attempted to resist him. But Conrad remained firm; his practices had the unequivocal sanction of his Holiness the Pope, and he did not hesitate to begin proceedings even against these three highest dignitaries of the Church in Germany. Wherever Conrad appeared, the fagots were lit, and many innocent people became the victims of his fanaticism. The Archbishop of Mayence, bent on stopping this fiend, wrote a letter to the Pope, in which he said:

"Whoever fell into his hands had only the choice between a ready confession for the sake of saving his life and a denial, whereupon he was speedily burnt. Every false witness was accepted, but no just defence granted,—not even to people of prominence. The person arraigned had to confess that he was a heretic, that he had touched a toad, that he had kissed a pale man, or some monster. Many Catholics suffered themselves to be burnt innocently rather than confess to such vicious crimes, of which they knew they were not guilty. The weak ones, in order to save their lives, lied about themselves and other people, especially about such prominent ones whose names were suggested to them by Conrad. Thus brothers accused their brothers, wives their husbands, servants their masters. Many gave money to the clergy for good advice as to how to protect themselves, and the greatest confusion originated." (*Alberici Monachi chron. ad. a.* 1233.)*

The Archbishop's letter failed to impress his Holiness and did not in the least change the course of things. On the contrary, Rome pursued more vigorously than ever its old policy, which was at last definitely formulated by Pope Urban V. in his bull "*In cœna Domini*," proclaimed in 1362, which sounded the slogan against all who ventured to dissent from Rome, and solemnly condemned heresy in strong and unequivocal terms.

Meanwhile the success of the Inquisition had been greatly imperilled by the opposition which Conrad of Marburg encountered in Germany. When the Inquisitor General indicted Count Henry of Sayn for heresy, he was cited before the German Diet that was held in Mayence. The Diet was not inclined to respect Conrad's authority and passed a vote of censure. Bent on vengeance for the insult received, the Inquisitor left for Paderborn, but before he could do further mischief he was overtaken by several noblemen on the 30th of July, 1233, near Marburg,

---

* Roskoff, *Geschichte des Teufels*, II, pp. 215–216.

on the Lahn, and slain.* Thus he fell a martyr to his bloody profession. The Germans breathed more freely, but Gregory IX canonised him as a saint and martyr, and ordered that a chapel be built on the spot on which he was killed.

While the establishment of the Holy Office in Germany met with serious difficulties, the inquisitors were welcomed in France by Louis the Pious, Philip the Fair, and Charles IV.

The Inquisitor Hugo de Beniols had a number of prominent people burned alive at Toulouse, in 1275, among them Angèle, Lady of Labarthe, a woman of sixty-five years accused of sexual intercourse with Satan. It is stated that she had borne a monster with a wolf's head and a serpent's tail, whose sole food consisted of babies. Under the rule of Charles IV the ill-famed Bastile was built, because the prisons no longer sufficed to hold the indicted heretics.

The reign of Charles VI is distinguished by a temporary lull in the witchcraft-prosecution in France, mainly due to the weakness of the papacy arising from the great schism between Rome and Avignon. The curses which the two popes mutually visited on their adherents appeared to change into blessings. The Synod of Langres (1404) speaks of soothsayers as impostors, and holds out to those who are in the power of Satan the hope of salvation through repentance and penance. The tribunal of Toulouse (1606) enacted no other punishments upon thirteen persons than fines, fasts, pilgrimages, and almsgiving, while the Inquisitor was tried and convicted for the misappropriation of confiscated property. King Charles VI ordered that he be deprived of his salary.†

In Spain the Inquisition prospered best. The *Directorium inquisitorum* of N. Eymerich (Rome 1587), the inquisitor-general for Castile, affords us a complete insight into the proceedings of the Holy Office, its spy-system, its modes of cross-examination and torture, and

---

* See *Konrad von Marburg*, by Henke (Marburg, 1861), and another work of the same title by Beck (Breslau, 1861).

Conrad was the father confessor of Elizabeth, the widow of the Landgrave of Thuringia. The poor woman submitted to most indecent corporal punishments, and was sainted as a reward. If the same events happened today, both the Land-gravine and her father confessor would probably have been transferred from the Wartburg to an insane asylum. It is scarcely credible, but nevertheless true, that a book appeared in defense of Conrad as an inquisitor and of his fiendish deeds by Kaltner under the title *Konrad von Marburg und die Inquisition in Deutschland.* Prague, 1882.

† Lamothe-Langon, III, p. 299, and Soldan, p. 193.

its spoils. Torquemada and Ximenes were the most determined and unrelenting successors of Eymerich.* The wealthiest, the most powerful, the most learned, were threatened alike, and even Archbishop Carranza, the primate of the Church of Spain, could not escape the prosecution of the inquisitors.

In the beginning of the fifteenth century, Johannes Nider, a German and a Dominican monk, published a book on *Witches and Their Deceptions.*† At the same time Pope Eugene IV (1431–1447) encouraged the inquisitors in a circular letter to proceed with severity, "summarily, without ado, and without any judiciary form."‡

The Prior of St. Germain, William von Edelin, who had preached against the reality of witchcraft, had to beg pardon publicly in the Episcopal Chapel at Evreux on September 12, 1453, and to confess that he himself had worshipped Satan, had renounced his faith in the cross, and preached that witchcraft was an illusion at the especial command of the Devil for the propagation of the Satanic dominion.§ Edelin remained incarcerated and was soon released from further persecution by death.

In 1458 J. Nicolaus Jaquerius appeared in the field with another publication called the heretics' scourge or *Flagellum heriticorum fascinariorum*¶ (Frankfort, 1581) in which Edelin's case is reported** as one argument among many others for the reality of witchcraft. And now at last all opposition to the practices of witch-prosecutors were put down.

The Inquisitor Pierre le Broussart, member of the Dominican order, cited during the absence of the Bishop of Arras a number of persons before his tribunal and made them confess on the rack that they had been with the Waldenses; he promised to spare their lives if they agreed publicly to confess all the abominable crimes of which the Waldenses had been accused. At a public meeting the accused persons appeared on a scaffold; they wore caps exhibiting pictures of Devil-worship. The

---

* F. Hoffmann, *Geschichte der Inquisition*, Bonn, 1878. Llorente, *Geschichte der spanischen Inquisition*. German, from the Spanish.

† Fr. Joannes Nider, *Suevi ordin. praedicat. s. theolog. profess, et hereticae pestis inquisitoris, liber insignis de maleficiis et eorum deceptionibus.*

‡ "Summarie simpliciter et de plano, ac sine strepitu et figura judicii."—Pope Eugene in his circular letter to the Inquisitors of 1437.

§ See Raynald ad. ann. 1451.

¶ The book is frequently appended to the *Malleus Maleficarum.*

** Chapter IV contains the abjuration formula.

various ceremonies of obscene demonolatry were read to them, and they were asked whether they were guilty. All the accused affirmed their guilt, whereupon, in utter neglect of previous promises, they were sentenced and turned over to the secular authorities to be burned alive. In vain did they now shout that they had been cheated, that they knew nothing of the crimes of which they had been accused, and that they had only confessed because they had been promised to be let off with a nominal punishment. Broussart was determined to set an example, and had them executed in 1560 in spite of the protestations of their innocence.

The Witch-Hammer

WITCH-PROSECUTIONS RECEIVED A NEW IMPULSE in the year 1484 through the bull of Pope Innocent VIII, beginning with the words *Summis desiderantes affectibus.* The inquisitors of Germany, Heinrich Institoris (whose German name was Krämer) and Jacob Sprenger, complained of having met with resistance while attending to their duties, and the Pope afforded them the desired assistance for the sake of strengthening the Catholic faith* and of preventing the horrible crimes and excesses of witchcraft.†

The bull of Pope Innocent VIII had reference to Germany only; but other popes, Alexander VI, Julius II, Leo X, and Hadrian IV, issued bulls written in the same spirit, instigating the zeal of the inquisitors to do their best for the purification of the faith and the supression of witchcraft.

The heinous bull of Pope Innocent VIII was the immediate cause of the writing of the *Malleus Maleficarum,* or *Witch-Hammer,* which

---

* ". . . ut fides catholica nostris potissime temporibus ubique augeatur et floreat, ac omnis heretica pravitas de finibus fidelium procul pellatur. . . Sane nuper ad nostrum non sine ingenti molestia pervenit auditum quod. . . complures utriusque sexus personæ . . . cum dæmonibus incubis et succubis abuti, ac suis incantationibus. . . mulierum partus, animatium fœtus, terræ fruges. . . periri, suffocari et extingui facere. . . ." (See Soldan, *Hexenprocesse,* p. 222. Roskoff, I, pp. 226–292.)

† Giovanno Ballista Cibo, when elected pope in 1484, chose the name Innocent, probably in commemoration of Innocent VII. The people of his time, thinking that he did not deserve the name, called him *Nocens.* He had seven natural children, perhaps more. A humorous distich castigates him as follows:

> *"Octo Nocens pueros genuit, totidenique puellas.*
> *Hunc merito poterit dicere Roma patrem."*

received the sanction of the Pope, and a patent from Emperor Maximilian. With the *Witch-Hammer* in hand, Sprenger and Institoris appeared in 1487 before the theological faculty of Cologne and demanded their approbation, which was given with reluctance and after long hesitation. The original form of the document is very guarded and approves of the principles of punishing witchcraft only "in so far as they do not contradict the sacred canons." This did not appear sufficient and the inquisitors insisted upon a more decisive verdict. There are four further articles which contain an unequivocal request to the secular authorities to assist the inquisition in the interest of the Catholic faith.

In addition the inquisitors secured a notary's certificate concerning the Emperor's patent and the approbation of the theological faculty; but it is noteworthy that the Emperor's patent is not literally reproduced; nor has it (according to Soldan's[*] opinion) ever been published. The notary declares merely that the Emperor promises to protect the papal bull and to assist both inquisitors.

Such is the first introduction of the *Witch-Hammer* in Germany, and the book was at once recognised by zealots as the main source of information on witchcraft. Damhouder, the great criminalist of the sixteenth century, esteemed its authority as almost equal to the law;[†] and its baneful influence extends over a period of three centuries.

The *Malleus Maleficarum*, or *Witch-Hammer*, is one of the most famous and infamous works ever written. Its name indicated that it was intended to crush witchcraft. No author is mentioned but Sprenger's spirit is recognised in both its preface (the *Apologia*) and the various chapters of the book. Its style is poor, its ideas are foolish, its intentions are villainous, and the advice given to the inquisitors concerning their procedure betrays a diabolical perfidiousness. The book contains the most confounded nonsense, often self-contradictory, and is throughout irrational and superstitious. The *Witch Hammer* advises beginning the trial with the question "whether or not the person on trial believes in witchcraft." The statement is added: "Mind that witches generally deny the question." If the culprit denies, the inquisitor continues: "Well, then, whenever witches are burnt, they are innocently condemned." A denial of witchcraft sealed the doom of the accused at once, for

---

[*] *Hexenprocesse*, p. 222.

[†] "Ita recepta est in hoc scribendi genere eorum authoritas ut pro lege apud omnes habeatur."—Damhooder's *Praxis rerum criminalium*.

the *Witch-Hammer* declares: "The greatest heresy is not to believe in witchcraft" (*haeresis est maxima opera maleficarum non credere*). However, if the accused affirmed the question, the tortures made him confess all that he knew about it and whether or not he had learned and practised the black art. To plead ignorance would not avail, for the very refusal of a confession was counted a crime under the name *maleficium taciturnitatis.* There was no escape, and the best course for the victim on the rack was to confess all at once without a relapse into denials, for that at least abbreviated the procedure and ended the tragedy without its incidental terrors. As a rule the prisoners of the inquisition ask for death as a boon and wherever possible commit suicide; for torture made of every one a hopeless cripple unfit for either work or enjoyment of life, even though he might be released. Acquittals, however, were rare and the *Witch-Hammer* advises the inquisitors never to acquit, but only temporarily to stop proceedings. A *nolle pros* was recommended as the safer way. The culprit should be handed over to the secular authorities for capital punishment, especially if the sentence of being burned alive was mitigated to decapitation,* a penalty which the Church avoided inflicting; for "the Church thirsts not for blood" (*ecclesia non sitit sanguinem*). A confessor and even the judge himself is advised to speak in private with the prisoner and upon the promise of pardon and mercy to extort a confession. The *Witch-Hammer* suggests that the judge may say: "'If you confess, I shall not condemn you to death,' for he may at any time call in another judge to take his place, who is at liberty to pronounce the sentence."

The victims of the Inquisition were practically without any assistance, for witchcraft was regarded as an exceptional crime (*crimen atrocissimum* and *crimen exceptum*) for which the usual rules of procedure were not binding. It belonged before the secular and also the ecclesiastical tribunal (*crimen fori mixti*). The culprit must be dealt with according to the maxim of Pope Boniface VIII (1294–1303), "simply and squarely, without the noise and form of lawyers and judges."†

---

* "Saecularem curiam affectuose deprecamur quatenus citra sanguinis effusionem et mortis periculum suam sententiam moderatur," was the usual clause when the inquisition handed their victims over to the secular authorities.

† "Simpliciter et de plano, absque advocatorum et judiciorum strepitu et figura,"—a phrase, which, as we saw, was almost literally repeated by Pope Eugenius IV.

To us who live in an age of calmer thought and more exact investigation, it is difficult to understand how the *Witch-Hammer* could ever have been believed.

The Torture

Witch-prosecution appears to us as rascality pure and simple, but it was not. It was the result of a firm and deep-seated religious conviction, as may be learned from the *Antipalus maleficiorum*, a work of John Trithemius, Abbot of the Monastery of Spongheim (1442–1516), who at the request of Joachim, Markgrave of Brandenburg, investigated the subject, and after years of conscientious study presented to the world his views in a book of four volumes, which was completed October 16, in the year 1508, when the pious abbot had reached the mature age of sixty-six years.

Trithemius distinguishes four classes of wizards and witches: (1) Those who hurt and kill others through poison and other natural means. (2) Those who injure others by the art of magic formulas. (3) Those who converse with the Devil personally. (4) Those who have actually concluded a contract with the Devil and have thus procured his assistance for evil designs. Trithemius believes that there is no other way of protecting the commonwealth against the obnoxious influence of these malefactors than by extirpating them, but best by burning them alive. He says:

> "It is to be lamented that the number of witches in all countries is very great, for indeed there is not a village, be it ever so small, which does not harbor at least one of the third and of the fourth class. But how rare are the judges who punish these crimes against God and nature."

And in another passage the abbot utters the complaint:

> "Men and animals die through the infamy of these women, and none considers that it is due to the malignity of witchcraft. There are many who suffer from serious diseases and do not even know that they are bewitched."

The great dangers of witchcraft seemed to demand extraordinary means for combating its evils; and thus the torture, which had formerly been applied only in exceptional and special cases, began to be developed in a most formidable and barbaric way.

Suspected persons were subjected to fire and water ordeals, but the latter test was preferred; and this is the reason, as we read in König's work on the subject:

"A case is known in which the accused person successfully passed through the fire ordeal. It happened immediately before the appearance of the *Witch-Hammer*. In the archives of Donau-Eschingen there is a document according to which a certain Anna Henne from Röthenbach, in the Black Forest, in 1485, cleared herself of the suspicion of witchcraft by carrying a hot iron."

Concerning the water ordeal the same author says:

"The water ordeal is very old. Ludwig, the Pious, abolished it, but Hinkmar of Rheims defended its practice. In the times of Bernhard of Clairvaux, it was used against the Manichees. Pope Innocent III. again abolished it in the Lateran Council, 1215. The famous law book, *The Saxon Mirror*, written by Eike von Repkow, in the year 1230, provides that if two men lay claim to the same thing and the neighbors can bear no witness, the water-ordeal shall decide."

The *Mirror of the Swabians*, also of the thirteenth century, contains the same proposition. In the sixteenth century the practice was almost universally established. As to the underlying idea, König says:

"There are opposite views applied to the ordeal of water. According to the one, the question was how long the accused could remain under water; according to the other the innocence of the accused was proved by sinking, the guilt by swimming. In both cases, the view prevailed that witches possessed a specific levity, and the rule was adopted that 'The water refused to receive in its depths those who had shaken off the baptismal water through a renunciation of their faith.'" (*Ausgeb. d. Menschenwahns*, pp. 100 ff.)

Who can contemplate without indignation and holy wrath the instruments of torture used by inquisitors in their infamous vocation?

There are thumbscrews, there are blacksmith's tongs and pincers to tear out the fingernails or to be used red-hot for pinching; there is the rack, Spanish boots, collars, chains, etc., there are boards and rollers covered with sharp spikes; there is the "Scavenger's Daughter," also the "Iron Virgin," a hollow instrument the size and figure of a woman, with knives inside which are so arranged that, when closing, the victim would be lacerated in its deadly embrace.

Incredible ingenuity was displayed in the invention of these instruments of torture; and one of the executioner's swords, which still hangs in the Torturers' Vault at Nuremberg on the left side of the entrance, exhibits in bad Latin the blasphemous inscription, "*Solo Deo Gloria!*"*

The hangmen took pride in their profession and regarded themselves as disgraced if they could not make their victims confess whatever the inquisitors wanted. Their usual threat, when a heretic, a wizard, or a witch was handed over to them, was: "You will be tortured until you are so thin that the sun will shine through you." The instruments look horrible enough, but the practice was more horrible than the wildest imagination can depict.

Before the torture began, the accused were forced to drink the witch-broth, a disgusting concoction mixed with the ashes of burnt witches, and supposed to protect the torturers against the evil influence of witchcraft. The filth† of the dungeons was a very effective means of making the prisoner despondent and preparing him for any confession upon which he could be condemned. He was frequently secured by iron manacles fixed in the wall or placed under heavy timbers which prevented the free use of his limbs, rendering him a helpless prey to rats, mice, and vermin of all sorts.

Consider only the fiendish details of the torture applied to a woman in the year 1631 on the first day of her trial:‡

"(1) The hangman binds the woman, who was pregnant, and places her on the rack. Then he racked her till her heart would fain break, but had no compassion. (2) When she did not confess, the torture was repeated, the hangman tied her hands, cut off her

---

* It ought to be *Soli Deo Gloria*.

† *Carceris squalores* is the expression used by the author of the *Witch-Hammer*.

‡ Translated from König, *Ausgeburten des Menschenwahns*, p. 130. See also Soldan, *Hexenprocesse*, pp. 269–270.

hair, poured brandy over her head and burned it. (3) He placed sulphur in her armpits and burned it. (4) Her hands were tied behind her, and she was hauled up to the ceiling and suddenly dropped down. (5) This hauling up and dropping down was repeated for some hours, until the hangman and his helpers went to dinner. (6) When they returned, the master-hangman tied her feet and hands upon her back; brandy was poured on her back and burned. (8) Then heavy weights were placed on her back and she was pulled up. (9) After this she was again stretched on the rack. (10) A spiked board is placed on her back, and she is again hauled up to the ceiling. (11) The master again ties her feet and hangs on them a block of fifty pounds, which makes her think that her heart will burst. (12) This proved insufficient; therefore the master unties her feet and fixes her legs in a vise, tightening the jaws until the blood oozes out at the toes. (13) Nor was this sufficient; therefore she was stretched and pinched again in various ways. (14) Now the hangman of Dreissigacker began the third grade of torture. When he placed her on the bench and put the 'shirt' on her, he said: 'I do not take you for one, two, three, not for eight days, nor for a few weeks, but for half a year or a year, for your whole life, until you confess: and if you will not confess, I shall torture you to death, and you shall be burned after all. (15) The hangman's son-in-law hauled her up to the ceiling by her hands. (16) The hangman of Dreissigacker whipped her with a horsewhip. (17) She was placed in a vise where she remained for six hours. (18) After that she was again mercilessly horsewhipped. This was all that was done on the first day."

This is not barbarous, this is not bestial, it is satanic. And such deeds could be done in the name of God, for the sake of the religion of Jesus, and by the command of the highest authorities of the Christian Church!

From the great number of prosecutions for witchcraft we select one instance only, which, however, is neither typical nor extraordinary in its horrors.

We read in König's popular exposition of human superstitions,[*] p. 240:

---

[*] *Ausgeburten des Menschenwahns,* ein Volksbuch, Rudolstadt.

"There was a farmer by the name of Veit, living in a village of Southern Bohemia. He was famous for his wit and unusual humor. At the same time he was physically strong, and whenever there was a quarrel at the inn he came off victor. The rumor spread that he was inviolable, as sometimes hunters are supposed to be bullet-proof, and Veit never denied it. By and by he was regarded as a wizard, and as his cattle prospered best and his fields yielded the richest crops, he was soon supposed to be in league with the Evil One. Now it happened that the village was troubled with mice, and Veit was suspected of having caused the plague. When questioned about it, he granted in a moment of humor that he had sent the mice but would soon drive them away again, and he promised to prove at the next church-fair that he could actually make mice. When the day appointed came, the inn was overcrowded, and farmer Veit appeared with a big bag under his arm, into which he requested the company to throw twenty pebbles. They did so without noticing that the bag was double. And while one part was empty the other contained twenty mice. When the pebbles were put in the bag, Veit murmured a magic formula and let the mice loose in the presence of his frightened audience.

"This performance, however, had unexpected and tragic results. The people were convinced that it was the work of hell, and Veit escaped with difficulty from the inn. Veit was arrested the next night and delivered to the criminal court. A mole on his body was thought to be a stigma of the Devil, and all the witnesses agreed that he was a genuine wizard. His case was thoroughly investigated, and even the University of Prague was consulted; the verdict signed by the Rector Magnificus with his own hand was against him, and Veit, who stoutly maintained his innocence, had to endure all the tortures of the inquisition. At last he was burned alive and the ashes of his body were thrown to the winds. We read in the records of the law-suit that Veit mounted the stake 'without showing repentance or doing penance.' And when chains were put on his neck, around his body, and around his feet, he cried with a loud voice, 'My God, I die innocently.' Judges, professors, physicians, and theologians agreed unanimously in the conviction of this innocent man."

Volumes might be filled with accounts of the many thousand various instances of witch-prosecutions, and every single case is so soul-harrowing that we prefer to pass them by in silence. The accusations are almost always very circumstantial and definite, mostly of brutal indecency and ridiculously impossible.

The Angel of Augsburg

WITCH-PROSECUTION WAS A CONVENIENT WEAPON in the hands of unscrupulous men for accomplishing crooked ends or satisfying some private vengeance. One of the most tragic and pathetic cases is the sad death of Agnes Bernauer, a beautiful woman, the daughter of a barber and the sweetheart of Albrecht, Duke of Bavaria.

Agnes was born about 1410 in Biberach, and it appears that she was a mere servant girl in Augsburg at the time Duke Albrecht of Würtemberg, the son of Duke Ernest, made her acquaintance. The story that Agnes was of patrician birth and that the lovers met at the great tournament is mere legend, but this much is sure that Agnes was extraordinarily beautiful, with golden hair, and delicate, noble features. Even her enemies could not help praising the nobility of her appearance. We know little or nothing about the relations between Duke Albrecht and Agnes, except that he courted her and took her with him to his residence in the County Vohnburg.

Duke Ernest, Albrecht's father, knew about Agnes's presence at Vohnburg but he cared little, until he became anxious about having a legal heir to his duchy. Then he requested his son to marry the daughter of Duke Erik of Brunswick, but Albrecht refused on account of the love he bore to Agnes.

When persuasion appeared to be without avail, Duke Ernest thought of other means to separate his son from the lowly-born maiden. At a public tournament, he ordered the judges to refuse admittance to Albrecht on the ground that for the sake of a concubine he neglected his filial duties. Albrecht was greatly exasperated and as soon as he returned to Vohnburg he recognised Agnes as his wife. With the consent of his uncle, Duke William, he moved to the castle Straubing, which he donated to her and surrounding her with a ducal court, called her henceforth Duchess Agnes.

The poor woman did not enjoy the splendor of the court. She feared the wrath of the old Duke, and built, in a melancholy presentiment of her sad fate, her own burial chapel, in the monastery of the Carmelites at Straubing. Her happiness was of short duration.

In Albrecht's absence, Duke Ernest seized Agnes, had her imprisoned and denounced her as a witch. Her condemnation had been decided upon before the trial began, and the verdict pronounced her guilty of having bewitched Duke Albrecht and thus committed a criminal offence against Duke Ernest. The judgment ordered her to be drowned in the river, and Duke Ernest signed the verdict.

The hangmen carried the young woman to the bridge at Straubing and thrust her, in the presence of a multitude of spectators, into the water. But the current drifted her ashore and she held up her white arms appealing to the people for help. The people were moved and she might have been saved, had not one of the hangmen, fearing the wrath of the old duke, seized a pole and catching her long golden hair held her under water until she expired. This happened in the year 1435.

She was buried in St. Peter's cemetery of Straubing.

When the young Duke on his return was informed of the terrible death of his beloved Agnes he swore vengeance, and in alliance with his cousin Duke Ludwig of Bavaria-Ingolstadt, began to wage a vigorous war against his own father. Through the mediation of the Emperor, however, he was reconciled with his father at the council of Basel.

Duke Ernest built a chapel over the grave of his innocent victim and had an annual mass read over her for the welfare of her soul. Duke Albrecht thereupon agreed to marry Anna, Princess of Brunswick, by whom he had ten children, although it cannot be said that his married life was a happy one.

In 1447 Duke Albrecht had the body of Agnes transferred to the chapel which she had built for herself in the Carmelite monastery; and he had the resting-place of her remains adorned with a beautiful marble image of her in full figure with the simple inscription:

"Obiit Agnes Bernauerin. Requiescat in pace."

Poets who have immortalised her name,[*] and the people of Bavaria among whom her memory is still cherished, call her "the angel of Augsburg."

---

* Folksong on Agnes die Pernawerin. Count Törring (1780), Böttger (1846), Melchior Meyr (1862). Friedrich Hebbel (1855), Otto Ludwig (a posthumous fragmentary design

ONE OF THE MOST COMICAL witch-prosecutions took place in 1474 against a diabolical rooster who had been so presumptuous as to lay an egg. The poor creature was solemnly tried, whereupon he was condemned to die at the stake and publicly burned by order of the authorities of the good city of Basel.

We abstain from entering further into the details of the prosecution of witches, which gradually developed into a systematic business involving great emoluments to judges, torturers, hangmen, inquisitors, denouncers, witnesses, and all persons connected with the process. It is a doleful work to go over the mere statistics of the *autos-da-fé*, and every single story of a trial for witchcraft cannot but rouse our deepest indignation; and even now the belief in witchcraft is not yet extinct among the so-called civilised races of mankind.

---

of a drama begun in 1852). König, *Ausgeburten des Menschenwahns* recapitulates the story as the legend has it. For a critical review and an exposition of the historical facts see Dr. Christian Meyer's article on Agnes Bernauer in *Die Gartenlaube*, 1873, p. 454.

THE AGE OF THE REFORMATION

The Reformation, although in many respects a great advance did not introduce a sudden change in the belief in the Devil. Nevertheless, the tendency becomes more and more apparent to interpret Satan in psychological terms, and instead of expecting him in the horrors of nature or in the objective reality of our surroundings, to find him in our own hearts where he appears as temptation in all forms, as allurement, ambition, vanity, as the vain pursuit of fortune, power, and worldly pleasures.

Christianity was split up into two parties, the conservatives who remained faithful to Rome's spiritual supremacy and the progressive Protestants who opposed the traditional authorities of the Church and clamored for reform in the various ways of life. Restless times of this kind are favorable for satire and sarcasm, and the Devil therefore naturally played an important part in the polemics on either side.

At the same time, the moral earnestness of the reformers forced the authorities of the Church to abandon many of the worst misuses, and thus the reform of the Reformation did not remain limited to the reformed Churches, but extended its blessings to the Roman Church itself. The anti-reformation, whose backbone was the Jesuits, was a most serious and rigorously pure movement born of a deep religious piety; but it was darkened in its very start by a mysticism verging on coarse superstition, and lacked that love of freedom, of progress, of scientific investigation, and the desire to learn the truth which characterises the exponents of Protestantism. It is noticeable, however, that the moral element is pushed into the foreground, and both parties begin to agree in this that morality is the ultimate test of religion.

The idea of conceiving Satan as sin and temptation is not new (think only of the illustrations in the *Hortus Deliciarum*), but the conception of sin and temptation begins now to be better understood as a psychological condition of subjective states.

Luther

LUTHER WAS, IN HIS DEMONOLOGY, a real child of his time; he saw the Devil everywhere, he struggled with him constantly, and overcame him by his confidence in God. He regarded the Pope as an incarnation of Satan, or as the Anti-Christ, and the Roman Church as the kingdom of the Devil. He sang of him:

> *"And were this world with devils filled*
> *That threaten to undo us;*
> *We will not fear, for God hath willed*
> *His truth to triumph through us.*
> *Our ancient vicious foe*
> *Still seeks to work his woe.*
> *His craft and power are great*
> *And armed with cruel hate.*
> *On earth is not his equal.*
>
> .   .   .   .   .
>
> *"The Prince of this world*
> *His banner has unfurled;*
> *And yet he will harm none*
> *For he is all undone;*
> *One little word defeats him."*

The Devil was to Luther a real, living power, a concrete personality, and he used to characterise him as the good Lord's hangman, and the instrument of his anger and punishment.[*] God needs the Devil for a servant and utilises his malignity for the procreation of the good (x, 1259).

Luther's belief in the Devil was not only very realistic but also almost childishly ingenuous. When at work he was prepared for his incessant interference, and when going to rest he expected to be disturbed by him. Luther was not afraid of him, yet the efforts he made in conquering the Evil One are sufficient evidence that he regarded him as very powerful. He protested he would go to Worms though every tile on the roofs of the city were a Devil; he saw the fiend grinning at him while he translated the Bible, and threw his inkstand at his Satanic Majesty.[†]

By and by the familiarity between Luther and the Devil increased: "Early this morning," Luther tells us in his *Tischreden*, "when I awoke

---

[*] Walch, *Tischreden*, v, 839; v, 1109; viii, 1234, x, 1257; xii, 481, and 2043.

[†] The story has been doubted, yet, considering the character of Luther, it is not only possible but probable. If Luther did not throw the inkstand at the Devil, the anecdote is, to say the least, *ben trovato;* it characterises excellently his attitude toward Satan.

the fiend came and began disputing with me. 'Thou art a great sinner,' said he. I replied, 'Canst not tell me something new, Satan?'"

Luther was inclined to believe in the Devil's power of assisting wizards and witches in their evil designs. Following St. Augustine's authority he conceded the possibility of *incubi* and *succubi*, because Satan, in the shape of a handsome young man, loves to decoy young girls. He also accepted the superstition of changelings and declared that witches should suffer death; but when once confronted with a real case, he insisted, when his counsel was sought, on the most scrupulous circumspection. He wrote to the judge:

> "I request you to explore everything with exactness so as to leave no trace of fraud. . . for I have experienced so many deceits, frauds, artifices, lies, treacheries, etc., that I can scarcely make up my mind to believe. Therefore see and convince yourself to your own satisfaction, lest you be mistaken and I may be mistaken through you."*

Although it is true that Luther's views of the Devil were as childish as those of his contemporaries, it would be rash to denounce the Reformation for having accomplished no progress and having done nothing to suppress the barbarous superstitions of demonology. Luther's God-conception was purer and nobler than the God-conception of the leading churchmen and popes of his time, and thus his faith, in spite of its crudities, led, after all, to purer conceptions, which were destined gradually to overcome the old traditional dualism.

Luther demanded that Christ should not only be recognised as the Saviour of mankind, but that every man should be able to say, "He has come to save me personally and individually." Luther thus carried the religious life into the very hearts of men and declared that there was no salvation in ceremonies, absolutions, or sacraments; unless one had individually, in one's own nature and being, vanquished the temptations of Satan. The most dangerous idols are, according to Luther, the pulpit and the altar, for sacraments and ceremonies

---

* *Angeli Annales Marchiæ Brandenburgicæ*, p. 326 (quoted by Soldan, p. 302). The original reads: "Rogo te, omnia velis certissime explorare, ne subit aliquid doli. . . Nam ego tot fucis, dolis, technis, mendaciis, artibus, etc., hactenus sum exagitatus ut cogar difficilis esse ad credendum. . . Quare vide et prospice tibi quoque ne fallare et ego per te fallar.

cannot save. They are symbols instituted to assist us. Those who believe that ceremonies possess any power of their own are still under the influence of the pagan notion that evils can be averted by sacrifices and exorcisms.

Luther's Successors

WHILE LUTHER INSTINCTIVELY ABHORRED PERSECUTIONS of any kind, he still retained those beliefs which were the ultimate cause of witch prosecution. We must, therefore, not be astonished to see even in Protestant countries a revival of the horrors which had been inaugurated by the Inquisition.

The most curious work of Protestant demonology is the *Theatrum Diabolorum* by Sigmund Feyerabend, a voluminous collection of the orthodox views of Luther's followers concerning the existence, power, nature, and demeanor of devils.

Luther's belief in the Devil was crude, but he was even here morally great, strong in his religious sentiment, and serious in his demand that every one personally should honestly wage a war with the powers of evil, and that no church, no intercession of saints, no formulas or rituals had any saving power. Luther's followers retain all the crudities of their master and to some extent his moral seriousness, but they fall below the manliness of his spirit.

Feyerabend's *Theatrum Diabolorum*, "which," as the title says, "is a useful and sensible book," contains a great number of essays written by such prominent little authorities as Jodocus Hockerus Osna-burgensis, Hermannus Hamelmannus, Andreas Musculus, Andreas Fabricius Chemnicensis, Ludovicus Milichius, and others. The Reverend Hocker explains in forty-eight chapters almost all possible problems connected with devils whose number in Chapter VIII is, according to Borrhaus, calculated to be not less than 2,665,866,746,664. Others describe special kinds of devils, such as the devil of blasphemy, VI; the dance-devil, VII; the servant's devil, VIII; the hunting devil, IX; the drink-devil, X; the wedlock-devil, XI; the devil of unchastity, XII; the miser's devil, XIII; the devil of tyranny, XIV; the laziness devil, XV; the pride devil, XVI; the pantaloon devil, XVII; the gambling devil, XVIII; the courtier's devil (represented in a drama of five acts, the scene being at the court of Darius), XIX; and the pestilence devil, XX. The author of this last chapter, the Rev. Hermann Strack, concludes by saying: "When we can obtain medicine let us not have a contempt for God's valuable gifts, but withal let us always and all the time rest our confidence and main comfort upon the only God."

The same conception of the Devil is presented with somewhat more poetical skill by Jacob Ruffs who dramatised the story of Job and the parable of the vineyard. The latter, which was performed at Zürich, Switzerland, in 1539, May 26, introduces Satan as he sows the seeds of sedition in the minds of the servants of the vineyard and induces them to slay the son of their master.

Almost all these treatises, poor though they may he as literary, theological, or pastoral exhortations, yet show the rationalistic tendency of discovering the Devil in the vices of man, and this method became more and more established until in these latter days Satan himself was boldly and directly by Protestant theologians declared to be a mere abstract idea and a personification of evil. Yet this step was not taken at once, and mankind had to pass first through a long period of wavering opinions, of conflicting propositions, uncertainties, venomous controversies, and anxious research for the truth.

Shakespeare

THE PROTESTANT DEVIL BECAME SOMEWHAT more cultured than the Catholic Devil, for the advancement noticeable in the civilisation of Protestant countries extended also to him. Says Mephistopheles in Faust:

> *"Culture which smooth the whole world licks*
> *Also unto the Devil sticks."*

To note the progress, let us compare Wyntoun who wrote early in the fifteenth century and Shakespeare. Wyntoun's witches are ugly, old hags; Shakespeare's, although by no means beautiful, are yet interesting and poetical; they are "so withered and so wild in their attire that look not like the inhabitants o' th' earth and yet are on it." It is a poetical fiction representing temptation. And in this same sense the very word Devil is frequently used by Shakespeare. We are told, "'tis the eye of childhood that fears a painted Devil," and one fiend, as we read in Shakespeare, is the invisible spirit of wine. "The Devil," we read in Hamlet, "hath power to assume a pleasing shape." And the meaning of this sentence is plainly psychological, as we learn from another passage in which Polonius says to his daughter:

> *"With devotion's visage*
> *And pious action we do sugar o'er*
> *The Devil himself."*

Milton

THE PROTESTANT DEVIL, AS A poetical figure, received his finishing touches from Milton. And Milton's Devil acquires a nobility of soul, moral strength, independence, and manliness which none of his ancestors possessed, neither Satan, nor Azazel, nor his proud cousins the Egyptian Typhon and the Persian Ahriman. The best characterisation of Milton's Satan is given by Taine. He ridicules Milton's description of Adam and Eve, who talk like a married couple of the poet's days. "I listen, and hear an English household, two reasoners of the period—Colonel Hutchinson and his wife. Heavens! Dress them! Folk so cultivated should have invented first of all a pair of trousers." The picture of the Good Lord is still more severely criticised. He says: "What a contrast between God and Satan!" Taine continues:

> "Milton's Jehovah is a grave king who maintains a suitable state, something like Charles I.
>
> "Goethe's God, half abstraction, half legend, source of calm oracles, a vision just beheld after a pyramid of ecstatic strophes, greatly excels this Miltonic God, a business man, a schoolmaster, a man for show! I honor him too much in giving him these titles. He deserves a worse name.
>
> "He also talks like a drill-sergeant. 'Vanguard to right and left the front unfold.' He makes quips as clumsy as those of Harrison, the former butcher turned officer. What a heaven! It is enough to disgust one with Paradise; one would rather enter Charles the First's troop of lackeys, or Cromwell's Ironsides. We have orders of the day, a hierarchy, exact submission, extra duties, disputes, regulated ceremonials, prostrations, etiquette, furbished arms, arsenals, depots of chariots and ammunition."

How different is the abode of Satan. Taine says:

"The finest thing in connexion with this Paradise is Hell.

"Dante's hell is but a hall of tortures, whose cells, one below another, descend to the deepest wells."

Milton's hell is the asylum of independence; it may be dreary but it is the home of liberty that scorns abject servility. Milton describes the place as follows:

> *"'Is this the region, this the soil, the clime,'*
> *Said then the last Archangel, 'this the seat*
> *That we must change for heaven? this mournful gloom*
> *For that celestial light? Be it so, since he,*
> *Who now is Sovran, can dispose and bid*
> *What shall be right: farthest from him is best,*
> *Whom reason has equal'd, force hath made supreme*
> *Above his equals. Farewell, happy fields,*
> *Where joy for ever dwells! Hail, horrors hail,*
> *Infernal world! and thou, profoundest hell*
> *Receive thy new possessor; one who brings*
> *A mind not to be changed by place or time.*
> *The mind is its own place, and in itself*
> *Can make a heaven of hell, a hell of heaven.*
> *What matter where, if I be still the same,*
> *And what I should be; all but less than he*
> *Whom thunder hath made greater? Here at least*
> *We shall be free; the Almighty hath not built*
> *Here for his envy; will not drive us hence:*
> *Here we may reign secure; and in my choice*
> *To reign is worth ambition, though in hell:*
> *Better to reign in hell, than serve in heaven.'"*

It has been frequently remarked that Milton's Satan is the hero of *Paradise Lost*, and, indeed, he appears as the most sympathetic figure in the greatest religious epic of English literature. His pride is not without self-respect which we cannot help admiring; Satan exclaims:

> *"Is there no place*
> *Left for repentance, none for pardon left?*

None left but by submission: and
That word disdain forbids me. . ."

And how noble appears Milton's Satan! Milton personifies in Satan the spirit of the English Revolution; Milton's Satan represents the honor and independence of the nation asserted in the face of an incapable government. Satan's appearance shows strength and dignity:

"He above the rest
In shape and gesture proudly eminent
Stood like a tower."

And his character is distinguished by love of liberty. Taine describes him as follows:

"The ridiculous Devil of the Middle Ages, a horned enchanter, a dirty jester, a petty and mischievous ape, band-leader to a rabble of old women, has become a giant and a hero.

"Though feebler in force, he remains superior in nobility, since he prefers suffering independence to happy servility, and welcomes his defeat and his torments as a glory, a liberty, and a joy."

The Devil naturally acquires noble features which make him less diabolical and more divine in the measure that the God-conception of an age becomes the embodiment of the conservatism of the ruling classes. When the name and idea of God are misapplied to represent stagnation, Satan might change places with God. A new sect of Devil-worshippers who aspire for advancement and progress in the name of Satan might have arisen had not Protestantism, decried centuries ago as the work of the Devil, gained so much influence that in time it became itself a great conservative power in the world; and that its noble aspirations were first attributed to the influence of the Devil is only preserved in verse and fable.

The Devil in the Human Heart

THE COMMON PEOPLE IN PROTESTANT countries knew nothing of the mighty hero of *Paradise Lost;* they knew Satan only through the

New Testament, and, being little affected by the progress of the natural sciences, took him as seriously as did the early Christians and the Dominicans of the Inquisition. But there is this difference; the spirit of the Reformation rested upon them with both its moral earnestness and its subjectivism. The middle classes as a rule did not fall a prey to the aberrations of former times; they practised no exorcisms and showed no inclination to prosecute, but confined their endeavors to the salvation of their own souls

The classical productions of the literature of this type are *Pilgrim's Progress* and *The Heart of Man*, both highly interesting from a psychological standpoint, for both exhibit the subjective methods of introspection in a high degree, and will, as instances of a naïve but extraordinary self-observation and analysis, retain a lasting value.

While the author of *Pilgrim's Progress*, his name and the vicissitudes of his life, are well known, *The Heart of Man* appeared anonymously, first in French and then in German. The French original seems to be lost and with it the date of its first appearance. The first German translation was published in Würzburg, in the year 1732, under the title *Geistlicher Sittenspiegel.* It was reprinted once more in 1815 under the more appropriate title *Das Herz des Menschen*, exhibiting a series of illustrations which represent the human heart as the battlefield of the powers of good and evil.

The first picture shows the human heart in its natural perversity, but the sinner repents in the second picture, and the Holy Ghost takes possession of his soul, in the third picture. The fourth picture shows us a contemplation of the sufferings of the Saviour and the Holy Trinity resides in the soul as is illustrated in the fifth picture. But worldly temptations and prosecutions, represented the former by a man with a goblet and the latter by another man with a dagger, prevail upon the heart and shake its good resolutions, which is seen in the sixth picture; until at last, in the seventh picture, Satan with seven other spirits more wicked than himself re-enters, and the last state of that man is worse than the first. The practical application of this analysis of the human heart is given in two illustrations picturing the death of the pious and impious man. The former, whose heart is depicted in the ninth picture, is portrayed in the tenth picture, as being called by the Saviour to enjoy the eternal bliss of Heaven; while the eighth picture exhibits the doom of the latter who is lost forever in Hell.

The interesting feature of these illustrations consists in the method of showing the elements of man's soul, his passions and aspirations as foreign powers which enter, pass out, and re-enter. The heart itself appears as an empty blank and its character is established by the tendencies which dwell in it. The psychology which lies at the bottom of the author's belief, is not clearly pronounced; it may be either the Brahmanical theory of the self, as a being in itself, or the Buddhist doctrine of the illusoriness of the self, but it appears that the self, as represented in the head above the heart, is a mere reflex of the process that takes place within the human soul, and should therefore be regarded merely as the principle of unity, the moral worth of which depends upon the nature of its elements. The author of these drawings has in his naive analysis of the human heart, approached a scientific conception of the soul more closely than presumably he was aware of himself.

A Revival of Witch Prosecution

AT THE TIME OF THE Reformation witch prosecution ceased for a while. It made room for another mania not less ugly and condemnable. Its place was filled by heresy persecution. Not only did Roman Catholic governments worry their Protestant subjects almost to death by confiscating their property, chasing them with hounds to mass, exiling entire districts, and ignominiously executing their leaders; but Protestants in their turn, too, regarded it as their religious duty to do the same to all dissenters. Luther himself, be it said to his everlasting honor, did not persecute; and so long as he lived he succeeded in preventing among his followers all persecutions. Calvin, however, ordered Servetus to be burned alive, because his belief in the trinity differed from his own; and King Henry VIII. of England resolutely suppressed with a high hand all opposition to the religious views he happened to hold at the time; nor did he shrink from shedding blood, although we must grant that he exercised much judgment by confining his persecution to a comparatively few powerful opponents.

While the fear of witchcraft was thus set aside for a time, the dangerous belief in the power of Satan continued and lay hidden like burning coals under ashes. The religious superstitions remained practically the same, and it is natural that the epidemic reappeared, although in a less virulent form. Even Protestant countries (North Germany, Sweden, England, Scotland, and the English colonies in North America) were visited by this spiritual plague, and a number of lay judges appeared who showed the same zeal as the Dominican inquisitors in Catholic countries.

With the waning of the zeal for burning witches the defenders of witchcraft grew rather more numerous than before. Among them are Dr. Thomas Erastus of Heidelberg,[*] and Jean Bodin, a Frenchman.[†] The Suffragan Bishop Peter Binsfeld[‡] and Justice Nicolaus Remigius[§] defended in voluminous books with new arguments the policy of the *Witch-Hammer*, and King James I. of England wrote a demonology[¶] filled with all the superstition of the Middle Ages; Martin Delrio,[**] a Jesuit, deems a revision of the belief in witchcraft in order, but comes to the conclusion that the evil exists and that there is no remedy save the use of relics, holy water, exorcisms, the holy sacraments of the Roman Catholic Church.

The National Museum of Germanic Antiquities at Nuremberg possesses a large poster which contains an account of three women who were burned as witches at Dernburg in the year 1555. Although they were not burned on the same day, the illustration represents them as standing on the fagots together and the statement is made that in one instance, when the fire was lit, Satan appeared and visibly carried away his paramour through the air.

The tragedy of Dernburg is one case only among many. Mayor Pheringer, of Nördlingen, swore to exterminate the whole brood of sorcerers, and Judge Benedict Carpzov, Jr. (1595–1666), of Leipsic, following in the footsteps of his father, condemned more than a hundred persons to die at the stake for witchcraft.

Sensible Prelates

THE PROTESTANTS OF THE SIXTEENTH and seventeenth centuries were on the average perhaps more serious in their religious beliefs than the Roman Catholics of the same period, and thus it happened that

---

[*] *De Lamiis et strigibus*, 1577.

[†] *De Magorum dæmonomania seu detestando lamiarum et Magorum cum Satana commercio*, 1579.

[‡] *Tractatus de confessionibus maleficorum et sagarum*, 1589.

[§] *Dæmonolatria*, which appeared in Latin and in German. See Soldan, p. 351.

[¶] *Demonologie*, 1597. See also the advice to suppress witchcraft, given to his son in the second book of his *Basilicon Doron*, 1599.

[**] *Disquisitiones magicæ*, 1599.

some French prelates of the Roman Church, being more worldly wise and more deeply imbued with the advancing spirit of the age than many bigoted Protestants, displayed infinitely more common sense than their brethren of the Reformed Churches.

This became particularly patent in the famous case of Martha Brossier, a French peasant girl, who, in 1588, claimed to be possessed of a devil. The excitement was great, and the pulpits resounded with alarming denunciations apt to renew all the terrors of former witch prosecutions. But Bishop Miron of Angers, and Cardinal De Gondi, Archbishop of Paris, retained their tranquillity, and had the case investigated not only according to a truly rational method, but even in a spirit of humor. When the never-failing tests with exorcisms through sacred books and holy water were administered, Bishop Miron so arranged matters that the possessed girl was induced to draw wrong conclusions, and lo! simple spring water and the reading of a line from Virgil regularly brought on epileptic fits, while neither the old reliable exorcisms nor the holy water produced any effect when the girl did not apprehend the sacred texts.

Believers in Satanic possession were not satisfied with Bishop Miron's experiments, for they regarded them as a proof of the cunning of the Devil who thus slyly deceived his enemies. The case was brought before the Archbishop De Gondi, but he, too, proved sceptical and declared after some judicious experiments that the demeanor of the possessed girl was a mixed result of insanity and simulation.

Urban Grandier

IN SPITE OF THE SOUND judgment shown by these and other prelates, the prosecutions of witches continued. In the case of Urban Grandier, a priest, who was accused by the Ursuline nuns at Loudun in Western France of having exercised Satanic powers upon their minds, the Archbishops of Bordeaux recognised the malicious hostility and hysterical bitterness with which the nuns bore witness against their preacher. Grandier was not innocent in other respects, but there were many priests whose morals were no better. Considering the innumerable contradictions in the statements of his enemies, the Archbishop dismissed the case and he was honorably reinstalled in his position. But that was not the end of it. It happened that M. de Laubordemont, a cousin of the prioress, while attending to some business of the French

Government in Loudun, heard of the story and gave a highly-colored report to Cardinal Richelieu, at whose instance the investigation was renewed. In the second trial Grandier had no chance; for Laubordemont was appointed judge. He accepted the most ridiculous evidence. The devils who spoke out of the mouths of the obsessed nuns were called upon as witnesses, and two documents were produced which purported to be the original pact of Grandier with Satan. One of them is signed by Grandier, the other bears the signature of six devils, the authenticity of which is vouched for by Baalbarith, the Secretary of his Satanic Majesty. The script is in mirror writing. Four expert Doctors of the Sorbonne, although they never doubted either the documents or the reality of the devils of the obsessed nuns, saw fit to caution the judges not to admit the testimony of Satan, because the slanderer and liar could not be a trustworthy witness. But the exorcising fathers, all of whom were Carmelite monks, laid down the principle that a properly exorcised devil cannot help confessing the truth. Grandier was cruelly tortured and executed on August 18; but Peter Lactantius, the chief exorcist whom the dying Grandier had challenged to appear before the tribunal of God, died a raving maniac exactly one month after the death of his victim, on September 18.

A Protestant Witch-Execution

MUCH HAS BEEN SAID AND written about the cruelty of the Roman Catholic methods of witch-prosecution, but the Protestants were not a whit better, except perhaps that they added to the proceedings a good deal more of pious cant and accompanied executions with a religious unction which made their conduct the more detestable. As a typical case we quote an abbreviated report of the execution of three witches, Susanna, Ilse, and their mother Catharine, which took place at Arendsee, 1687, August 5:[*]

> "The case was submitted for another revision, during which time six clergymen attended daily upon the three prisoners and exhorted them to pray and sing and repent. Then they were cited before the court one after the other and the clergymen stood

---

[*] See Horst, *Zauberbibliothek*, 2, pp. 411–413, quoted from Reichardt, Vol. I, pp. 100–126.

behind them. The president of the court asked them once more, first Susanna, whether she had received an incubus; (answer: Yes!) Secondly Ilse, whether her mother had given her an incubus; (answer: Yes!) and thirdly Catharine, whether she had given an incubus to Ilse; (answer: Yes!) Thereupon the Notary, Mr. Anton Werneccius, read the judgment, and the executioner went to the court and asked for mercy in case he should not succeed at once in decapitating Susanna and Ilse. The question was asked whether there was any additional grievance. Then the rod was broken, table and chairs of the court upset, and the procession moved out to the Köppenberg, the place of execution.

"Part of the guards opened the way. Each one of the three witches was accompanied on either side by a clergyman and led with a rope by a hangman. At the same time six armed citizens surrounded her. Another part of the guard closed the procession.

"On the way prayers alternated with exhortations and singing of hymns.

"Before the Seehausen gate a circle was made and Susanna was led round until the public had finished singing the hymn 'God our father, dwell with us.'

"When her head was taken off, the people sang, 'To thee we pray, O Holy Ghost.'*

"Next came Ilse who was killed in the same way, accompanied by the singing of the same hymns.

"While the singing continued Catharine was placed upon the fagots and her neck fastened with an iron chain, which was drawn so tight that her face swelled and became suffused with a brown color. The fagots were lit and all present, clergy, school-children, and spectators sang until her body was consumed in the fire."

Witch-Prosecution in America

NOT LESS TERRIBLE FRUIT THAN in Europe did the belief in witchcraft bear on the free soil of Protestant America. Death-sentences

---

* Especially the latter song, *Nun bitten wir den Heilgen Geist*, was believed to afford protection against witchcraft. When a pious superintendent in the University of Giessen was once surrounded by students dressed as devils he chanted in his anxiety this hymn in the hope of driving away thereby his tormentors.

for witchcraft occurred several times after the foundation of the New England colonies; but the last and most terrible outbreak took place in Salem, Massachusetts, as recorded in Upham's *History of Salem Witchcraft*, and in Drake's *Witchcraft Delusion in New England*. Under the baneful influence of the religious teachings of Increase Mather and his son, Cotton Mather,* two Boston clergymen, the Rev. Samuel Parris, minister of the Church in Salem, began to have a case of witchcraft investigated, which, as says President Andrew Dickson White,† "would have been the richest of farces had they not led to events so tragical." The possessed behaved like maniacs in court and charged a poor old Indian woman with having bewitched them. Her husband, an ignorant fool, was induced to testify against her. This easy success emboldened the believers in witchcraft, among whom the Putnam family played a prominent part. They began to prosecute some of the foremost people of New England; several men and women were executed, many fled for their lives, and a reign of terror ensued. Any person once suspected and accused was doomed. As an instance we quote the case of Mr. Burroughs, a clergyman, who on account of petty parish quarrels with the Putnam family had been dismissed from the ministry. President White says:

"Mr. Burroughs had led a blameless life, the only thing ever charged against him by the Putnams being that he insisted strenuously that his wife should not go about the parish talking of her own family matters. He was charged with afflicting the children, convicted, and executed. At the last moment he repeated the Lord's Prayer solemnly and fully, which it was supposed no sorcerer could do, and this, together with his straightforward Christian utterances at the execution, shook the faith of many in the reality of diabolical possession."

President White continues:

"Ere long it was known that one of the girls had acknowledged that she had belied some persons who had been executed, and especially Mr. Burroughs, and that she had begged forgiveness;

---

* Compare Cotton Mather, *The Wonders of the Invisible World; being an Account of the Tryals of Several V Vitches, lately Ex[e]cuted in New England* (first London edition, 1693).
† See his "New Chapters in the Warfare of Science," *Popular Science Monthly*, May, 1889, p. 11. Compare also König, *Ausgeburten des Menschenwahns*, pp. 488–494.

but this for a time availed nothing. Persons who would not confess were tied up and put to a sort of torture which was effective in securing new revelations.

"In the case of Giles Cory the horrors of the persecution culminated. Seeing that his doom was certain, and wishing to preserve his family from attainder and their property from confiscation, he refused to plead. He was therefore pressed to death, and, when in his last agonies his tongue was pressed out of his mouth, the sheriff with his walking-stick thrust it back again."

Increase and Cotton Mather were the last defenders of diabolical possession and witchcraft on American soil; the latter saw in his later years a new era dawning upon his country. Vigorously and successfully censured by Robert Calef, a courageous Boston merchant, he bemoaned the decay of the religious spirit among the growing generation, and even to his dying hour regarded the mere unbelief in witchcraft as an attack upon the glory of the Lord.

The present generation may well smile at his mistaken religious notions; but granting him that the old conception of God as a miracle-worker and an individual ego-being after the fashion of pagan personifications be right, his idea of the importance of a belief in witchcraft is logically correct. If witchcraft is impossible, then there can be no wizard-god who changes sticks into serpents, who stops the sun in his course, reverses the shadow of the dial, is jealous of other gods and of the familiar spirits of witches. The abandonment of the belief in witchcraft tacitly implied the abandonment of a belief in God as a miracle-worker, and prepared the way for a nobler religious faith which surrendered the idea of seeking God in the suppositious possibility of breaking the laws of nature, and finally found him in the cosmic order itself, i.e., in the unity, the harmony, the rightness of those eternal factors of existence which are the conditions of reason, of truth, and of justice.

The Abolition of Witch-Prosecution

Molitor and Erasmus

THE HORRORS OF DEVIL WORSHIP, of the Inquisition, and of witch-prosecution were the natural consequences of a misconception of the nature of evil. They were the visitations that necessarily followed in the footsteps of a most abandoned ignorance. They oppressed mankind like a dreadful nightmare, like ghastly hallucinations of a feverish brain, and the disease passed away slowly, very slowly, only when the light of science, which is the divine revelation that is taking place now, gradually began to dispel the gloomy shadows of the night and revealed the superstitious character of the belief that had begotten the crimes of the dark ages.

The first protests against witch-prosecution were raised at the time when the two inquisitors Sprenger and Institutoris, fortified with the unequivocal authority of his Holiness the Pope, carried on their criminal profession in the boldest way. The outrages of the Inquisition were pointed out in a pamphlet entitled *Dialogus de lamiis et pythonibus mulieribus*, written in 1489 by Dr. Ulrich Molitoris, an attorney of Constance. Two other prominent men of the juridical profession, Alciatus and Ponzinibius, expressed themselves in the same spirit; they declared bodily excursions of witches and similar things to be pure imagination. But their arguments were of no avail, for Bartholomæus de Spina, the master of the holy palace, declared that jurists could not understand the case of witchcraft.

The time was not yet ripe; the people still clung to the belief in visions and miracles, dreams, apparitions and sorcery. Most insane productions (such as, e.g., Grünbeck's *New Interpretation of Strange Miracles*, which appeared in the year 1507) attracted the attention of the world and passed for divine revelations. The more uncanny they were, the higher was the credit they received.*

There is a remarkable instance on record that the hangman of Vienna refused to perform his office on Oct. 21, 1498. The execution

---

* Crosses were seen everywhere; in the dress of the people and in the sky; also crowns of thorns, nails, scourges, etc., which caused the Bishop of Liège to order special fasts and call the emperor's attention to the dangers that threatened the world.

had to be delayed until another hangman could be procured.* Another case is mentioned by Soldan.† Katharine Hensel of Feckelberg was sentenced to die in June, 1576, but when at the place of execution she pleaded her innocence, the hangman refused to execute her. The case was referred to the Palsgrave George John of Veldenz who after a careful examination of the trial ordered an acquittal and condemned the township Feckelberg to bear the costs.‡

The famous Erasmus of Rotterdam published a letter in the year 1500 in which he spoke of devil-contracts as an invention made by the witch-prosecutors; but his satire had no effect; for, in the meantime, fagots were constantly burning all over Europe.

Weier, Meyfart, and Loos

THE FIRST SUCCESSFUL ATTEMPT—SUCCESSFUL only temporarily and in a limited degree—of stopping witch-prosecution came from a Protestant physician, Johannes Weier (Latin "Wierus" or "Piscinarius"). He was born in Grave, 1515, had studied medicine in Paris, and travelled in Africa, where, as he tells us, he had had a good opportunity of studying sorcery. Then he went to Crete, and on his return was elected body-physician to Duke William of Cleves. His work of six books, *De præstigiis Dæmonum et incantationibus ac Veneficiis*, appeared in 1563. He still believes in the Devil and in magic, but he rejects the possibility of witchcraft and compacts with the Devil. He boldly accuses monks and clergymen of being, under the pretext of serving religion, most zealous servants of Beelzebub. William, Duke of Cleves, Frederic, Count of Palatine, and the Count of Niurwenar followed Weier's advice and suppressed all witch-prosecution.

Twenty years after Weier another heroic man, a Protestant, named Meyfart, rector of the Latin school of Coburg, raised his voice of warning. His booklet was a sermon of "Admonitions to the powerful princes and the conscientious preachers," by which words he meant the Dominican fathers who were the official witch-prosecutors. He reminded them of the day of judgment, when they would be held to account for every torture and tear of their victims.

---

* Schlager, *Wiener Skizzen aus dem Mittelalter*, II, n. F., p. 35; mentioned by Roskoff, II, p. 294; König and others.

† *Hexenprocesse*, p. 255.

‡ Quoted in *Neue Zusätze* of the German translation of Weier's *De præstigiis dæmonum*

Weier and Meyfart made a deep impression. But a reaction followed. How little, after all, Weier succeeded in conquering the belief in witchcraft, which he had temporarily shaken, can be learned from the fact that in the Protestant Electorate of Saxony a criminal ordinance was issued in the year 1572, which threatened all people making a compact with the Devil "to be brought from life to death on the fagot."

Cornelius Loos, a canonicus and professor at the University of Treves and a devout Catholic Christian, was unfortunate enough to be more clear-headed than his bishop, Peter Binsfeld. Recognising the baseness of judges in the cases of witchcraft, he wrote a book *De vera et falsa magia*. The book was never published; it was stopped in the press and its author sent to prison. In 1593 Loos was forced to recant on his knees before the assembled dignitaries of the Church. He died in 1595 of the plague, which probably saved him from an execution at the stake. Loos's manuscript was supposed to be lost but was recently discovered by Prof. George Lincoln Burr of Cornell University.*

Three Noble Jesuits

ADAM TANNER† (1572–1632) AND PAUL Laymann (1575–1635), two Jesuits of South Germany, strongly advised the judges to be very careful in lawsuits against witches. When death overtook Tanner on a journey, in a little place called Unken, the parishioners refused to grant him a Christian burial, because a "hairy little imp" on a glass plate was found among his things. It was an insect prepared for the microscope.‡ The curate of Unken, however, succeeded in convincing his congregation of the harmless nature of the "imp," and they at last consented to the interment in their cemetery.

Most touching is the narrative of another Jesuit, a noble-minded man, who takes a prominent place among the strugglers against the dreary superstition of burning witches. This man is Friedrich Spee von Langenfeld (1591–1635), a poet and the author of a collection of songs called *Trutznachtigall* (spite-nightingale), whose warnings remained unheeded, "as a voice crying in the wilderness." His *Cautio criminalis*

---

* See *The New York Evening Post*, November 13, 1886.
† Sometimes spelled "Thanner." See König, *ib.*, II, p. 572, and Roskoff, II, p. 308.
‡ König says it was a mosquito, and Roskoff a flea.

(published anonymously* in 1631) was an appeal, much needed at the time, to the German authorities anent their legal proceedings against witches.

Spee was engaged in Franconia as pastor, and had prepared for their death at the stake not fewer than two hundred persons accused of witchcraft. Scarcely thirty years of age, he was asked one day by Philip of Schoenborn, Bishop of Würzburg, why his hair had turned gray. "Through grief," he said. "Of the many witches whom I have prepared for death, not one was guilty." The reply must have burnt into the soul of the questioner, for ever after Philip of Schoenborn remained under its influence. Spee confessed to the Bishop that he was the author of the *Cautio criminalis*, and the Bishop did not betray the confidence of the young Jesuit.

Says Spee in his *Cautio criminalis:*

"In these proceedings no one is allowed to have legal assistance or defence, however honestly it may be conducted. For it is claimed that the crime is a *crimen exceptum*, one not subject to the rules of ordinary legal proceedings. And even if an attorney were allowed to the prisoner, the former would from the outset be suspected himself, as a patron and protector of witches, so that all mouths are shut and all pens are blunted, and one can neither speak nor write. . . I swear solemnly that of the many persons whom I accompanied to the stake, there was not one who could be said to have been duly convicted; and two other pastors made me the same confession from their experience. Treat the heads of the Church, the judges, myself, in the same way as those unfortunate ones, make us undergo the same tortures, and you will convict us all as wizards."

Spee did not deny the possibility of witchcraft; he was a faithful believer in the dogmas held by the Church of his age. He merely objected to the abuses of witchcraft and recommended clemency.

Philip of Schoenborn became Archbishop of Mayence and to his honor be it said that under his government no fagots were lit.

---

* That Spee von Langenfeld was the author of the *Cautio criminalis* was discovered by Leibnitz.

Horst (in his *Zauberbibliothek*, VI, 310) publishes a strange instance of the fanaticism of the seventeenth century which appeared anonymously under the title *Druten-Zeitung*, in 1627, praising in poor verses the great deeds of the Inquisition. According to Horst's authority, they are written by a Protestant who expresses his joy and gratitude to God that in the adjoining Catholic countries the extirpation of witchcraft was carried on with unabating vigor. Thus it is apparent that in spite of Weier and Spee the idea of witchcraft and of the necessity of witch-prosecution was still deeply rooted in the minds of many people. Still, the authorities began to lose faith in the necessity of witch-prosecution, and the champions of the lost cause deem it wiser to seek the shelter of anonymous publication.

In Holland witch-prosecution was abolished in 1610; in Geneva, Switzerland, it ceased in 1632.

Christina, Queen of Sweden, as the first act after her accession to the throne, issued a proclamation on February 16, 1649, which applied also to all the Swedish possessions on German soil, to stop all proceedings of witch-prosecution. Gabriel Naudé, a Frenchman (he died 1680) wrote against witch-prosecution, and, although the Parliament of France which convened at Rouen insisted on the existence of witchcraft and on the necessity of the capital punishment of witches, Louis XIV. decreed in 1672 that all cases of witchcraft be dismissed. He was obliged to re-introduce the law of capital punishment of witches in 1683, but did not fail to limit the power of the judges.

Matthias Hopkins, commonly called "witchfinder general," took advantage of the disorders of the English civil wars of the seventeenth century and made a special business of the discovery of witches. He was quite successful, until his own methods were tried on his own person, and as he did not sink in the water ordeal, the people declared him to be a wizard and slew him (1647).* Butler describes Hopkins's career in Hudibras as follows:

> *"Hath not this present Parliament*
> *A lieger to the devil sent,*
> *Fully empower'd to treat about*

---

* For details see *Letters on Demonology and Witchcraft*, by Walter Scott.

Finding revolted witches out?
And has he not within a year
Hang'd threescore of them in one shire?
Some only for not being drown'd,
And some for sitting above ground
Whole days and nights upon their breeches,
And feeling pain, were hang'd for witches.
And some for putting knavish tricks
Upon green geese or turkey chicks;
Or pigs that suddenly deceased
Of griefs unnatural, as he guess'd,
Who proved himself at length a witch
And made a rod for his own breech."

Witch-prosecution was finally abolished in England in the year 1682. Glanville, a fanatic Englishman of Somerset, felt himself called upon to refute the writings of Gabriel Naudé and found many followers, but Dr. Webster, a physician, stood up against Glanville's superstitious propositions. Glanville thereupon proceeded to hunt witches, but the English government ordered Mr. Hunt, a justice of the peace of Somerset, to stop him.

At the end of the seventeenth century the polemics against the belief in the Devil began to grow bolder and ever bolder. A Dutch physician, Anton van Dale, no longer attributes the pagan oracles to the influence of the Devil, but to priestly fraud (*De oraculis Ethnicorum*, Amsterdam, 1685), and set the people to thinking on witch-prosecution (see his work *Dissertationes de origine ac progressu Idolatriæ*, etc., 1696). He thus prepared the way for the two great reformers Bekker and Thomasius, who openly and squarely denounced witchcraft as a superstition and at last succeeded in abolishing the official prosecutions of witches by the authorities of State and Church.

Balthasar Bekker, a Dutch clergyman of German descent, published in 1691–1693 a work entitled "The Enchanted World" (*De betoverde Weereld*), which was a thorough and careful examination of the belief in devils, witches, and the legal suits conducted against witches. Bekker is a faithful Christian who undertakes to prove that the existence of a personal Devil is a superfluous assumption. His book is a formidable attack upon the Inquisition and its habits of ensnaring its innocent victims. And the success of the book was as great as it was deserved.

Within two months four thousand copies were sold. And yet did Bekker fail to convince his contemporaries. A flood of refutations appeared, and the synod to whom he presented his work, a Protestant body, condemned his views and discharged him from the ministry.

The seeds sown by Bekker were reaped by Christian Thomasius (1656–1718), professor at the University of Halle, who waged a relentless war against witch-prosecution. In the year 1698 a case of witchcraft was submitted to him and against the advice of one of his colleagues he condemned a poor woman to death. However, when the judgment had been executed, the arguments of his opponent gained on him until he became convinced of his own error; and now he deemed it his duty to devote the whole influence of his authority to the abolition of witch-prosecution. He came out boldly and squarely in condemnation of the practice and denied the bodily corporeality of the Devil, which served him as an argument to disprove the possibility of making a compact with him. His main writings are *Dissertatio de crimine magiæ* and *De origine et progressu processus inquisitorii contra sagas*.

Thomasius was more successful than his predecessors. All official witch-prosecutions ceased, and the Devil was no longer an object of universal awe.

The Last Traces

THE INQUISITION WAS STILL IN existence during the first quarter of the nineteenth century in Spain, a country distinguished by its ultra-Roman conception of Christianity. When in 1808, after the battle of Ramosiera, the French troops under General La Salle conquered Toledo, they opened the dungeons of the Inquisition. The cells were dark and unclean holes, scarcely large enough to allow a man to stand upright, and most of the prisoners that were brought up to daylight had become stiff and crippled by the maltreatment of their torturers. Unhappily they and their liberators, a detached troop of lancers, were cut off by a furious mob of Spaniards from the main body of the French army. General La Salle hurried to their rescue but came too late; he found only the mangled bodies of the slaughtered.

In a subterranean vault General La Salle found a wooden statue of the holy virgin dressed in silk, her head surrounded with a golden halo, her right hand holding the standard of the Inquisition. She was fair to look at, but her breast was covered with spiked armor; and her arms and hands were movable by machinery concealed behind the statue. The servants of the Inquisition explained to General La Salle that it was used for bringing heretics to confession. The delinquent received the sacrament at the altar in the presence of the dimly illumined statue, and was once more requested to confess. Then two priests led him to the statue of the *Madre dolorosa* which miraculously seemed to welcome him by extending her arms. "She beckons you to her bosom," they said; "in her arms the most obdurate sinner will confess," whereupon the arms closed, pressing their victim upon the spikes and knives.

Napoleon I. suppressed the Inquisition (in Spain December 4, 1808, and in Rome one year later), but it was revived by Ferdinand VII, King of Spain, June 21, 1813. Its last victims were a Jew who was burned, and a Quaker school-master who was hanged in 1826.

Descriptions of Hell

THE JESUIT FATHER, CAUSSIN, THE father confessor of King Louis XIII. writes on hell in his book, *La Cour Sainte*,—a work which attained considerable fame in his days, as follows:

> "What is hell? A silence; for all that which is said of hell is less than hell itself. No just man can think of it without shedding thousands of tears. But do you want to know what hell is? Ask Tertullian. He will tell you that hell is a deep, dark pit of stench in which all the offal of the whole world flows together. Ask Hugo of St. Victor. He will answer: 'Hell is an abyss without a bottom, which opens the gates of despair, and where all hope is abandoned.' 'It is an eternal pool of fire,' says St. John the divine (Rev. xiv. 20); 'its air comes from glowing coals, its light from flickering flames. The nights of hell are darkness; the places of rest of the damned are serpents and vipers; their hope is despair. O, eternal death! O, life without life! O, misery without end!'"

Justus Georg Schottel,* whilom member of the Consistory of Brunswick-Lüneburg, and councillor to the duke, doctor of jurisprudence, and a learned man who was not without merit in German poetry and literature, took special interest in the mysteries of

---

* This as well as the quotations following are taken from J. Scheible, Vol. I, pp. 196 ff.

the infernal regions, and published his views in a book of 328 pages, in which he explained the tortures of the iron wheel of eternal hell torture:

"Dear reader," he says, "look at this wheel all round and read carefully what is written on it. How much time and suffering, how much anxiety and torture of despair, must be gone through in hell, must be endured, borne, experienced and realised, by hundreds, by thousands, by hundreds of thousands, by millions of years in burning pitch, in flaming sulphur, in red hot iron, in poignant blow-pipe flames, with weeping and wailing and gnashing of teeth infinite; with hunger and thirst miraculous; in stench and darkness cruelly; before this wheel be turned around only once. But now this wheel of eternity is made of purely everlasting iron, and must turn round many hundred, yea million, and millions of millions of times, and can never wax old, never perish, never be worn out, and can never stand still in all eternity. Whereas you can conclude and find out by reflexion this all-discomforting, all-terrible, and all-cruelest infinity of hell-torture. One might grow mad and insane when considering this fiery eternity and these iron eternal years, etc., etc."

Dr. Schottel's Wheel of Life is of special interest as it reminds one of the Buddhist Wheel of Life which the Evil Spirit holds in his clutches.[*]

Similar ideas as to the awfulness of the sufferings in hell are offered in the sermons of Abraham a Sancta-Clara who was the most influential preacher in Vienna in the beginning of the eighteenth century.

The eighteenth century is the age of an intellectual dawn, but while the rays of light begin to spread the shadows of the night linger and their darkness seems rather more intense than before.

The Rev. Father Gilbert Baur, writes in the year 1785 as follows:

"You know what happens when meat is salted. The salt enters all parts, every nerve and every bone, and communicates to all parts its acrid qualities; and yet the meat is not dissolved nor annihilated by the salt, but on the contrary preserved from decay. In the same way the hellish fire will enter into the innermost marrow, and be distributed throughout the entrails. It will take

---

[*] Compare the illustrations on pp. 119, 121, and 123.

hold of all the arteries and nerves and make the brain boil with furious pains, without causing death or annihilation."

Some theological geographers have placed hell in the sun, others in the moon, still others in the center of the earth. But the question as to which of the three opinions is right has not yet been decided.

A Slavonian folk song sings of hell as follows:*

"Look at the terrible maw! How fiery and deep is the place of torture! No eye can discover its bottom.

"A spark alone causes immense pain, but against the fury of this fire it is but a dewdrop.

"Reason cannot comprehend and tongue cannot utter what it may be to be in the fires of Hell.

"Devils transform themselves into dogs, into wild animals, into snakes and dragons; they howl, and they bellow, and they bawl; what terrors they cause!

"Every poor sinner must pay tribute here to the justice of God; and for every vicious deed he must suffer special pain."

After an enumeration of the sufferings for various sins and vices, the poem continues:

"Can there be worse misery? Indeed, there is not; for from this place of darkness the eye of the damned will never see the face of God.

"'Woe, woe!' thus they howl; 'Whither have we gone, we miserable creatures? Oh! that men would believe us; they would never fall into sin.'

"'Death, where art thou? O, thunder-bolts, slay us! O, God, we want to die, for we cannot endure these pains!'

"Alas! In vain you wish for death, ye souls lost in eternity. You are damned to live, eternally dying.

"Even a toothache you could not endure forever. How much more terrible must be the fire everlasting!

"Consider then, O sinner, the misery that awaits you. Who knows whether you may not reach your destiny tomorrow?

---

* Quoted in a German translation by Scheible, Vol. I, p. 208 ff.

"Tonight you go to bed in your sin, and tomorrow you may wake up burning in the fires of Hell."

These descriptions of hell are, in all their essential features, still current in "darkest Europe" and also in "darkest America." The picture of hell, here reproduced, surpasses in drastic beauty and grandeur of stage-effect the paintings of the famous Hell Breughel. It possesses the additional interest of being still in the market, being even now advertised and sold among other religious pictures.

No wonder that there are good Christians who would gladly change places with brute animals. A young Jesuit who afterwards turned Prostestant said in his memoirs that he used to envy the watch dog in the courtyard to whom death meant annihilation without the terrors of hell.

There is a good deal of moral courage in the comfort which, as the story goes, an old infidel farmer gave to his dying son, saying: "We do not go to church, and the parson hates us; now, when you die you will go to hell; but don't shame our family by howling and gnashing of teeth. What others can stand we can stand too." Must not the Lord have been better pleased with infidel grit than with the submissiveness of the slavish believer?

Schwenter and Kircher

THE JESUIT ORDER CARRIES THE principle of Romanism and obedience to church-authorities to extremes. It was founded for the purpose of creating and sustaining a counter-reformation to Protestantism, and to Protestants therefore it is the most objectionable Roman Catholic order. But whatever may be said against the Jesuits, their methods and narrow principles, we must acknowledge that some of their members have been very prominent and scholarly men; and Athanasius Kircher is one of the greatest scientists they have produced. Born at Geisa, near Fulda, Germany, in 1601, he was professor of philosophy and mathematics at the University of Würzburg, which he left during the Thirty Years' War, for Avignon, in France. He journeyed with Cardinal Frederick of Saxony to Malta, and ended his life as professor of mathematics and Hebrew at Rome. His investigations have no direct, but only an indirect, bearing on witchcraft-prosecutions. He made some curious experiments with hens and pigeons, which remained a problem to psychologists, and are still repeated by them today. He placed a hen on the floor, and made a stroke of chalk along its bill, whereupon the hen lay quiet as if paralysed, remaining in this awkward position until she was released by some motion of the hands of the experimenter.

We ought to add here that although Kircher is generally credited with the invention of this experiment because it became known mainly through him,[*] Professor Preyer has proved that he simply reproduced the experiment made by Daniel Schwenter,[†] who published his discovery ten years before the appearance of Kircher's *Ars Magna Lucis et Umbræ.*

The attitude of the hen, which Kircher ascribes to her imagination, was later, in the eighteenth century, called a phenomenon of magnetism or mesmerism, and in the nineteenth century, hypnotism. Whatever scientific value this isolated fact may possess, its discovery marked the beginning of a scientific treatment of psychical phenomena which naturally tended to a better comprehension of the abnormal conditions of the human mind, and thus could not but exercise a wholesome influence.

Diabolism Developing Into Pathology

IN THE MIDDLE OF THE eighteenth century Pater John Joseph Gassner, vicar of Klösterle in Chur, a Roman Catholic clergyman, acted on the theory that the majority of diseases arose from demoniacal possession and he cured himself and his parishioners by exorcism. The success of his cures made a great stir in the world and threatened a dangerous reaction. Some declared he was a charlatan, while others believed in him.

Mesmer, at the request of the Elector of Bavaria, made investigations and said that he explained his miracles as spiritualistic magnetic influences, while Lavater maintained that the curative element consisted solely in the glorious name of Jesus. Gassner lived some time in Constance, afterwards in Ratisbon, partly protected, partly distrusted by his ecclesiastical superiors. In 1775 he went to Amberg, then to Sulzbach, where the halo of his miraculous cures waned. The

---

[*] See the chapter "A Marvellous Experiment with the Imagination of a Hen (*Experimentum Mirabile de Imaginatione Gallinæ*), in Kircher's *Ars Magna Lucis et Umbræ*, Rome, 1646.

[†] See Daniel Schwenter, *Deliciæ Physico-Mathematicæ*, etc. Nürnberg, 1636.

Prince-Bishop of Ratisbon declared in his favor, but Emperor Joseph II. forbade his exorcisms in the whole Roman empire. The Archbishops of Prague and Salzburg rejected him, and even Pope Pius VI. disapproved of him.

Gassner's exorcisms renewed the interest taken in the problem of the existence of the Devil. The question was discussed in several publications, among which we mention "a humble petition for information to the great men who do no longer believe in a Devil," written anonymously from the orthodox standpoint by Professor Köster, of Giessen, editor of a religious periodical. It was answered in another pamphlet: "Humble reply of a country-clergyman," whose author claims that the biblical Satan is an allegory, idols are called "nothings" in Hebrew, and the Devil is one of these nothings. He offers rationalistic explanations of the Bible, representing, for instance, the tempter of Christ as "a sly messenger and spy of the synagogue," and declaring the theory of a Devil to be idolatry disguised in orthodoxy, and a sublimated Manicheeism. The author concludes: "I had rather that the people fear God than the Devil. The fear of God is the beginning of wisdom, but the fear of the Devil, whatever be its results, is no Christian adornment."

The number of anti-diabolists increased rapidly, even among the clergy; yet the belief in a personal Devil remained the orthodox view, and if we are not mistaken it is still regarded as an essential dogma of the Christian faith by many theologians, especially among those who display a contempt for worldly culture and secular science.

The worst superstitions had grown harmless, but the hankering after miracles had not yet ceased. Diabolism had lost its hold on mankind, but mysticism reappeared in new forms; and the contrasts that prevailed in the eighteenth century cannot be better characterised than by the visions of Swedenborg as against the refutation of the dreams of visionaries by Kant.

The belief in mysticism begets frauds; and the boldest, wiliest, and most successful imposter of the eighteenth century was Giuseppe Balsamo of Sicily, who travelled under the assumed name of Count Cagliostro, finding easy victims among the credulous of all descriptions, especially the Free Masons. His tricks, however, were exposed by Countess Elizabeth von der Recke, and being thereafter exiled from every country which he entered, he fell at last into the hands of the Inquisition, as whose prisoner he died in the year 1795.

Demonology of the Nineteenth Century

THE FREE-THOUGHT MOVEMENT OF THE eighteenth century and a better scientific conception of nature relieved mankind of the unnecessary fear of the Devil, and the nineteenth century could begin to study the question impartially in its historical and philosophical foundations.

Kant found the principle of evil in the reversal of the moral world-order. "The Scriptures lay down," he says, "man's moral relation in the form of a history, representing the opposite principles in man as eternal facts, as heaven and hell. The significance of this popular conception, dropping all mysticism, is that there is but one salvation for man, which lies in his embracing in his heart the moral maxims."

Following the example of Kant, theologians began to give a rational explanation of the Devil. Daub, a disciple of Schelling, attempted to construct a philosophical devil, in his book *Judas Iscariot, or Evil in its Relation to Goodness*, defining Satan, the Antichrist and enemy of God, as the hatred of all that is good.

Schenkel regards the Evil One as a manifestation that appears in the totality of things, and characterises him as that which is collectively bad. "Satan, accordingly, is a 'juridical person,'" and this explains his extraordinary and superindividual power; but he has not as yet succeeded in becoming a single, concrete personality, and let us hope that he probably never will. Hase does not deny the possibility of an influence of spiritual powers, good as well as evil, upon man, "but," says he, "the Devil appears only when he is believed to exist; and the effects of his influence being explicable only in the light of man's nature, the reality of such beings remains problematic."

Reinhard, although inclined to supernaturalism, doubts whether the Scriptural Devil is to be taken seriously; and De Wette speaks of the Devil as a popular conception (*Volksvorstellung*). Schleiermacher in his famous work *The Christian Faith According to the Doctrines of the Evangelical Church* (1821; fourth edition, 1842) declares the idea of the Devil, as historically developed, to be "untenable" and "unessential to a Christian's belief in God."

Martensen believes in the Devil not as an idea, but as an "historical person." He is in the beginning only the principle of temptation; as such he is a cosmical principle. He is not yet bad, but the potentiality of badness. He does not really become the Devil until man has allowed him to enter his consciousness. Man, accordingly, gives existence to the Devil. Lücke opposes Martensen: "The Devil as a symbol is absolutely bad, but as a fallen creature he cannot be absolutely bad. We have no other conception of the Devil than as the representative of sin." This is an attempt to reconcile the theological conception with the philosophy of his time.

David Friedrich Strauss did not consider it necessary to refute the doctrine of Satan's personality, which he regarded as utterly overthrown. Modern mysticism, on the other hand, shows an inclination to emphasise the importance of the traditional Satanology.

Dogmatic theologians in the ranks of English and American Protestants endeavor to preserve the traditional views of hell and the Devil, without, however, making much practical use of these doctrines. They no longer discuss the problem at length but still uphold the belief in the personality of the Evil One. For instance, Professor Schaff scarcely enters into a detailed exposition of the subject, and Dr. William G. T. Shedd, who devotes in his great work *Dogmatic Theology* one or several chapters to every Christian dogma, omits a particular discussion of Satan. Passages in the chapter on hell nevertheless prove that he believes in both a personal Satan and an eternal personal punishment on the ground of scriptural evidence.

The liberal theology of today urges that Jesus makes thirst for justice, love of God and man, the conditions for entering into the Kingdom of God. A belief in the Devil, it is claimed, is nowhere demanded and can, to say the least, not be regarded as essential; it is not so much Christian and Jewish, as pagan; it is a survival of polytheistic nature-worship and of pagan dualism, quite natural at a time when the sciences were still in their infancy, characterised by astrology and alchemy, and when the irrefragability of nature's laws was not as yet understood. The belief in a personal Devil, accordingly, and all the practices resulting therefrom, were rather due to ignorance than to religion.

There are still plenty of believers in a personal Devil among those who call themselves orthodox, but their influence has ceased to be of any consequence. Vilmar regards the belief in an individual devilish personality as an indispensable qualification of a real theologian, saying: "In order rightly to teach and take charge of souls, one must have seen the Devil gnashing his teeth, and I mean it bodily, not figuratively; he must have felt his power over poor souls, his blasphemy, especially his sneer." Similarly, another German theologian, Superintendent Sanders, shows great zeal in defence of the Biblical Devil in his pamphlet *The Doctrine of the Scriptures Concerning the Devil* (1858), and Dr. Sartorius, following Hengstenberg's orthodoxy, says that, "he who denies Satan cannot truly confess Christ." Twesten, however, although accepting the belief in a personal Devil, concedes that the necessity of his existence cannot be deduced from the contents of our religious consciousness. Fr. Reiff (in *Zeitfragen des christlichen Volkslebens*, VI, 1, 1880) declares that there is a Kingdom of Evil as much as there is a Kingdom of God. The belief in a personal Prince of Darkness is the counterpart of a personal God. And Erhard wrote an apology of the Devil, not so much for the sake of the Devil as for the traditional idea that evil and sin are actualities.

Present Conditions

THE ROMAN CATHOLIC CHURCH OF today still holds in theory the same views as in the Middle Ages; but the secular authorities will never again allow themselves to be influenced in their legal proceedings by the opinions of inquisitors.

Görres,* one of the ablest and most modern defenders of the Roman Church, complains about "the purely medical view" of historians who regard witch-prosecution as a mere epidemic. He finds the ultimate cause of witchcraft and sorcery in apostasy from the Church, which had become fashionable in those days. Dr. Haas, another Roman Catholic, takes the same view in his inquiry into witch-prosecution.† He concedes that witchcraft is a revival of pagan notions mixed with a false conception of Christianity (p. 68), but he still shares with the inquisitors of yore and with Pope Innocent III the belief in the actuality of witchcraft. Like Görres, Haas regards "witchcraft as the product of heresy," and calls the former "a cousin" and "a daughter" of the latter. Both to him result from "unbelief, unclearness, pride, eccentricity." Both are manias or illusions (*Wahngeschöpfe*); "they maltreat and are maltreated, and thus they increase until they are opposed with reason and vigor." The only trouble was that the remedy of inquisitorial "reason and vigor" was worse than the disease. Haas continues: "For the minds of many were not yet free from error (i.e., heresy), and when the house

---

* *Die Hexenprocesse, ein culturhistorischer Versuch.* Tübingen. 1865.
† Quoted from Roskoff, p. 239. from *Christliche Mystik*, III, 66.

was swept and cleaned worse spirits entered, and matters were worse than ever."

The Inquisition, the natural result of a belief in the Devil, is now powerless; "still," says the Rev. G. W. Kitchin, in the *Encyclopedia Britannica:*

"Its voice is sometimes heard; in 1856 Pius IX issued an encyclical against somnambulism and clairvoyance, calling on all bishops to inquire into and suppress the scandal, and in 1865 he uttered an anathema against freemasons, the secular foes of the Inquisition."

The Rev. Mr. Kitchin sums up the present state of things as follows:

"The occupation of Rome in 1870 drove the papacy and the Inquisition into the Vatican, and there at last John Bunyan's vision seems to have found fulfilment. Yet, though powerless, the institution is not hopeless; the Catholic writers on the subject, after long silence or uneasy apology, now acknowledge the facts and seek to justify them. In the early times of the 'Holy Office' its friends gave it high honor; Paramo, the inquisitor, declares that it began with Adam and Eve ere they left Paradise; Paul IV announced that the Spanish Inquisition was founded by the inspiration of the Holy Spirit; Muzarelli calls it 'an indispensable substitute to the Church for the original gift of miracles exercised by the apostles.' And now again, from 1875 to this day, a crowd of defenders has risen up: Father Wieser and the Insbruck Jesuits in their journal (1877) yearn for its re-establishment; Orti y Lara in Spain, the Benedictine Gams in Germany, and C. Poullet in Belgium take the same tone; it is a remarkable phenomenon, due partly to despair at the progress of society, partly to the fanaticism of the late pope, Pius IX. It is hardly credible that any one can really hope and expect to see in the future the irresponsible judgments of clerical intolerance again humbly carried out, even to the death, by the secular arm."

Roman Catholic authors are, as a rule, too worldly wise to precipitate or provoke a discussion of the history of either the Inquisition or the doctrine of the Devil, hut whenever they cannot avoid a discussion of the subject they claim that the Inquisition was a secular institution (so Gams of Ratisbon and Bishop Hefele), or defend the measures taken by the Inquisition. They have not as yet acquired sufficient insight, or, if they have the insight, they do not possess the moral courage to condemn the whole institution, and with it the policy of the Popes Innocent III, Gregory IX, Urban IV, John XXII, and others whose names are compromised in matters of witch-prosecution.

Devil-exorcism is not yet extinct in Roman Catholic countries. The exorcism performed in Germany by Father Aurelian on Michael Zilk, the son of a Catholic Father and Protestant mother, with the especial permission of the Bishop Leopold von Eichstadt, is a sufficient evidence of the Egyptian darkness that still penetrates the minds of a great mass of our Christian brethren, among them members of the higher clergy.[*]

Mr. E. P. Evans, who quotes the curious occurrence,[†] furnishes another interesting fact. He says:

"Pope Leo XIII is justly regarded as a man of more than ordinary intelligence and more thoroughly imbued with the modern spirit than any of his predecessors, yet he composed and issued, November 19, 1890, a formula of an '*Exorcismus in Satanam et Angelos Apostatas.*' His Holiness never fails to repeat this exorcism in his daily prayers, and commends it to the bishops and other clergy as a potent means of warding off the attacks of Satan and casting out devils."

The holy coat of Treves is still exercising its power over the minds of many credulous people and works miracles that are seriously believed, while the dancing-procession of Echternach is not only not abolished but encouraged by the Church. Pope Leo XIII has granted a six years' absolution to all those who take part in the performance. There are on an average about ten thousand persons who annually join in this stupid survival of the Middle Ages.

THE PERSONAL DEVIL IS DEAD in science, but he is still alive even in Protestant countries among the uneducated, and the number of those

---

[*] *Die Teufelsaustreibung in Werndive.* Nach den Berichten des P. Aurelian für das Volk critisch beleuchtet von Richard Treufels. Munich, Schuh & Co. 1892. This curious treatise can no longer be obtained in the book-market.

[†] *Popular Science Monthly*, December, 1892, p. 161.

who belong to this category is legion. The Salvation Army is still in our midst singing:

> "Come join our army, the foe must be driven;
> To Jesus, our captain, the world shall be given.
> If hell should surround us we'll press through the throng.
> The Salvation Army is marching along."

The following vigorous verse reminds one of Parseeism:

> "Christian, rouse thee, war is raging.
> God and fiends are battle waging,
> Every ransomed power engaging,
> Break the Tempter's spell.
> Dare ye still lie fondly dreaming,
> Wrapt in ease and worldly scheming,
> While the multitudes are streaming
> Downwards into hell?"

A good illustration of their personal attitude towards the Evil One appears in these lines:

> "The Devil and me, we can't agree,
> I hate him and he hates me.
> He had me once, but he let me go,
> He wants me again, but I will not go."

The Devil of the Salvation Army proves that there is still a need of representing spiritual ideas in drastic allegories; but though Satan is still painted in glaring colors, he has become harmless and will inaugurate no more witch-prosecutions. He is curbed and caged, so that he can do no more mischief. We smile at him as we do at a tiger behind the bars in a zoological garden.

The Religious Import of Science

THE INQUISITORS AND WITCH-PROSECUTORS WERE by no means scoundrels pure and simple. Most assuredly there were scoundrels among them; but there is no doubt that the movement of the Inquisition and witch-prosecution took its origin from purer motives. It was to the popes and grand inquisitors and to many princes and other people who promoted the policy, a matter of conscience; they simply attended to it as a religious duty, sometimes even with a heavy heart and not without great pain.

Torquemada, the grand inquisitor of Spain, was in his private life one of the purest and most conscientious of men, and he was so tender-hearted that he was obliged to leave the inquisitorial tribunal and quit the room as soon as the torture of a heretic began. He would cry about the obstinacy of those who had given themselves over to Satan; but though his heart was bleeding, he condemned thousands and thousands to the cruelest tortures and the most dreadful death for the sake of salvation and the glory of God—of that monster-god in whom he believed, that abominable idol which was worse than the Moloch of ancient Phœnicia.

When complaints reached Pope Innocent III about the cruelty of Conrad of Marburg, the first Inquisitor General of Germany, he said, "the Germans were always furious and therefore needed furious judges." Pope Leo X, referring to cases of witchcraft that happened in Brixen and Bergamo, grieves in a brief of 1521 at "the obstinacy of the culprits, who would rather die than confess their crimes." In the same document the Holy Father complains about the impiety of the Venetian Senate who prevented the inquisitors from performing their duties. And similar expressions are not infrequent in later papal bulls and briefs, all of which prove that the horrors of the Inquisition are ultimately due, not to ill will or even to the desire for power, but to error which had assumed the shape of a deep-seated religious conviction.

Among the Protestants, the Calvinists come nearest in zeal to the Roman Catholic inquisitors. In Geneva, Switzerland, the home of Calvin, five hundred persons were, within three months, executed for heresy and witchcraft. The protocols of the city in the year 1545 declare that the labor of torture and execution exceeded the strength of the hangman; and the complaint is made that, "whatever torture be applied, the malefactors still refuse to confess."

The facts of witch-prosecution with its kindred superstitions are an object lesson. How mistaken are those who believe that religion has nothing to do with ethics, and that a religious conviction exercises no influence upon a man's conduct! There are ethicists, professors of ethics, and ethical preachers, who imagine that ethics may be taught without teaching religion, and that the morality of the people can be improved without an interference with their convictions as to the nature of the world and the import of life. But a wrong world-conception will beget a wrong morality; a false religion will unfailingly produce bad and injurious ethics; and the grossest errors will, if they have their way, find expression in the grossest abominations of misguided conduct. A radical cure on the other hand must go to the root of the evil. It is not sufficient to remove the symptoms of the disease, you must replace false religion by true religion.

It would not do to say with our agnostic friends that religion is concerned with matters unknowable; and that therefore we must leave it alone! Religion is the most important problem of life, and we can ignore it as little as a reckless storage of dynamite in crowded parts of great cities. We must investigate the religious problem and replace the old errors with their dualistic superstitions by sound and scientifically correct views. At the bottom of all the terrors of the Inquisition and witch-prosecution lies a serious endeavor to do what is right; and this power can be utilised as well for the progress and elevation of mankind as for the suppression of reason and sound judgment.

Religion is the strongest motive power in the world; nothing therefore is more injurious than false religious convictions, and nothing more desirable than truth.

Let us make the love of truth our religion. Beware of mysticism and endeavor to be clear and exact. There is as little truth in mysticism as there is light in fog. Nor should we rely on tradition, for tradition is uncertain, but the truth (i.e., generalised statements of facts or laws of nature) can be made unequivocally certain and will remain verifiable to every competent inquirer. It is man's duty, in all departments of life, to seek the truth with the best and most scientific methods at his disposal, and the adherence to this principle is "the Religion of Science."

It is a fact that the confidence in science has already become a religious conviction with most of us. The faith in scientifically provable truth has slowly, very slowly, and by almost imperceptible degrees, but steadily and surely, taken root in the hearts of men. Today it is the most powerful factor of our civilisation, in spite of various church-dogmas which are declared to be above scientific critique and argument; for these dogmas are becoming a dead letter. There are several conservative and prominent churchmen who publicly confess that the dogmas of the

Church must be regarded as historical documents and not as eternal verities.

Those who doubt the religious import of science need only consider what science has done for mankind by the radical abolition of witch-prosecution, and they will be convinced that science is not religiously indifferent, but that it is the most powerful factor in the purification of the religions of mankind.

The world-conception of our industrial and social life, of international intercourse, and all serious movements on the lines of human progress, has even now to a great extent practically become the Religion of Science, although the fact is not as yet definitely and openly acknowledged; and any sectarian faith that endeavors to set forth its claim of recognition does it and can do it only on the ground that it is one with scientific truth. For there is nothing universally true, nothing catholic, nothing genuinely orthodox, except those truths that are positively demonstrated by science.

In Verse and Fable

The devil in folklore is entitled to our ungrudging admiration for his indefatigable energy. There are innumerable devil-stones thrown at churches, there are devil-walls, devil-bridges, cathedrals, monasteries, castles, dikes, and mills, built by him for the purpose of seducing and gaining souls. He has had his finger in the pie everywhere and appears to be all but omnipresent and omniscient.

In popular literature the Devil plays a most important rôle. While he is still regarded as the incarnation of all physical and moral evil, his main office has become that of a general mischief-worker in the universe; without him there would be no plot, and the story of the world would lose its interest. He appears as the critic of the good Lord, as the representative of discontent with existing conditions, he inspires men with the desire for an increase of wealth, power, and knowledge; he is the mouth-piece of all who are anxious for a change in matters political, social, and ecclesiastical. He is identified with the spirit of progress so inconvenient to those who are satisfied with the existing state of things, and thus he is credited with innovations of all kinds, the aspiration for improvement as well as the desire for the overthrow of law and order. In a word, he is characterised as the patron of both reform and evolution.

Devil-Stories

The literature of devil-stories is very extensive. We select from them a number of the most representative tales.

Several legends indicate an origin by hallucination: For instance, St. Hilarion when hungry, saw a number of exquisite dishes. St. Pelagia, who had been an actress in Antioch, lived the life of a religious recluse in a cave on the Mount of Olives. Once the Devil offered her a number of rings, bracelets, and precious stones, which disappeared as quickly as they came. Rufinus of Aquileja relates the story of a monk, a man of great abstinence, living in a desert. One evening a beautiful woman appeared at his hermitage asking for a night's shelter. She conducts herself with modesty at first, but soon begins to smile, to stroke his beard, and to caress him. The monk grows excited and embraces her fervently, when, lo! the whole apparition vanishes, leaving him lonely in his cell. He hears the laughter of devils in the air, and, despairing of salvation, he goes back into the world and falls an easy prey to the temptations of Satan.

While Christianity was still under the influence of orientalised Gnosticism, the Church believed in the perversity of bodily existence, and therefore clung to the notion that all nature was the work of the Devil. Thus the monk retired from the world, but he took with him into his solitude the memory-pictures of his life. Memory-pictures are part of our soul, and a man who suddenly cuts off all new impressions so that his present life becomes a blank, will have hallucinations as naturally as a man who falls asleep will have dreams. The darkness of the present throws into strong relief the most vivid recollections of the past; the emptiness of a solitary mode of existence causes the slumbering memory-images to appear almost in bodily reality.

A very interesting letter of St. Jerome to the virgin Eustochia, which exemplifies the truth of this explanation, is still extant. St. Jerome writes:

"Alas! how often, when living in the desert, in that dreary, sunburnt loneliness, which serves as an habitation to the monks, did I believe myself revelling in the pleasures of Rome. I sat lonely, my soul filled with affliction, clothed in wretched rags, my skin sunburnt like an Ethiopian's. No day passed without tears and sighs, and when sleep overcame me I had to lie on the naked ground. I do not mention eating and drinking, for the monks drink, even if sick, only water, and regard cooking as a luxury. And if I, who had condemned myself from fear of hell to such a life, without any other society than scorpions and wild beasts, often imagined myself surrounded by dancing girls, my face was pale from fasting, but in the cold body the soul was burning with desires, and in a man whose flesh was dead the flames of lust were kindled. Then I threw myself helpless at the feet of Jesus, wetted them with tears, dried them again with my hair, and subdued the rebellious flesh by fasts of a whole week. I am not ashamed to confess my misery; I am rather sorry for no longer being such as I was. I remember still how often, when fasting and weeping, the night followed the day, and how I did not cease to beat my breast until at the command of God peace had returned."

The legend of Merlin, as told by Bela in the old chronicles, characterises a whole class of stories.

The defeated Satan proposes to regain his power by the same means by which God has vanquished him. He decides to have a son who shall undo Christ's work of redemption. All the intrigues of hell are used to ruin a noble family until only two daughters are left. The one falls into shame, while the other remains chaste and resists all temptations. One night, however, she forgot to cross herself, and thus the Devil could approach her,—even against her will. The pious girl underwent the severest penance, and when her time came she had a son whose hairy appearance betrayed his diabolical parentage. The child, however, was baptised and received the name Merlin. The excitement in heaven was great. What a triumph would it be to win the Devil's own son over to the cause of Christ. The Devil gave to his son all the knowledge of the past and the present; God added the knowledge of the future, and this proved the best weapon against the evil attempts of his wicked father. When Merlin grew up, he slighted his father and performed many marvellous things. He was full of wisdom, and his prophecies were reliable. It is generally assumed that after his death he did not descend into hell but went to heaven.

Similar is the story of Robert the Devil, the hero of a modern opera. The Duchess of Normandy, the old legend tells us, had no children. Having implored the help of God in vain, she addressed herself to the Devil who satisfied her wish at once. She had a son who was a rogue from babyhood. Being very courageous and strong, he became the chief of a band of robbers. He was knighted, to temper his malignity, but this appeal to his feeling of honor failed to have any effect. In a tournament he slew thirty knights; then he went out into the world to seek adventures. On his return he became a robber again. One day, when he had just strangled all the nuns of a cloister, he remembered that he had a mother and decided to visit her. But when he made his appearance, her servants dispersed in wild fear. For the first time in his life he was impressed with the idea that he had become odious to his fellow-men, and becoming conscious of his evil nature, he wanted to know why he was worse than others. With his sword drawn, he forced his mother to confess the secret of his birth. He was horror-struck, but did not despair. He went to Rome, confessed to a pious hermit, submitted willingly to the severest penance and combated the Saracens who happened to be laying siege to Rome. The emperor offered him his daughter as a reward. And now the two records of Robert's fate become contradictory. Not knowing the truth, we state both impartially. Some say that Robert married the emperor's daughter who was in love with him; others declare that he refused the match and crown, and returned to his hermit confessor, into the wilderness where he died blessed by God and mankind.

Not all the sons of the Devil, however, join the cause of the good Lord. Eggelino, the tyrant of Padua, forces his mother to confess the secret, that he and his brother Alberico were sons of Satan. Eggelino boasts that he will live as befits the son of the Evil One. He succeeds with the assistance of his brother in becoming the tyrant of Padua, commits terrible crimes and dies at last in misery and despair. The story is dramatised by Albertino Mussato in his *Eccerius*.

On the right side of the high altar of the church of St. Denys, near Paris, a bas-relief illustrates the legend of St. Dagobert's death, which proves the soul-saving power of Christian saints. We are told that "a hermit on an island in the Mediterranean was warned in a vision to pray for the Frankish King's soul. He then saw Dagobert in chains, hurried along by a troop of fiends, who were about to cast him into a volcano. At last his cries to St. Denys, St. Michael, and St. Martin, brought to his assistance those three venerable and glorious persons, who drove off the devils, and with songs of triumph conveyed the rescued soul to Abraham's bosom."*

Among the romances which represent the struggle of man with temptation and the powers of evil Spenser's *Faerie Queene* and Bunyan's *Pilgrim's Progress* are well known and need no further comment. The underlying idea, however, is not original with these authors of the sixteenth and seventeenth centuries, but dates back to the fourteenth and thirteenth centuries. A manuscript-copy of *Le Romant des trois Pélerinages* by Guillaume de Guillauille describes the adventures of man in his pilgrimage through life. In a deep valley the pilgrim meets covetousness, which Didron[†] describes as follows:

"The idol worn upon her head is 'the peny of gold or of silver whereon is emprinted the figure of the hye Lord of the countree.' The false God that blindeth him that turneth his eyes towards

---

* *Gesta Dagob.* (cc. 23, 44). Baronius (647. 5). D. Bouquet. *Rec. des histoires de France*, t. ii. p. 593. Didron, *Christian Iconography*, ii. p. 132.

† A manuscript-copy of an old English translation exists in the University Library of Cambridge, England.

him and maketh fools to bend their eyes downwards. This God by whom she hath been disfigured and defamed is Avarice. The hands behind like griffin's claws are to symbolise 'Rapine, Coutteburse, and Latrosynie.'

"In the next pair of hands she holds a bowl for alms, or for the money she extorts through beggary, and a hook, with which she enters the house of Christ and seizes his servants. Taking their croziers and shepherds' crooks, she furnishes them with this devil's prong instead, fished up by her out of the darkness of Hell, and this hand is named Simony. In the next hands she holds a yard-measure, purse, and scales. With the measure she deals out false lengths, with the balances she weighs false measure, and into the purse she puts the ill-won gains of her treachery, gambling, and dishonesty. Round her neck hangs a bag, and nothing that is put therein can ever come out again; all things remain there to rot."

Devil-Contracts

THE DEVIL, FIGHTING WITH GOD for the possession of mankind, was supposed to have a special passion for catching souls. Being the prince of the world he could easily grant even the most extravagant wishes, and was sometimes willing to pay a high price when a man promised to be his for time and eternity. Thus originated the idea of making compacts with the Devil; and it is worthy of note that in these compacts the Devil is very careful to establish his title to the soul of man by a faultless legal document. He has, as we shall learn, sufficient reason to distrust all promises made him by men and saints. Following the authority of the old legends, we find that even the good Lord frequently lends his assistance to cheating the Devil out of his own. He is always duped and the vilest tricks are resorted to to cheat him. While thus the Devil, having profited by experience, always insists upon having his rights insured by an unequivocal instrument (which in later centuries is signed with blood); he, in his turn, is fearlessly trusted to keep his promise, and this is a fact which must be mentioned to his honor, for although he is said to be a liar from the beginning, not one case is known in all devil-lore in which the Devil attempts to cheat his stipulators. Thus he appears as the most unfairly maligned person, and as a martyr of simple-minded honesty.

The oldest story of a devil-contract is the legend of Theophilus, first told by Eutychian, who declares he had witnessed the whole affair with his own eyes.

Theophilus, an officer of the church and a pious man, living in Adana, a town of Cilicia, was unanimously elected by the clergy and by the laymen as their bishop, but he refused the honor from sheer modesty. So another man became bishop in his stead. The new bishop unjustly deprived Theophilus of his office, who now regretted his former humility. But in his humiliation Theophilus went to a famous wizard and made with his assistance a compact with Satan, renouncing Christ and the Holy Virgin. Satan at once causes the bishop to restore Theophilus to his position, but now Theophilus repents and prays to the Holy Virgin for forgiveness. After forty days of fasting and praying he is rebuked for his crime but not comforted; so he fasts and prays thirty days more, and receives at last absolution. Satan, however, refuses to give up his claim on Theophilus, and the Holy Virgin then actually castigates the enemy of God and men so severely that he at last surrenders the fatal document. Now Theophilus relates the whole story in the presence of the bishop to the assembled congregation in church; and after having divided all his possessions among the poor dies peacefully and enters into the glories of Paradise.

Even popes are said to have made compacts with the Devil. An English Benedictine monk, William of Malmesbury, says of Pope Sylvester II, who was born in France, his secular name being Gerbert, that he entered the cloister when still a boy. Full of ambition, he flew to Spain where he studied astrology and magic among the Saracens. There he stole a magic-book from a Saracen philosopher, and returned flying through the air to France. Now he opened a school and acquired great fame, so that the king himself became one of his disciples. Then he became Bishop of Rheims, where he had a magnificent clock and an organ constructed. Having raised the treasure of Emperor Octavian which lay hidden in a subterranean vault at Rome, he became Pope. As Pope he manufactured a magic head which replied to all his questions. This head told him that he would not die until he had read Mass in Jerusalem. So the Pope decided never to visit the Holy Land. But once he fell sick, and, asking his magic head, was informed that the church's name in which he had read Mass the other day was "The Holy Cross of Jerusalem." The Pope knew at once that he had to die. He gathered all the cardinals around his bed, confessed his crime, and, as a penance, ordered his body to be cut up alive and the pieces to be thrown out of the church as unclean.

Sigabert tells the story of the Pope's death in a different way. There is no penance on the part of the Pope, and the Devil takes his soul to hell. Others tell us that the Devil constantly accompanied the Pope in the shape of a black dog, and this dog gave him the equivocal prophecy.

The historical truth of the story is that Gerbert was unusually gifted and well educated. He was familiar with the wisdom of the Saracens, for Borrell, Duke of Hither Spain, carried him as a youth to his country where he studied mathematics and astronomy. He came early in contact with the most influential men of his time, and became Pope in 999. He was liberal enough to denounce some of his unworthy predecessors as "monsters of more than human iniquity," and as "Antichrist, sitting in the temple of God and playing the part of God;" but at the same time he pursued an independent and vigorous papal policy, foreshadowing in his aims both the pretensions of Gregory the Great and the Crusades.

The most famous, most significant, and the profoundest story among the legends of devil-contracts is the saga of Dr. Johannes Faustus. Whether the hero of the Faust legend derives his name from the Latin *faustus*, i.e., the favored one, or from the well-known Mayence goldsmith Fust, the companion of Gensfleisch vom Gutenberg, the inventor of printing, or whether he was no historical personality at all, is an open question. Certain it is that all the stories of the great naturalists and thinkers whom the people at the time regarded as wizards were by and by attributed to him, and the figure of Dr. Faustus became the centre of an extensive circle of traditions. The tales about Albertus Magnus, Johannes Teutonicus (Deutsch), Trithemius, Abbot of Sponheim, Agrippa of Nettesheim, Theophrastus, and Paracelsus, were retold of Faust, and Faust became a poetical personification of the great revolutionary aspirations in the time immediately preceding and following the Reformation.

The original form of the Faust-legend represents the Roman Catholic standpoint. Faust allies himself with the Devil, works his miracles by the black art, and pays for its practice with his soul. He begins his career in Wittenberg, the university at which Luther taught, and is the embodiment of natural science, of historical investigation, of the Renaissance, and of modern discoveries and inventions. As such he subdues nature, restores to life the heroes of ancient Greece, gathers knowledge about distant lands, and revives Helen, the ideal of classic beauty.

As the fall of the Devil is, according to Biblical authority, attributed to pride and ambition, so progress and the spirit of investigation were denounced as Satan's work, and all inquiry into the mysteries of nature was regarded as magic. Think only of Roger Bacon, that studious, noble monk, and a greater scientist than his more famous namesake, Lord Bacon! In the thirties of the thirteenth century, at the University of Paris, when Roger Bacon, making some experiments with light, made the rainbow-colors appear on a screen, the audience ran away from him terrified, and his life was endangered because he was suspected of practising the black art.

The Faust Legend

FAUST IS THE REPRESENTATIVE OF scientific manliness. He investigates, even though it may cost him the Christian's title to heavenly bliss; he boldly studies nature, although he will be damned for it in hell; he seeks the truth at the risk of forfeiting his soul. According to the mediaeval theology Satan fell simply on account of his manly ambition and high aspiration, and yet Faust dares to break and eat of the forbidden fruit of the tree of knowledge. According to Marlowe's Faustus, Lucifer fell, not only by insolence, but first of all "by aspiring pride." Mephistopheles seems to regret, but Faustus comforts him, saying:

> *"What is great Mephistopheles so passionate,*
> *For being deprived of the joys of heaven?*
> *Learn thou of Faustus manly fortitude,*
> *And scorn those joys thou never shalt possess."*

The oldest Faust book, dated 1587 (called the *Volksbuch*) exists in one single copy only which is now carefully preserved in Ulm, and Scheible has re-published it in his work *Dr. Johannes Faust* (3 Volumes, Stuttgart, 1846).

The preface of the *Volksbuch* states that the publisher had received the manuscript from a good friend in Speyer, and that the original story had been written in Latin. The contents of this oldest version of the Faust legend are as follows:

Faust, the son of a farmer in Rod, near Weimar, studied theology at Wittenberg. Ambitious to be omniscient and omnipotent like God, he dived into the secret lore of magic, but unable to make much progress, he conjured the Devil in a thick forest near Wittenberg. Not in the least intimidated by the Devil's noisy behavior, he forced him to become his servant. Faust, having gained mastery over demons, did not regard his salvation endangered, and when the Devil told him that he should nevertheless receive his full punishment after death, he grew extremely angry with him and bade him quit his presence, saying: "For your sake I do not want to be damned." When the Devil had left, Faust felt an uneasiness not experienced before, for he had become accustomed to his services. Accordingly, he ordered the Devil to return, who now introduced himself as Mephistopheles. The name is derived from the Greek μὴ τό φῶς φιλής, "not-the-light-loving," and was afterwards changed to Mephistopheles. He now made a compact with the Devil who consented to serve him for twenty-four years, Faust to allow him afterwards to deal with him as he pleased. The contract was signed by Faust with his blood, which he drew with a penknife from his left arm. The blood, running out of the wound, formed the words: *Homo fuge* (man, fly!). This startles Faust, but he remains resolute.

Mephistopheles entertained his master with all kinds of merry illusions, with music and visions. He brought him dainty dishes and costly clothes stolen from royal households. Faust became luxurious and desired to marry. The Devil refused, because marriage is a sacrament. Faust insisted. Then the Devil appeared in his real shape which was so terrific that Faust was frightened. He gave up the idea of marriage, but Mephistopheles sent him devils who assumed the shape of beautiful women, and made him dissolute.

Faust conversed with his servant about eschatological subjects, and heard many things which greatly displeased his vanity. Mephistopheles said, "I am a devil and act according to my nature. But if I were a man, I would rather humiliate myself before God than before Satan."

Faust became sick of his empty pleasures. His ambition was to be recognised in the world as a man who could explain nature, presage future events, and so excite admiration. Having received sufficient information concerning the other world, he wanted to come into direct contact with it, and Mephistopheles introduced to him a number of distinguished devils. When the visitors left, the house was so full of vermin that Faust had to withdraw. However, he did not neglect his new acquaintances on that account, but paid them a visit in their own home. Riding upon a chair built of human bones, he visited hell and contemplated with leisure the flames of its furnaces and the torments of the damned.

Having safely returned from the infernal region, he was carried in a carriage drawn by dragons up to heaven. He took a ride high in the air, first eastwards over the whole of Asia, then upwards to the stars, until they grew before his eyes on his approach into big worlds, while the earth became as small as the yolk of an egg.

His curiosity being satisfied in that direction, he concentrated his attention upon the earth. Mephistopheles assumed the shape of a winged horse upon which he visited all the countries of our planet. He visited Rome and regretted not having become Pope, seeing the luxuries of the latter's life. He sat down invisible at the Pope's table and took away his daintiest morsels, and the wine from his very lips. The Pope, believing himself beset by a ghost, exorcised its poor soul, but Faust laughed at him. In Turkey he visited the Sultan's harem, and introduced himself as the prophet Mohammed, which gave him full liberty to act as he pleased. Beyond India he saw at a distance the blest gardens of Paradise.

Faust, being invited in his capacity of magician to visit the Emperor Charles the Fifth, made Alexander the Great, the beautiful Helen, and other noted persons of antiquity appear before the whole court. Faust fell in love with Helen, so that he could no longer live without her. He kept her in his company and had a child by her, a marvellous boy who could reveal the future.

When the twenty-four years had almost elapsed, Faust grew melancholy, but the Devil mocked him. At midnight, on the very last day, some students who had been in his company heard a frightful noise, but did not dare to enter his room. The next morning they found him torn to pieces. Helen and her child had disappeared, and his famulus Wagner inherited his books on magic art.

This briefly is the contents of the *Volksbuch* on Faust.

A transcription of the Faust-legend in rhymes was published as early as 1587 in Tübingen. Another version by Widman appeared in Hamburg in 1599. It is less complete than the first Faust-book and lacks depth of conception while it abounds rather more in coarse incidents. Widmann's edition became the basis of several further renderings, one in 1674 by Pfitzer in Nuremberg, another in 1728 in Frankfort and

Leipsic. Faust must have appeared on the stage in the seventeenth century, for the clergy of Berlin filed a complaint that Faust publicly abjured God on the stage. The puppet-play Faust was compiled for the amusement of peasants and children, in fairs and market places. Yet it was powerful enough to inspire Goethe who saw it still performed when a boy, to write the great drama which became the most famous work of his life.

The Faust-legend found a continuation in the story of Christoph Wagner, Faust's famulus and companion. The Wagner-story, however, contains nothing new and is nothing but a bare repetition of Faust's adventures and sorry end.

English editions appeared very early, and Marlowe, the greatest pre-Shakespearian dramatist, used the Faust-story for one of his dramas, which is still extant.

Goethe's Faust

GOETHE'S CONCEPTION OF FAUST REPRESENTS the Protestant standpoint. Faust allies himself with the spirit of negation and promises to pay the price of his soul on condition that he shall find satisfaction; but Faust finds no satisfaction in the gifts of the spirit that denies. However, he does find satisfaction, after having abandoned the chase for empty pleasures, in active and successful work for the good of mankind. Goethe's Faust uses the Devil but rises above his negativism. However, he inherits from the revolutionary movement of the age that gave birth to the legend, the love of liberty. Says the dying Faust:

> *"And such a throng I fain would see,—*
> *Stand on free soil among a people free."*

This Faust cannot be lost. His soul is saved. Mephistopheles now ceases to be a mere incarnation of badness; his negation becomes the spirit of critique. The spirit of critique, although destructive, leads to the positive work of construction; and thus Faust becomes a representative of the bold spirit of investigation and progress which characterises the present age.

The Devil of the *Volksbuch* is real; actors and spectators believe in his power and are afraid to fall into his clutches. In Goethe's Faust the mythology of the story is felt to be mere allegory and has become part of the dramatic machinery. This is plainly seen in the Walpurgis night scene which has become a satirical intermezzo of Goethe's time.

Humorists

THE FIGURE OF THE EVIL One began slowly to lose the awe which it exercised during the Middle Ages upon the imagination of the people, and Hans Sachs treats the Devil in his poems as a being of whom no courageous man need be afraid. Thus the German halberdier, he says, laughs at him, for Old Nick would not dare to admit a *Landsknecht* of their rank into his kingdom.

The first man, however, who (so far as I am aware) was wise enough to take, as a matter of principle, a humorous view of the Devil and hell was Dionysius Klein. In his *Tragico-Comœdia*, published in the year 1622, he describes his trip both to heaven and to the infernal region, which latter place is reported to be well equipped with water-power and good machinery, as these were used in the beginning of the seventeenth century.

In modern times the humorous character of Satan develops in the degree that he is no longer regarded as an individual being but changes to the principle of evil.

In the British Islands where the majority of the people still believe in a personal Devil, there exists an unwritten law which reads, "Thou shalt not take the name of the Devil in vain." In Germany and France, however, and in all other countries of the European continent, people use the word freely in a way that must shock the feelings of a well-bred Englishman.

Victor Hugo uses the Devil as a setting for his political satire. No more trenchant sarcasm in poetic form can be imagined than his lines on Napoleon III. and Pope Pius IX. He says:

> "One day the Lord was playing
> For human souls (they're saying)
> With Satan's Majesty.
> And each one showed his art:
> The one played Bonaparte,
> The other Mastaï.

> "An abbot sly and keen,
> A princelet wretched mean,

And a rascal, upon oath.
God Father played so poorly,
He lost the game, and surely
The Devil won them both.

"'Well, take them!' cried God Father,
'You'll find them useless rather!'
The Devil laughed and swore:
'They'll serve my cause, I hope.
The one I'll make a pope,
The other emperor!'"*

["Un jour Dieu sur la table
Jouait avec le diable
Du genre humain haï;
Chacun tenait sa carte,
L'un jouait Bonaparte
Et l'autre Mastaï.

"Un pauvre abbé bien mince,
Un méchant petit prince,
Polisson hasardeux!
Quel enjeu pitoyable!
Dieu fit tant que le diable
Les gagna tous les deux.

"'Prends! cria Dieu le pére,
Tu ne sauras qu'en faire!'
Le diable dit: 'erreur!
Et, ricanant sous cape,
Il fit de l'un un pape,
De l'autre un empereur.'"]

The Devil in the literature of today is of the same kind: a harmless fellow at whose expense the reader enjoys a hearty laugh. Lesage's novel *The Devil on Two Sticks* is a poor piece of fiction, and Hauff's *Memoirs of Satan* are rather lengthy.

---

* Translation specially made by E. F. L Gauss.

Heinrich Heine said jestingly:

> *"Don't, my friend, scoff at the Devil,*
> *For the path of life is short;*
> *And eternal reprobation*
> *Is not merely parson sport."*

> *["Freund verspotte nicht den Teufel,*
> *Kurz ist ja die Lebensbahn;*
> *Und die ewige Verdammniss*
> *Ist kein blosser Pöbelwahn."]*

In another poem Heine tells how he made the acquaintance of Satan and what impression he made on the poet. According to Miss Emma Lazarus's translation Heine says:

> *"I called the Devil and he came,*
> *His face with wonder I must scan;*
> *He is not ugly, he is not lame,*
> *He is a delightful, charming man;*
> *A man in the prime of life, in fact,*
> *Courteous, engaging, and full of tact.*
> *A diplomat, too, of wide research*
> *Who cleverly talks about State and Church.*
> *A little pale, but that is en règle*
> *For now he is studying Sanskrit and Hegel.*

> *"He said he was proud my acquaintance to make*
> *And should prize my friendship, and bowed as he spake.*
> *And asked if we had not met before*
> *At the house of the Spanish ambassador.*
> *Then I noted his features line by line,*
> *And found him an old acquaintance of mine."*

In modern times it has become quite customary in French, German, and American papers to picture the Devil without fear and in good humor, and few are they who would take offence at the sight.

Hell Up to Date is a genuine Chicago production of modern style. The author introduces himself as a newspaper reporter who interviews

"Sate," and is shown round the Inferno. He finds that "Hell is now run on the broad American plan." "Captain" Charon, who began his career as a ferryman with a little tub of a "rowboat," is now running big steamers on the Styx, "the only navigable river in hell." Judge Minos sits in court, and an Irish policeman introduces the poor wretches one by one. The lawyers are condemned to be gagged, and their objections are overruled by Satan; the inventor of the barbwire fence is seated naked on a barbwire fence; tramps are washed; policemen are clubbed until they see stars; quack doctors are cured according to their own methods; poker fiends, board of trade gamblers, and fish-story tellers are treated according to their deserts; monopolists are baked like pop-corn, and clergymen are condemned to listen to their own sermons which have been faithfully recorded in phonographs.

DEVIL-STORIES ARE MYTHS IN WHICH Christian mythology is carried to the extreme. Symbols are taken seriously, and from the literal belief of the Christian dogma the imagination weaves these pictures which to our ancestors were more than mere tales that adorn a moral.

The Philosophical Problem of
Good and Evil

The question as to the nature of evil is by far the most important problem for philosophical, religious, and moral consideration. The intrinsic presence of suffering is the most obvious feature that determines the character of existence throughout, but gives at the same time origin to the most important blessings that make life worth living. It is pain that sets thoughts to thinking; a state of undisturbed happiness would make reflexion, inquiry, and invention redundant. It is death which begets the aspiration of preserving oneself beyond the grave. Without death there would be no religion. And it is sin that imparts worth to virtue. If there were no going astray, there would be no seeking for the right path; there would be no merit in goodness. Blame and praise would have no meaning. In this absence of want, imperfection, and all kinds of ill, there would be no ideals, no progress, no evolution to higher goals.

The Mythology of Evil

MYTHOLOGY BEING ALWAYS A POPULAR metaphysics, it is a matter of course that the idea of evil has been personified among all nations. There is no religion in the world but has its demons or evil monsters who represent pain, misery, and destruction. In Egypt the powers of darkness were feared and worshipped under various names as Set or Seth, Bess, Typhon, etc. Though the ancient Gods of Brahmanism are not fully differentiated into evil and good deities, we have yet the victory of Mahâmâya, the great goddess, over Mahisha, the king of the giants.* Buddhists call the personification of evil Mâra, the tempter, the father of lust and sin, and the bringer of death. Chaldean sages personify

---

* As to the myth of the origin of Mahâmâya, who is identified with Durgâ, see "the Chandi" in the *Mârkandeya Purâna*. Vishnu, beholding the wretchedness of the gods to which the powers of the victorious giant-king Mahisha had reduced them, grew so enraged that streams of glory issued from his countenance taking shape in the figure of Mahâmâya. Similar effulgences came forth from the other gods and entered into the system of the goddess who then went forth and slew the buffalo-shaped monster Mahisha. Another account of the same myth is contained in the *Vâmana Purâna*. For details see Hindu mythologies under Mahisha and Mahishamardini (the slayer of Mahisha).

the chaos that was in the beginning, in Tiamat, the monster of the deep. The Persians call him Angra Mainyu or Ahriman, the demon of darkness and of mischief, the Jews call him Satan the fiend, the early Christians, Devil (διάβολος), i.e., slanderer, because, as in the story of Job, he accuses man, and his accusations are false. The old Teutons and Norsemen called him Loki. The Middle Ages are full of devils, and demonologies of the Japanese and Chinese are perhaps more extensive than our own.

The evolution of the idea of evil as a personification is one of the most fascinating chapters in history, and the changes which characterise the successive phases are instructive. While the old Pagan views survive in both Hebrew and Christian demonologies, we are constantly confronted with accretions and new interpretations. Franz Xaver Kraus, in his *History of Christian Art** concedes that our present conception of the demons of evil is radically different from that of the early Christians. He says:

> "The popular conceptions of the early Christians concerning devils are essentially different from those of the present time. The serpent or the dragon as a picture of the Devil appears not only in the Old Testament (Genesis iii. 1), but also in Babylonian literature, in the Revelation of St. John (xii. 9), and in the Acts of the Martyrs. We read in the Vision of Perpetua: 'Under the scales themselves [i.e., for weighing the souls] the dragon lies, of wonderful magnitude.'"[†]

The intellectual life of mankind develops by gradual growth. The old views are, as a rule, preserved but transformed. There is nowhere an absolutely new start. Either the main idea is preserved and details are changed, or *vice versa*, the main idea is objected to while the details remain the same. Gunkel has proved[‡] that the splendid description of Leviathan (in Job xli) as a monster of the deep protected by scales is a reproduction of Chaldæan mythology, and God's fight with the monsters of the deep is a repetition of Bel Merodach's conquest

---

* *Geschichte der christlichen Kunst,* Vol. I, p. 210.

† *Sub ipsa scala draco Cubans mirae magnitudinis.*

‡ *Schöpfung und Chaos.* Göttingen, 1891.

of Tiamat. Changes of a radical nature take place in the religious conceptions of mankind, yet the historical connexion is preserved.

The conception of evil in its successive personifications would be humorous if most of its pages (especially those on witch-prosecution) were not at the same time very sad. But for that reason we must recognise the prestige of the Devil. The pedigree of the Evil One is older than the oldest European aristocracy and royal families; it antedates the Bible and is more ancient than the Pyramids.

Having outlined in the preceding chapters the history of the Devil, we shall now devote the conclusion of this book to a philosophical consideration of the idea of evil; and here we are first of all confronted with the problem of the objective existence of evil.

The Era of Subjectivism

THE QUESTION PRESENTS ITSELF: "Is not evil the product of mere illusion? Is it not a relative term which ought to be dropped as a one-sided conception of things? Does it not exist simply because we view life from our own subjective standpoint, and must it not disappear as soon as we learn to comprehend the world in its objective reality?" The tendency to regard evil as a purely negative term is at present very prevalent, for it agrees with the spirit of the times and is one of the most popular notions of today.

In ancient times man was in the habit of objectifying the various aspirations and impulses of his soul. In order to understand beauty the Greek mind fashioned the ideal of Aphrodite, and the moral authority of righteousness appeared to the Jew as Yahveh the Lord, the Legislator of Mount Sinai. Religious aspirations were actualised in the Church by means of ceremonials and ecclesiastical institutions.

Things changed at the opening of that era in the evolution of mankind which is commonly called modern history. A new age was prepared through the inventions of gunpowder, the compass, and printing, and began at the end of the fifteenth century with the discovery of America, and the Reformation. The more the horizon of the known world grew, the more man began to comprehend the importance of his own subjectivity. The tendency of philosophy since Descartes and of religion since Luther, has been to concentrate everything in man's individual consciousness. That alone should have value which had become part of man's soul. Man's consciousness became his world, and thus, in religion, conscience began to be regarded as the ultimate basis of conduct. Men felt that religion should not be an external, but an internal, factor. Toleration became a universal requirement, and subjectivity was made the cornerstone of public and private life. Thus the era of the Reformation showed itself as a revolutionary movement, which, proclaiming the right of individualism and subjectivity, overthrew the traditional authority of an external objectivity.

The originators of this movement did not intend to discard all objective authority, but the spirit of nominalism which dominated them prevailed over their movement in its further progress. The last consequences of the principle of subjectivity, which starts with the famous assumption *cogito ergo sum,* were not anticipated by Descartes, for he naïvely assumes objective existence on one of the most trivial arguments. Nor would Luther with his peculiar education and stubborn narrowness, which were by no means inconsistent accompaniments of his greatness, ever have endorsed later theories based upon the purely subjective aspect of conscience; but the fact remains that the last consequence of the recognition of the supremacy of the subjective principle is a denial of any objective authority in philosophy, politics, religion, and ethics, which leads in politics to anarchism, i.e., individualism pushed to its extreme; in philosophy to agnosticism, i.e., the denial of any cognisable objectivity, worked out most systematically in Kant's critical idealism. In ethics it is the refusal to recognise any objective authority in morals; which leads either to Bentham's ethical egotism and hedonism or to intuitionism, and finally to Nietzsche's immoralism.

Our present civilisation is based upon the Protestant ideal of individualism, and nobody who lives and moves in our time can be blind to the enormous benefits which we derive from it. Nevertheless, we must beware of the onesidedness of subjectivism. Objectivism is not so utterly erroneous in principle as it appears from the point of view of modern subjectivism. The external methods of the Roman Church are mistaken; the tyranny of its hierarchical system which substitutes the priest's authority and an infallible papacy for God's authority is radically wrong; and the main task of Protestantism consisted in protesting against this authority, which, in spite of its self-asserted catholicity, is based upon the human authority of fallible mortals, an authority that was more frequently misused through bigotry and ignorance than through malice and selfishness.

There are Protestants who might object that Protestantism is not merely negative; it is also positive. It is not only a protest, but also an affirmation. True, indeed! But most of the Protestant affirmations are simply relics of the old Romanism which bound the consciences of man and crippled his reasoning power. The fanatics among the Protestants are by no means friends of liberty and free inquiry; and the positive power, the new factor in history that was destined to build up a new civilisation, was nothing else than Science. Therefore, Protestantism is not as yet the last word spoken in the religious development of mankind. We must look to higher aims and more positive issues, and a new reformation of the Church will obtain them only on the condition of its again recognising the importance of objectivity.

Mankind will not return to the dogmatic system of hierarchical institutions, which would only bind again the consciences of men by man-made authority. But the fact must be recognised that truth is not a mere subjective conception; it must be seen that truth is a statement of facts, and, accordingly, that it contains an objective element, and that this objective element is the essential part of established truth.

In the old period of objectivism, the ultimate authority was lodged in great men, prophets, reformers, and priests, whose spirit, after it had been adapted to the needs of the powerful, was embodied in Church institutions. The new objectivism discards all human authority; it rests ultimately upon science, which is an appeal to facts. Truth is no longer what the Church teaches, or what some infallible man may deem wise to proclaim; nor is it what appears to me as true, or to you as true; but it is that which according to methodical critique has been proved to be objectively true, i.e., so proved that everybody who investigates it will find it to be so.

Objective truth, demonstrable by evidence and capable of revision, or, in a word, Science, is the highest, the most reliable and the most valuable revelation of God. God reveals himself in the facts of life, among which we include our afflictions and personal experiences; God speaks in our conscience, which is, as it were, the moral instinct, the result of all our inherited and acquired experiences, and this is the reason why the voice of conscience makes itself heard in our soul with that automatic force which is characteristic of all deep-seated subconscious reactions. God also appears in our sentiments, our ideal aspirations, our devotions, our hopes and our yearnings. All these various manifestations are important and must not be lost sight of; but above them all is the objectivity of truth which speaks through science.

It is impossible for all men to be scientists, but for that reason it is not necessary that their minds and hearts should be enslaved by blind faith. The faith of every man should be the trust in truth, not in fairy tales that must be taken for granted, but in the truth,—the truth which in its main outlines is simple enough to be comprehensible to all,—the truth that this world of ours is a cosmic harmony in which no wrong can be done without producing evil effects all around.

Faith in the objective authority of truth is the next step in the religious evolution of mankind. We stand now at the threshold of the third period which will be, to characterise it in a word, an era of scientific objectivism. The tendency of the second era was negative, revolutionising, theorising; the tendency of the third will be positive, constructive, practical.

Negativism and subjectivism appear from the standpoint of the positivism and objectivism of the first period as the work of the destroyer, of the negative spirit, the Devil. It is a reaction. This explains why Milton's Satan actually became a hero. Milton was a Protestant, a revolutionist, a subjectivist, and he unconsciously sympathised with Satan, who in the terms of a philosopher of the age declares:

> *"The mind is its own place and in itself*
> *Can make a heaven of hell, a hell of heaven.*
> *What matter where, if* I *be still the same*
> *And what I should be."*

The negativism of the second period is not a mistake. It was an indispensable condition of the third period; for it manufactured the tools for a higher and better positivism,—criticism. But criticism is insufficient for positive construction; we must have actual results, methodical work, and positive issues; and the prophet of the twentieth century finds it necessary again to emphasise the importance of objectivity.

Is Evil Positive?

A MODERN FABLE CHARACTERISES THE relativity of good and evil in the story of a farmer, who, weeding his field with a cultivator, curses the morning-glories which grow luxuriantly on his maize stalks as being created by the Devil. In the meantime his little daughter weaves a wreath of the same flowers and praises the beauty of God's handiwork. Evil and good may be relative, but relativity does not imply non-existence. Relations are facts too. If mischief is wrought by good things being out of place, the evil does not become chimerical but is as positive as any other reality.

In the same way, the relativity of knowledge does not prove (as some agnostic philosophers claim) the impossibility of knowledge. Concrete things, such as stones and other material bodies, are not the only realities; relations, too, are actual, and the same thing may under different conditions be either good or evil.

A proper comprehension of the relativity of goodness and badness, far from invalidating the objectivity of the moral ideal, will become a great stimulus that will work for the realisation of goodness, for there ought to be nothing so bad but that it can by judicious management be turned to good account. Badness, however, is sometimes spoken of as a mere negation, and the assertion is made that it is not a positive factor. Looking for the most characteristic representative of this view among the ablest authors of our time, we find a statement written by the well-known author of the novel *Ground Arms!* Bertha von Suttner, one of the most prominent advocates of universal peace on earth. She knows as well as Schopenhauer that the ills of life are positive, for she describes all the horrors of war in their drastic reality. Nevertheless, Bertha von Suttner devotes in her ingenious book *The Inventory of a Soul* a whole chapter to the proposition "The Principle of Evil a Phantom."* She says:

"I do not believe in the phantoms of badness, misery, and death. They are mere shadows, zeros, nothingnesses. They are negations of real things, but not real things themselves. . . There is light, but there is no darkness: darkness is only the non-existence of light. There is life, death is only a local ceasing of lifephenomena. . . We grant that Ormuzd and Ahriman, God and Devil, are at least thinkable, but there are other opposites in which it is apparent that one is the non-existence of the other. For instance: noise and silence. Think of a silence so powerful as to suppress a noise. . . Darkness has no degree, while light has. There is more

---

* *Inventarium einer Seele.* Chap. XV.

light or less light, but various shades of darkness can mean only little or less light. Thus, life is a magnitude, but death is a zero. Something and nothing cannot be in struggle with each other. Nothing is without arms, nothing as an independent idea is only an abortion of human weaknesses... two are necessary to produce struggle. If I am in the room, I am here; if I leave it, I am no longer here. There can be no quarrel between my ego-present and ego-absent."

This is the most ingenious and completest denial of the existence of evil that we know of, and it is presented with great force. It is the expression of the negativism of philosophy from Descartes to Spencer. It seems to be consistent monism. And yet, we cannot accept it.

True enough, the idea of a personal Devil is as imaginary as a fairy, or an elf, or a hobgoblin; true also that there is no evil in itself, and no goodness in itself; the dualism of the Manichees is untenable. The evil principle cannot be conceived as an independent substance, essence, or entity. But for that reason we cannot shut our eyes to its real and positive existence. Granted that silence is the absence of noise; yet noise is not goodness, neither is silence badness. While I think or write, noise is to me an evil, while silence is bliss. Silence, where a word of cheer is expected or needed, may be a very positive evil, and a lie is not merely an absence of truth. The absence of food is a mere negation, but considered in relation to its surroundings, as an empty stomach, it is hunger; and hunger is a positive factor in this world of ours. Sickness can be considered as a mere absence of health, but sickness is caused either by a disorder in the system or the presence of injurious influences, both of which are unquestionably positive. A debt is a negative factor in the books of the debtor, but what is negative to the debtor is positive to the creditor.

If negative ideas were "mere abortions of human weakness," as Bertha von Suttner claims, how could mathematicians have any use for the minus sign? And if the idea of evil were an empty superstition, how could its influence upon mankind have been so lasting? On the one hand it is true that all existence is positive, but on the other hand we ought to know that existence in the abstract is neither good nor bad; goodness and badness depend upon the relations among the various existent things. And these relations may be good as well as evil. Some existences destroy other existences. Certain bacilli are destructive of human life, certain antidotes destroy bacilli. There are everywhere parasites living upon other lives, and what is positive or life-sustaining to the one is negative and destructive to the other, and every such negation is a reality, the effectiveness of which neutralises the action of another reality.*

The idea of goodness is by no means equivalent with existence, and badness with non-existence. Existence is the reality; it is the indivisible whole, the one and all. Good and evil, however, are views taken from a certain given standpoint, and from this standpoint good and evil are features forming a contrast, but as such they are always actualities; neither the one nor the other is a mere nothing. The question is only whether *we* have a right to regard *our own* standpoint as the positive one, representing that which is good, and all the powers that hinder human life as negative or evil.

The answer to this question seems to be that any and every being will naturally regard its own standpoint as the positively given fact, and every factor that destroys it as negative; his pleasure appears to him the standard of goodness.

And we grant that every being is entitled to take this standpoint, and that subjectivism naturally forms the initial stage of all ethical valuation. But we cannot rest satisfied with the principle of subjective autonomy as a solution of the problem of good and evil.

Is there an Objective Standard of Goodness?

SUPPOSING THAT GOOD WERE INDEED simply that which gives pleasure or enhances *my* life, and bad that which gives pain or threatens to destroy it, the standard of goodness and badness would be purely subjective. The famous savage chief quoted by Tylor, and from Tylor by Spencer, would have fathomed the problem of good and evil when he declared that "bad is if anybody took away his wife, but if he took away the wife of some one else, that would be good."† Good would be that which pleases *me;* and *the* good as an objective reality would not exist. There would be something good for me, for you, and for many others,

---

* This exposition appeared first in *The Monist*, Vol. VI, No. 4. pp. 585 ff. In reply the Baroness Bertha von Suttner wrote a few courteous lines of recognition which may indicate that she is inclined to accept the author's arguments.

† Tylor, *Primitive Culture*, Vol II, p. 318.

but what might be good for me might be bad for you. Goodness and badness would be purely subjective qualities without any objective value.

The view which bases ethics upon a consideration of pleasure and pain and defines goodness as that which affords the greatest amount of pleasurable feelings is called hedonism. The coarsest form of hedonism (as represented by Bentham) makes the pleasure of the individual supreme; it bases its ethics upon selfishness, and sees in altruism only refined egotism. The altruist is said to love but himself in others.

Let me add here that the intuitionalist basing ethics upon the voice of his conscience is, closely considered, also a hedonist, or at least a subjectivist, for he finds the ultimate authority for conduct in himself, viz., in the pleasure of those motor ideas of his which he calls his conscience: what he is pleased to consider as ethical, he thinks is ethical. His standard of morality is the subjectivity of his conviction, which he is unable either to analyse or to trace to its origin. He differs from Bentham's hedonism of ethical egotism only in this, that the pleasure of his conscience overrules the lower pleasures of the senses.

Modern utilitarianism, as represented by Mr. Spencer, remains a purely subjective ethics, for it makes the greatest happiness of the greatest number the maxim of ethics; and by doing so it introduces no objective principle, but it simply proposes to replace every single subjectivity by the sum total of all subjectivities; and subjective ethical maxims are not as yet truly ethical; they remain on the level of the world-conception of Tylor's savage.

All subjective ethical theories fail to see the cardinal point of ethics, for the very nature of ethics is objective. If there is no objective authority for moral conduct, we had better openly declare that ethics is an illusion and what we call ethics is simply an arithmetical calculation in which pleasures and pains are weighed against one another and morality is at best only a dietetics of the soul. As a matter of fact, however, he who opens his eyes will see that there is an objective authority for conduct in life. Life and the factors in life are not purely what we make them. Here we are to run a race, and the course of the individual as much as that of mankind and all living beings is prescribed in a very definite and unmistakable way on the lines of what since Darwin we have accustomed ourselves to call evolution. We must learn to recognise the necessity of progress which leads us onward on a straight and narrow path. Those who willingly obey the laws of progress advance on the path in spite of its thorns, joyously and gladly. The reluctant are urged forward and feel the smart of nature's whip, while he who obstinately refuses to heed the laws of the cosmic order goes to the wall.

Nature has no consideration for our sentiments, be they pleasures or pains. Happy is he who delights in acting according to her laws. But he who seeks other pleasures is doomed. Look at the situation from whatever standpoint you may, the criterion of right and wrong, of good and bad, of true and false, lies not in the greater or lesser amount of pleasure and pain, but in the agreement of our actions with the cosmic order; and morality is that which is in accord with the law of evolution. Ethics teaches us to do voluntarily what after all we must do whether or not it may please us.

In a word, ethics is unthinkable without duty, and the essential element of duty is its objective reality, its inflexible sternness, and its austere authority.

We say to the hedonist, a good action is not moral because it gives pleasure, but because it accords with duty; and we must not be on the search for that which gives us pleasure but must endeavor to find our highest pleasure in doing that which the cosmic law (or, religiously speaking, God) demands of us.

Those who deny that there is any objective norm of right and wrong in the universe, are inclined to claim with Huxley, that man survived not on account of his morality, but on the contrary, on account of his immorality. It has been said that man is more rapacious, more egotistical, more immoral, than brutes. Without denying that an immoral man may sometimes appear more brutish than a brute, we cannot see that man is as immoral as, or even more immoral than, brutes. But the case is worth considering.

Says the wolf in Æsop's fable: "Why is it right for you to eat the lamb, when for me it is supposed to be wrong?" Is not man in the same predicament as the wolf, and does not mankind slaughter more animals than all the wolves in the world ever ate?

Granted that the wolf's pleadings are substantiated, we observe that man lives, but wolves are exterminated, which seems good evidence in favor of man's being in greater accord with the cosmic laws. And yet the actions of both, the wolf and the man, seem to be identical; or rather, if the blackness of a crime depended upon quantitative measurement by addition, we should have to decide in favor of the wolves; for man at the present time kills more sheep, pigs, and other animals in one year than wolves could devour in a century. Yet man possesses the impudence to call the wolf a robber and to drive him from the fold whenever he attempts to imitate man's voracity. What is the justification of slaughter in the one case, and what its condemnation in the other?

In answering this question we shall not idealise man's mode of living on the flesh of his fellow-creatures. For it appears that from a moral standpoint it would be preferable to sustain life without slaughtering lambs and calves, fowl and fishes. The case must not be considered from an abstract or ideal standpoint, but simply treated as a comparison of the wolf's conduct with man's conduct; and we find that the more sheep a man eats, the more he raises. The wolf eats them without raising them. The wolf murders the lamb. However, the slaughter of the lamb by man is no murder, for it serves to increase and to sustain human souls, and the souls of man possess more truth and a higher insight into nature. The lamb dies as a sacrifice on the altar of humanity, and this sacrifice is right and good if, and in so far as, it substitutes higher life for lower life. Subjectively considered the wolf has the same right as man to kill a lamb; and also the same right as the lamb would have to kill wolves or men. The difference between man's and the wolf's actions appears only when we take into account the objective conditions of man's superiority, giving him a wider dominion of power which he can maintain because his soul is a better reflector of truth than are the notions of a wolf.

We must insist here that the attainment of a higher life, consisting in a fuller comprehension of truth and a greater acquisition of power, is one of the most essential requisites of morality. Morality is not a negative quality, but a very positive endeavor. We must abandon the old standpoint of negativism, that goodness consists in not doing certain things which are forbidden. Genuine goodness consists in daring and doing; and in doing the right thing. One genuine and positive virtue atones for many sins that consist in mere omissions. The sheep is by no means (as is frequently claimed) more moral than the wolf. The wolf is bad enough, but he is at least courageous and keen; the sheep is a coward, and with all its cowardice it is stupid. It is time to discard the ovine ideal of morality which praises all lack of energy and of accomplishments as the highest type of goodness. What we need is a positive conception of virtue based upon a careful consideration of the requirements of life.

What higher life and lower life is cannot be declared to be an arbitrary distinction. It is not purely subjective, but can be defined according to an objective standard. Good to the savage is that which pleases him, and bad that which hurts him. Good, to him who has deciphered the religious mystery of the universe and understands the nature of God, is that which produces higher life, and bad is that which hinders, or perverts, or destroys it.

The God-Idea

GOD IS A RELIGIOUS TERM, and it is often claimed that knowledge of God does not fall within the domain of science; the idea of God and all other religious terms are claimed to be extra-scientific. Thus there are two parties both of which are under the influence of nominalistic subjectivism: religious agnostics and infidel agnostics. The belief of the former is as irrational as the disbelief of the latter. If there is an objective authority for conduct, we must be able to know it; we can obey it only in so far as we know it. Now experience teaches us that there is an authority for conduct, and the theory of evolution promises to prove it by positive evidence. This authority for conduct is called in the language of religion "God." Our scientists formulate under the name "laws of nature" that which is immutable in the various phenomena, that which is universal in the variety of happenings, that which is eternal in the transient, and every law of nature is in its sphere a rigorous authority for conduct which in this sense is part and parcel of God's being.

The most important laws of nature in the ethical domain are those which regulate all the various and sometimes very delicate relations of man to man, which concatenate our fates and set soul to soul in a mutually helpful responsion.

Existence is one harmonious entirety; there is not a thing in the world but is embraced in the whole as a part of the whole. The One and All is the condition of every creature's being; it is the breath of our breath, the sentiency of our feelings, the strength of our strength. Nothing exists of itself or to itself. All things are interrelated; and as all masses are held together by their gravity in a mutual attraction, so there is at the bottom of all sentiment a mysterious longing, a yearning for the fulness of the whole, a panpathy which finds a powerful utterance in the psalms of all the religions on earth. No creature is an isolated being, for the whole of existence affects the smallest of its parts. Says Emerson:

> *"All are needed by each one,*
> *Nothing is fair or good alone."*

The unity of the whole, the intercoherence of all things, the oneness of all norms that shape life, is not a mere theory but an actual reality; and in this sense the scriptural saying "God is Love" is a truth demonstrable by natural science.

Science proves that the whole of existence presents itself throughout as regulated by law; that it is not a chaos, not an incomprehensible riddle, but a cosmos. As a cosmos it is intelligible, and sentient creatures can learn to understand its nature and adapt themselves to it. God is that feature in the world which condition; and produces reason; and reason is nothing but a reflexion of the world-order. The cosmic order of existence, the harmony of its laws, its systematic regularity, makes intelligence possible, and sentient beings will naturally develop into minds. God is that which changes individuals into persons, for reason and a rational will are the essential characteristic of personality.

Taking this ground we say, (adopting here, for the sake of simplicity, the religious term God,) those beings are good which are images of God.

The nature of progress is not (as Mr. Spencer has it) an increase of heterogeneity, but growth of soul. Evolution is not mere adaptation to surroundings, but a more and more perfect incarnation of truth. Adaptation to surroundings is, from an ethical point of view, an incidental blessing only of the power afforded by right conduct.*

All facts of experience are revelations, but those facts which teach us morality (man's conduct to his fellow-beings) embody truths of special importance. They exercise a wholesome influence upon the development of our souls, even though the primitive man was not able to fully understand their why and wherefore. In the lack of a clear comprehension of facts themselves, man's imagination clothes them in the garb of mythological imagery. In our own days the great teachers of morality are still regarded as the Indian regards the medicine-man, and the sacraments of the Church are treated like the totems of savages. Religion is now slowly passing out of the old stage of magic into the higher stage of a direct comprehension of facts. Myth changes into knowledge, and the allegory of the parable begins to be understood.

As astrology changed into astronomy, so the religion of miracles will give way to the religion of science.

---

* Cf. *Homilies of Science,* "The Test of Progress," p. 36, and "The Ethics of Evolution," p. 41.

We often hear God spoken of as good, and he is sometimes represented as goodness in general. But God is more than goodness. God is the objective reality of existence regarded as the ultimate authority for conduct. God is thus the standard of goodness; to call God good is an anthropomorphism. His creatures are more or less good, according as they are more or less faithful portraits of him, and as they obey his will. God is neither good nor bad, neither moral nor immoral, he is unmoral; yet, his nature and character is the ultimate criterion of goodness and of morality. And God's will can be learned from his revelations, which in the terms of science are called experiences, and which we formulate with exactness in what is called "the laws of nature."

God is not existence itself; He is not, either singly or collectively, the facts of the world; He is not the sum total of objects or existences. God is the norm of existence, that factor which conditions the cosmic order and is formulated by naturalists as laws of nature. Being the norm of existence, God is, above all, that omnipresent feature in the facts, in the objects of the world, in reality, which commands obedience. God's will appears as that something in experience to which we have to conform. In a word, God is the standard of morality and the ultimate authority for conduct. This is nomotheism, but not pantheism, for it recognises the distinction between God and the All or sum total of existence. God is something distinct and definite, not an indifferent omneity. This is monotheism, but not the old monotheism, for it no longer looks upon God as one individual ego-being. Yet it preserves the nucleus of the oldest conception of God, and accepts at the same time all that is true in pantheism.*

God was always an idea of moral import. God was and will remain (so long as the word is retained) the ultimate authority for conduct. Since the order of the world in its most general features is of intrinsic necessity, which means that under no conditions could it be imagined otherwise, God is the *raison d'être* not only of the world as it actually exists but of any possible world; and in this sense nomotheism teaches that God is supernatural. Supernaturalism may be untenable as it was

---

* *Pantheism* identifies God and the All. *Nomotheism* teaches that the laws of nature are not laws given by God as a lawgiver may issue ordinances, but that they are manifestations of God and as such parts of the Deity. They are particular aspects of the eternal and all comprehensive norm of existence. *Monotheism* is the theory that there is one God, and monotheism is commonly understood to mean that this one God is a personal being. See the author's *Religion of Science,* pp., 19 et seq., The Authority for Conduct.

understood by dogmatists, yet there is a truth in supernaturalism which will remain true forever.

Those who see in the facts of nature only matter in motion will naturally be surprised at the fact that a cosmos with living and morally aspiring beings can develop out of it. A deeper insight into the conditions of nature reveals to us that the world is a well regulated cosmos, having its own definite and immutable laws, and these laws are realities as much as material things. They are not concrete entities, but they are real, nevertheless, and indeed of greater importance than the existence of sense-perceptible objects. The cosmos is not only an enormous mass of innumerable atoms, and molecules, and masses of suns and stars, but its finer texture shows that down into its most delicate details it is a wonderful systematic whole, full of life and consistency, and possessing an outspoken and clearly intelligible character, and the world-order which makes the world a whole possesses objectivity, i.e., it is a reality independent of what we think it to be. The world is not as we think it to be, but we must think the world as it is, and our duty is to act accordingly.

These are the plain facts of science which even the man who has no idea of science must heed. Only those creatures can in the long run of evolution survive who act according to the truth. Thus, the truth became embodied in moral rules, even before science could deduce or explain them. Religion is a revelation in so far as it is an anticipation of certain truths which were at the time of their invention still uncomprehended. Religious ideas, accordingly, had to be symbols, and could be communicated only in parables. Now, the more science progresses, the better shall we learn to understand the meaning of these parables.

God is in all things, but he is best revealed in man,—especially in the morally aspiring man, and this is the meaning of the ideal of a God-man, or Christ,—a Saviour whose teachings are the way, the truth, and the life.

Every man's conception of God is a measure of his own stature. He pictures God according to his comprehension, and thus it is natural that every man has a different notion of God, every one's God being characteristic of his mental and moral caliber. On the lowest stages of civilisation devils and gods are almost indistinguishable, but while they become properly differentiated in the onward march of mankind we cannot fail to detect the parallelism between God and Satan which is never lost. The god of savages is a bloodthirsty chieftain; the god of sentimentalists is a good old papa; the god of the superstitious is a magician and a trickster; the god of the slave is a tyrannical master; the god of the egotist is an ego-world-soul; and the gods of the wise, of the just, of the free, of the courageous are wisdom, justice, freedom, and courage. The conception of evil in all these phases will always be the contrast to the ideal embodiment of all goodness.

Satan is at once a rebel and a tyrant. He proclaims independence but his rule bodes oppression and slavery. He himself is represented in chains, for the liberty of sin, which is licence, enthralls the mind. As Satan is a captive of his own making, so all the beings that belong to him are his prisoners. He is their torturer and destroyer.

A most drastic picture of Satan which is found in the missal of Poitiers,* is described by Didron as follows:

"He is chained to the mouth of hell as a dog to its kennel, and yet wields his trident sceptre as the monarch of the place which he guards. Cerberus and Pluto in one, he is yet a Cerberus of Christian art, a demon more hideous and more filled with energy than Pagan art has offered... This image figures the various aspects of infernal sin, by its many faces, having a face on the breast as well as on the head, a face on each shoulder and a face at each hip. How many more behind? With long ears like those of a hound, thick short horns of a bull, his legs and arms are covered with scales, and seem to issue from the mouths of the faces at his joints. He has a lion's head with tusks, and hands like the claws of a bear. His body, open at the waist, reveals a nest of serpents darting forth and hissing. In this monster we find all the elements of a dragon, leviathan, lion, fox, viper, bear, bull, and wild boar. It is a compound of each evil quality in these animals, embodied in a human form." Didron, *Iconography* II, p. 118.

While Satan is the rebel who seeks liberty for himself and oppression of others, God's kingdom signifies the establishment of right, which insures the liberties of all. Satan promises liberty, but God gives liberty. Schleiermacher, a learned and thoughtful man but of a

---

* See the illustration on p. 441.

weak constitution, physically as well as spiritually, still bows down in submissive awe before a God whom he conceived most probably after the model of the Prussian government, and defines religion as the "feeling of absolute dependence."

Poor Schleiermacher! What an abominable religion didst thou preach in spite of thy philosophical caution which, in the eyes of zealous believers, amounted to heresy!

It is worth while to criticise Schleiermacher's definition of religion, because it found favor with many people, especially in liberal circles; for it appealed to the free religious people as a definition which omitted the name of God and retained the substance of religion. Would it not be better to retain the name of God and purify its significance, than to discard the word and retain the substance and source of the old superstitions? But it is an old experience that the Liberals are iconoclasts of external formalities and idolators of reactionary thoughts. They retain the cause of obstruction, and discard some of its indifferent results, in which it happens to find expression. They cure the symptoms of the disease but are very zealous in extolling its cause as the source of all that is good.

Schopenhauer in comment upon Schleiermacher's definition, said that if religion be the feeling of absolute dependence, the most religious animal would not be man, but the cur.

To the lovers of freedom the feeling of dependence is a curse, and Sasha Schneider has well pictured it as a terrible monster whose prey are the weak—those whose religion is absolute submissiveness.

Truly if we cannot have a religion which makes us free and independent, let us discard religion! Religion must be in accord not only with morality but also with philosophy; not only with justice, but also with science; not only with order, but also with freedom.

Man is dependent upon innumerable conditions of his life; yet his aspiration is not to be satisfied with the consciousness of his plight; his aspiration is to become independent and to become more and more the master of his destiny. If religion is the expression of that which constitutes the humanity of man, Schleiermacher's definition is wrong and misleading, for religion is the very opposite. Religion is that which makes man more of a man, which develops his faculties and allows him more independence.

Monarchical Europe has generally characterised the Devil as the rebel in the universe, and in a certain sense he is. But he represents revolution only in its misguided attempts to gain liberty. Every rebellion which is not in its own nature self-destructive, is an expression of the divine spirit. Every dash for liberty is a righteous deed, and a revolutionary movement that has the power and inherent good sense to be able to stay, is of God.

Satan may be the representative of rebellion; God symbolises liberty. Satan may promise independence by a call to arms against rules and order; God gives independence by self-control and discretion. Satan is sham freedom, in God we find true freedom. Satan is an indispensable phase in the manifestation of God; he is the protest against God's dispensation as a yoke and an imposition, and thus revolting against the law prepares the way to the covenant of love and spontaneous good-will.

We must only learn that independence cannot be gained by a rebellion against the constitution of the universe, or by inverting the laws of life and evolution, but by comprehending them and adapting ourselves to the world in which we live. By a recognition of the truth, which must be acquired by painstaking investigation and by accepting the truth as our maxim of conduct, man rises to the height of self-determination, of dominion over the forces of nature, of freedom. It is the truth that makes us free.

So long as the truth is something foreign to us, we speak of obedience to the truth; but when we have learned to identify ourselves with truth, the moral ought ceases to be a tyrannical power above us, and we feel ourselves as its representatives; it changes into aspirations in us. True religion is love of truth, and being such it will not end in a feeling of dependence, but reap the fruit of truth, which is liberty, freedom, independence.

The Devil-Conception in Its Relation to the God-Conception

THE EVOLUTION OF THE CONCEPTION of evil is by no means an unimportant chapter in the history of religion, for the idea a man has of Satan is characteristic of his mental and moral nature.

While the Bible declares that man is made in the image of God, anthropologists say that men make their gods after their own image: and the truth is that every God-conception is characteristic of the man who holds it. It has been said: I will tell you who you are when you tell me what your conception of God is.

But the same observation holds good as to the conception of the Devil, and we might as well say, "I will tell you who you are when you tell me what your conception of the Devil is."

There is a similarity between our conceptions of good and evil which cannot be accidental, for it is natural that all our thoughts should possess a certain family likeness. Your idea of the Devil is your best interpretation of your idea of God. It will be interesting to compare one of the most famous representations of God, holding the universe in his hands with the pictures of Mara, the Buddhist Satan with the world-wheel in his clutches. (See pp. 119, 121, 123.)

This similarity can be proved from history.

The Trinity conception of Satan is as old as the Trinity conception of God. As we have Trinities among the Pagan deities, for instance among the Greeks, the three-headed Hecuba; so we have three-headed monsters as for instance, the three-headed Cerberus; and in the history of Christian art a similar parallelism obtains between God-representations and Devil-representations. The idea of representing the divine trinity as a person having three faces may have originated in a modification of the two-headed Janus.

Professor Kraus says concerning the trinitarian demons of Christianity:

"The diabolical dragon is described as a three-headed monster (probably in recollection of Cerberus) in the Apocryphal *Gospel of Nicodemus*, and in the *Good Friday Sermon* of Eusebius of Alexandria, who addresses the Devil 'Three-headed Beelzebul' (τρικέφαλε Βεελζεβούλ.). The idea of the Demon as a serpent with the head of a woman appears not earlier than the Middle Ages, in Bede, from whom it is quoted by Vincent de Beauvais."

Dante describes the three-faced Satan in these lines:

> *"Oh, what a sight!*
> *How passing strange it seemed when I did spy*
> Upon his head three faces: *one in front*
> *Of hue vermilion, the other two with this*
> *Midway each shoulder joined and at the crest;*
> *The right 'twixt wan and yellow seemed; the left*
> *To look on, such as come from whence old Nile*

Stoops to the lowlands. Under each shot forth
Two mighty wings, enormous as became
A bird so vast. No plumes had they,
But were in texture like a bat, and these
He flapped in the air, that from him issued still
Three winds wherewith Cocytus to its depth
Was frozen. At six eyes he wept: the tears
Adown three chins distilled with bloody foam.
At every mouth his teeth a sinner champed,
Bruised as with ponderous engine; so that three
Were in this guise tormented."

—(Hell. Canto xxxiv)

As according to Christian doctrine God is actualised in the God-man, so Satan in his turn is represented as the Antichrist and is pictured as a human caricature full of ugliness and wickedness. Professor Kraus continues:

"Simultaneously with the conception of the Devil as a dragon are found in the Acts of the Martyrs notions of him as an awful negro (a Moor or Ethiopian). The same views are found in Augustine, Gregory the Great, and the Apocryphal Acts of St. Bartholomew. In the latter, the idea is so far developed as to represent the Devil as the archetype of deformity: he becomes a negro with a dog's snout, covered with hair down to his toes, with glowing eyes, fire in his mouth, smoke issuing from his nostrils, and with the wings of a bat. We see that this pleasant description of the Evil One, which perhaps is based on Job xli. 9 et seq., contains all the elements of the grotesque conception of the Middle Ages. They are found also in the *Vita S. Antonii* where also the horns of the Devil are mentioned."

Compare for instance Milton's Satan with Goethe's Mephistopheles! The one heroic like the English nation, a Protestant, a rebel, a dissenter, a subjectivist (see p. 351 ff.), the other a sage, a scholar, a philosopher, like a German poet. Goethe's Mephistopheles is not as grand as Milton's Satan, but he is in his way not less interesting, for he is more ingenious, more learned, more poetical. He is a philosophical principle, being the spirit of criticism; and as such he plays an important part in the economy of nature.

Mephistopheles characterises himself in these words:

> *"I am the spirit that denies!*
> *And justly so: For all things from the void*
> *Called forth, deserve to be destroyed.*
> *T'were better, then, were nought created.*
> *Thus, all which you as sin have rated,—*
> *Destruction,—aught with evil blent,—*
> *That is my proper element."*

And what a sympathy exists between Mephistopheles, the spirit of criticism and the dignified author of the Universe. The Lord says in the Prelude to Faust:

> *"In self-indulgence man finds soon his level*
> *He seeks repose and ease; and stops to grow.*
> *Gladly on him the comrade I'll bestow*
> *Who will provoke and must create as Devil."*

As God, now and then, needs the Devil, so the Devil is anxious from time to time to pay his respects to the good Lord. After the heaven is closed Mephistopheles remains alone on the stage and says:

> *"At times the Ancient Gent I like to see,*
> *Keep on good terms with him and am most civil."*

Hobbling away, he stops before leaving the stage and turning to the audience adds:

> *"'Tis truly fine of such a grand grandee*
> *So humanly to gossip with the Devil."*

Conclusion

EVIL PERSONIFIED APPEARS AT FIRST sight repulsive. But the more we study the personality of the Devil, the more fascinating it becomes. In the beginning of existence the Evil One is the embodiment of everything unpleasant, then of everything bad, evil, and immoral. He is hatred, destruction, and annihilation incarnate, and as such he is the adversary of existence, of the Creator, of God. The Devil is the rebel of the cosmos, the independent in the empire of a tyrant, the opposition to uniformity, the dissonance in universal harmony, the exception to the rule, the particular in the universal, the unforeseen chance that breaks the law; he is the individualising tendency, the craving for originality, which bodily upsets the ordinances of God that enforce a definite kind of conduct; he overturns the monotony that would permeate the cosmic spheres if every atom in unconscious righteousness and with pious obedience slavishly followed a generally prescribed course.

The ingenuous question, "Why does not God kill the Devil?" is comical enough, because we feel instinctively that it is impossible. I know of a good old lady who prayed daily with great fervor and piety that God might have mercy on the Devil and save him. Think of it closely, and this attitude is touching! How many great theologians have seriously discussed the problem whether the Devil could be saved. Like that good old lady, they were so engrossed in the literal belief of their mythology that they did not see that the problem implied a contradiction. For God and Devil are relative terms, and God would cease to be God if there were no Devil.

The universe is such that the evolution of a higher life is possible only through great strain. The evolution of the warm glow of a soul out of the cold clay of the earth, of moral aspirations out of the fierce hatred that animates the struggle for existence, of intelligence, thought and foresight out of the brute indifference of that unthinking something which *we call* matter in motion, is due to extraordinary exertions; it is the product of work performed by the expenditure of enormous energy, and constant efforts are required merely to preserve the treasures already won. Difficulties to be overcome are called in the terminology of mechanics "the power of resistance," and this power of resistance is, closely considered, an essential and even a beneficial factor in the constitution of the universe.

If there were no power of resistance, if no efforts were needed to reach any end desired, if the world were pleasure and goodness throughout, we should have no evolution, no progress, no ideals; for all spheres of existence would float in one universal ocean of bliss, and all things would be intoxicated with heavenly delight.

Pain produces the want of something better, and deficiencies arouse the desire for improvement. If the feeling substance of moners had all their wants satisfied without further exertion, man would never have risen out of the bythos of amœboid existence, and if the man of today lived in a Schlaraffia, he would not trouble about new inventions, progress, or any amelioration; he would simply live on in unthinking enjoyment. There would be no need of making any effort, no need of struggling against evils, no need of virtue, no need of working out our salvation. There would be no badness, but there would be no goodness, either. All existence would be soaked with moral indifference.

Good is good only because there is evil, and God is God because there is a Devil.

As evil is not a mere negation, so the figure of Satan in religion is not an idle fancy. Goethe says:

> *"Ich kann mich nicht bereden lassen,*
> *Macht mir den Teufel nur nicht klein:*
> *Ein Kerl, den alle Menschen hassen,*
> *Der muss was sein!"*

> *["You have the Devil underrated.*
> *I cannot yet persuaded be!*
> *A fellow who is all-behated,*
> *Must something be."]*

Now, let us look at the mythical figure of Satan as represented in theology, folklore, and poetry. Is he not really a most interesting man? Indeed, in spite of being a representative of all kinds of crimes, he possesses many redeeming features so as to be great and noble. According to the account in the second chapter of Genesis, Satan is the father of science, for he induced Eve to make Adam taste of the fruit of knowledge, and the Ophites, a gnostic sect, worshipped the serpent for that reason. Satan produces the unrest in society, which, in spite of many inconveniences, makes the world move onward and forward; he is the patron of progress, investigation, and invention. Giordano Bruno, Galileo, and other men of science were regarded as his offspring and persecuted on his account by the Church. And when we glance over the records of the Devil-contracts, we learn to have respect for the old gentleman. Milton's Satan is a grand character, a noble-souled rebel, who would rather undergo an eternity of torture than suffer humiliation.

Consider but the fact that, taking the statement of his adversaries alone, the Devil is the most trustworthy person in existence. He has been cheated by innumerable sinners, saints, angels, and (according to various old Church legends) even by the good Lord himself; and yet he has never been found wanting in the literal and punctilious fulfilment of all his promises; and all the bad experiences he has had in the course of millenniums have not in the least lowered his character. His mere word is honored as the holiest oath, or as the best signature verified with seals and legal witnesses. The instances are rare in which it is known that persons with whom he has had business transactions have requested him to sign a contract, to give a pledge, or to show any proof that he would honestly abide by his word; his honesty was never doubted by anybody. And mind you, it is not the Devil who boasts of his integrity, but this is the conclusion at which we arrive from the evidences adduced by his enemies.

Our sympathy for this martyr of honest conduct, the dupe of God and man, grows when we consider our own nature and relation to his Satanic majesty. With our hands upon our hearts, must we not confess that every one of us, in spite of man's boastful claim of a likeness to God, has some trait or other that makes him kin to the Devil? I do not mean here to make reference to actual sin or grievous transgressions, but to things of which we scarcely think of repenting. Did we never in an hour of humor laugh at our neighbor? Did we never joke at the cost of somebody else? Did we never bulldoze, tease, or tantalise our very best friends? Did we never enjoy the awkward situation in which some poor innocent had been caught? And why should we not? If we took away from life its satire, jokes, and other "devil-tries," it would lose part of its most fragrant zest, and if we constructed a man consisting of virtues only, would not that fellow be the most unbearable bore in the world, wearisome beyond description? For it is a sprinkling of petty vices that makes even a great man human. A mere ethical machine would neither be attractive nor arouse our sympathies.

The Devil is the father of all misunderstood geniuses. It is he who induces us to try new paths; he begets originality of thought and deed. He tempts us to venture out boldly into unknown seas for the discovery of new ways to the wealth of distant Indias. He makes us dream of and hope for more prosperity and greater happiness. He is the spirit of discontent that embitters our hearts, but in the end often leads to a better arrangement of affairs. In truth, he is a very useful servant of the Almighty, and all the heinous features of his character disappear when we consider the fact that he is necessary in the economy of nature as a wholesome stimulant to action and as the power of resistance that evokes the noblest efforts of living beings.

God, being the All in All, regarded as the ultimate authority for conduct, is neither evil itself nor goodness itself; but, nevertheless, he is in the good, and he is in the evil. He encompasses good and evil. God is in the growth and in the decay; he reveals himself in life, and he reveals himself in death. He will be found in the storm, he will be found in the calm. He lives in good aspirations and in the bliss resting upon moral endeavors; but he lives also in the visitations that follow evil actions. It is his voice that speaks in the guilty conscience, and he, too, is in the curse of sin, and in this sense he is present even in the evil itself. Even evil, temptation, and sin elicit the good: they teach man. He who has eyes to see, ears to hear, and a mind to perceive, will read a lesson out of the very existence of evil, a lesson which, in spite of the terrors it inspires, is certainly not less impressive, nor less divine, than the sublimity of a holy life; and thus it becomes apparent that the existence of Satan is part and parcel of the divine dispensation. Indeed we must grant that the Devil is the most indispensable and faithful helpmate of God. To speak mystically, even the existence of the Devil is filled with the presence of God.

A Note About the Author

Paul Carus (1852–1919) was a German American author, scholar, and philosopher. Born in Ilsenburg, Germany, he studied at the universities of Strassburg and Tübingen, earning his PhD in 1876. After a stint in the army and as a teacher, Carus left Imperial Germany for the United States, settling in LaSalle, Illinois. There, he married engineer Mary Hegeler, with who he would raise seven children at the Hegeler Carus Mansion. As the managing editor of the Open Court Publishing Company, he wrote and published countless books and articles on history, politics, philosophy, religion, and science. Referring to himself as "an atheist who loved God," Carus gained a reputation as a leading scholar of interfaith studies, introducing Buddhism to an American audience and promoting the ideals of Spinoza. Throughout his life, he corresponded with Leo Tolstoy, Thomas Edison, Nikola Tesla, Booker T. Washington, and countless other leaders and intellectuals. A committed Monist, he rejected the Western concept of dualism, which separated the material and spiritual worlds. In his writing, he sought to propose a middle path between metaphysics and materialism, which led to his dismissal by many of the leading philosophers of his time.

A Note from the Publisher

Spanning many genres, from non-fiction essays to literature classics to children's books and lyric poetry, Mint Edition books showcase the master works of our time in a modern new package. The text is freshly typeset, is clean and easy to read, and features a new note about the author in each volume. Many books also include exclusive new introductory material. Every book boasts a striking new cover, which makes it as appropriate for collecting as it is for gift giving. Mint Edition books are only printed when a reader orders them, so natural resources are not wasted. We're proud that our books are never manufactured in excess and exist only in the exact quantity they need to be read and enjoyed.

bookfinity™

Discover more of your favorite classics with Bookfinity™.

- Track your reading with custom book lists.
- Get great book recommendations for your personalized Reader Type.
- Add reviews for your favorite books.
- AND MUCH MORE!

Visit **bookfinity.com** and take the fun Reader Type quiz to get started.

Enjoy our classic and modern companion pairings!

Classic & Modern